D1482210

THE
International Breakfast
BOOK

*Greet the Day with 100 Recipes
from Around the World*

MARTHA HOLLIS

Macmillan • USA

To all the earth's peoples who eat breakfast
with the hope that we can continue
to share with one another joyous love and peace.

MACMILLAN
A Simon & Schuster Macmillan Company
1633 Broadway
New York, NY 10019-6785

Macmillan Publishing books may be purchased for business or sales promotional use. For information please write: Special Markets Department, Macmillan Publishing USA, 1633 Broadway, New York, NY 10019.

Copyright © 1997 by Martha Hollis

Illustrations copyright © 1997 by Richard Fox

All rights reserved. No part of this book may be reproduced or transmitted in any form or by any means, electronic or mechanical, including photocopying, recording, or by any information storage and retrieval system, without permission in writing from the Publisher.

MACMILLAN is a registered trademark of Macmillan, Inc.

BOOK DESIGN BY KEVIN HANEK

Library of Congress Cataloging-in-Publication Data

Hollis, Martha
   The international breakfast book / Martha Hollis.
      p.   cm.
   Includes index.
   ISBN 0-02-861011-3
   1. Breakfasts.   2. Cookery, International.   3. Travel—Anecdotes.
I. Title.
TX733.H66   1997
641.5′2—dc21   97-19470
                                                   CIP

Manufactured in the United States of America
10 9 8 7 6 5 4 3 2 1

Contents

vii

What Is for Breakfast?

*T*he *International Breakfast Book* is a slice of morning life, about the ordinary folks and food professionals whom I encountered in my glorious search for breakfasts far and wide. Often a morning walk in a new land leads to delicious discoveries and encounters with wonderful people eager to share their everyday way of life.

"What did you have for breakfast?"

The answers to my question often lead to surprises. Nearly all types of foods are consumed in the morning somewhere in the world, and many unusual ones are related to dinner leftovers. Apple pie or some form of it is, oddly enough, very popular. I have even seen sliced duck with salad on the breakfast buffet in Prague, along with fancy dessert strudels.

Breakfast foods are as diverse as the peoples of the world. When it's midnight in New York, perhaps a Muslim is arising in Malaysia. After his morning prayers he may have chicken in a spicy curried sauce with coconut-infused rice. One culture's dinner may be another's breakfast or vice versa. The Dutch and Hungarians eat pancakes for desserts. The Belgians enjoy their waffles as desserts or as snack food. The French love omelets as a light lunch or dinner. The Spanish enjoy potato omelets (tortillas) for tapas. The Japanese take pleasure in miso soup with fish, seaweed, and rice for breakfast. Asians relish noodles for breakfast. Egyptians go for falafels.

Some practices boggle the mind. Skipping breakfast because of a late and heavy dinner may be common. But one man explained he breakfasted, including coffee with caffeine, before retiring for bed because his mornings were so hectic.

Children seem to be some of the most religious adherents to a regular breakfast— all that dreaming and growing demands sustenance. They seem unwilling to wait very long, and they demand the basics.

In Singapore, little ones love to slurp noodles with a light broth in the incredibly clean outdoor market stalls. Dutch children relish the light, crispy rusks spread with butter and sprinkled with a chocolate topping: *hagelslag,* also known as spaghetti or worms. North American and English children are major consumers of hot and cold cereals.

Older students and those heading off to work define the "grab-and-go" culture. Quick, no-effort items, such as a breakfast burrito or a sausage biscuit to eat with one hand while the other grabs the bus rail or steering wheel, exemplify this food genre. Street vendors sell quickies outside trains and buses with orders passed through windows. Japanese vendors offer beautiful wooden boxes with artfully arranged items, and on-the-spot fried breads in Thailand come in somewhat absorbent paper. Underground transportation shopping centers worldwide sport pastry and beverage shops rapidly dispensing sustenance to the hurried. A wide class of ready-to-eat sweets feed this world—pastries, cakes, doughnuts, croissants, and cookies.

I've hung around streets and alleys, watching busy morning eaters. In Bangkok, noodles in broth are eaten in a plastic bag; in Taipei, open-air snack shops cook delicate sesame pancakes over sidewalk charcoal cookers. Sidewalk seating, on small chairs covered in brightly colored plastic seats with tiny tables, turns over quickly. Malaysians love the huge thin rotis of Indian origin soused with eye-watering chilies, bought from vendors in the basements of office buildings or on street corners.

Those with the luxury of time have sustained and enhanced the rituals of breakfast worldwide. Fortunately I have been included in many of these "full" breakfasts, and I have tried to capture and share their essence. Many are associated with Sunday, holiday, or vacation mornings.

The full English breakfast, dominating the Victorian and Edwardian eras, set the standard morning fare that spread via the British attempts at colonization in the United States, Canada, Australia, Singapore, and parts of Africa. The British Empire's rise and fall enormously influenced the world's morning consumption of eggs, bacon and sausage, tomato, toast and marmalade, and English Breakfast and Earl Grey teas.

Upscale traditional breakfasts are still celebrated with the "Knightsbridge" at the Hyde Park Hotel in London. It starts with a split of Tattinger's champagne and moves on to sorbet from exotic fruits, Scottish salmon with scrambled eggs and mushrooms, and pressed coffees and mango tea infusions.

The Europeans, separated by more than the English Channel, enjoy their Continental breakfasts—a meal that is still popular in many Roman Catholic-dominated countries. The simplest Continental breakfast is a hard, white roll, with jam and butter, and coffee or tea. Often these are enhanced with fruit juices, hot chocolate, and croissants and pastries.

Cultures claiming only a Continental breakfast ingeniously deal with morning hunger. Just a roll with butter and jam does not handle the Roman prelunch appetite. The quick trip to the bakery for the paper-thin pizza with garlic and olive oil or a cappuccino with a ham and cheese sandwich can see one through to lunch. In prerevolutionary Sarajevo, the thick Turkish coffee contained enough sugar to be almost classified as food.

Reformation countries such as Germany and Holland expanded breakfast to include cheeses, eggs, chocolate, and meats, and the Scandinavian countries expanded with all manners of fish and open-faced sandwiches. After Europeans migrated to South America, the Continental breakfast became the dominant pattern of that continent.

Major changes have come about in the last two decades under the banner of "good nutrition." Today whole grain breads almost dominate the scene in Belgium and the Netherlands. Tons of these grain mixes (e.g., seven grain) are exported to the United States. Fewer eggs seem to be consumed. Fatty breakfast meats are yielding to leaner selections.

But every nation developed unique and exciting recipes, using local food stuffs, native cuisine ideas, and regional culture—jazzy eggs Sardou in New Orleans, traditional water-boiled bagels in New York, dosai in India, arepas in Venezuela, huevos rancheros in Mexico, fish in Sweden, oatmeal in Ireland, espresso and croissants in France, Smith-field ham in Virginia, hangtown fry in San Francisco, and ackee and codfish in Ocho Rios.

Morning beverages are also rituals—chocolate milk, spring water, coffees, teas, infusions, fresh juices, along with their myriad of varieties and manners of consumption. One morning in a health spa in Heviz, Hungary, I found a spraying fountain of fresh strawberry juice on the buffet.

An oriental teahouse provides a most delightful leisure morning. There, older men carrying cages of their prized songbirds gather and swap gossip. In Hong Kong, after morning tai chi chuan and aerobics in the park, many head directly for the teahouse. The unfermented green tea is sipped slowly under clouds of smoke while talk of neighborhood politics and people perpetuates the daily ritual.

Searching for food sources has always enhanced my travels. In addition to visiting the usual museums, historical sites, and restaurants, I search for tours by producers and growers of foods. Some have included a tea plantation in China, Blue Mountain coffee growers in Jamaica, cheese producers in Gouda, whole grain bread bakeries in Amsterdam, a national baking school near Frankfurt, an orange juice plantation in Florida, blueberry farms in Michigan, egg ranches in Virginia, peppercorn growers in the jungles of Borneo, tortilla makers in Mexico, chocolate factories in Switzerland, and dry cereal producers in both Battle Creek, Michigan, and Manchester, United Kingdom.

My careers as a magazine feature writer and a professionally trained chef have opened many kitchen doors for me. I have been given incredible access to food, people, and information through writing assignments, covering the crème de la crème of culinary events such as

the Culinary Olympics (held every four years), the American Culinary Federation competitions, and numerous food-related conferences, and special events. Chefs have permitted me to watch preparations, carefully explaining their techniques and even permitting hands-on involvement.

There is one rule for breakfasting—eat whatever is available, and eat anything you want. If you skip breakfast, you are missing a joyous way to begin every day.

TO THE COOK

*T*he International Breakfast Book could revolutionize the breakfasts you serve in your home. Serving unusual foods, particularly for morning parties, is a delightful way to entertain.

Usually I return home with a suitcase or two full of foodstuffs, eager to recreate the wonders I have experienced and to share them with my friends and readers. Initially, I develop a recipe using the original ingredients. Then, I experiment with ingredients available locally. Living in Williamsburg, Virginia (not a major international-food shopping Mecca), I often resort to mail-order sources or travel to a major city for shopping. Many

herbs special to particular cuisines, such as cilantro, lemon grass, and epazote, I now cultivate in my own gardens.

Mail-order sources are listed for unusual ingredients. Notes to recipes suggest possible ingredient substitutions and tricks to fashion special equipment from things found around the house.

An important practice always followed by professional chefs and cooks is *mise en place*, to have everything in place before beginning to cook. Plainly speaking, it is being organized for your adventure in cooking. After reading the entire recipe, arrange all ingredients, bowls, spatulas, cups, mixers, whisks, pans, vegetable sprays, and other special equipment on the counter. If you are satisfied that you have everything (or have suitable substitutes), give the recipe a go.

For perfect recipe followers, these recipes have been carefully tested in a home kitchen, and they work. For recipe personalizers, enjoy your changes and creative touches—that is how cooking becomes a delightful pastime for some. Do not stray too far from scientific formula suggestions in the baked goods, particularly ratios of flours, liquids, and leavening. But feel free to change some types of grains, spices, and flavoring extracts and to add dried fruits and nuts. Sometimes baking bread in an unusual shape (remember to change cooking time) makes a special change.

Ingredient quantities are listed with weights (where appropriate) and standard cups. The weights listed in recipes will help in buying sufficient quantities of ingredients. Those with scales will enjoy the increased accuracy and easier assembly. A quality set of kitchen scales, which costs about thirty dollars, is a good investment. As mentioned earlier, scales are especially useful for baking. All professional bakers weigh solid ingredients, such as flour and sugar, instead of using measuring cups.

THE BEGINNING—MY BREAKFAST CONSCIOUSNESS

I hated eggs, but loved school. These two institutions were creatively linked by my mother. She said, "You can't go to school until you've finished your eggs." Many a tortuous morning I forced down these cold, rubbery, unadorned scrambled gaggers.

When just barely old enough to reach a fry pan, I took over the chore of scrambling eggs. Reducing the number of units in the pan, I could readily respond to mother's query, "Have you eaten your eggs?"

"Yes, I had some egg." The plural of the word was worth getting around. Using a quark-sized quantity, before scientists were to discover this subatomic particle, I seemed to close the issue. Success in life is finding a way out of unpleasant realities.

Packaged cereals offered no respite. Why put milk on these crispy little technological wonders? But dry they scratch the throat and are dreadfully noisy.

Weekends, what joy! Pancakes and waffles appeared. On refrigerator defrosting days I valiantly volunteered to polish off the ice cream—my dream concept of an exciting breakfast.

Doughnuts, greasy fried dough with scaly glazes always left my fingers dirty. But in my late teens the rich fat-mouth feel of a buttery croissant in Europe was ethereal. There I also encountered the Continental breakfast: bread, jam, butter, and coffee, which I found to be not much use in quelling an appetite.

Still, in my world, the classic "American" breakfast seemed to prevail—two eggs any style, a strip of fatty bacon, buttered toast, juice, and coffee. This morning rite, a national bad habit, could be had at a diner for a mere ninety-nine cents, and fifty cents more for greasy potatoes. My periodic attempts to enjoy these meals failed. I found the standard breakfast lacking in texture, taste, color, and variety. Particularly variety!

Years later I began to celebrate the notion of prelunch eating. A quick glimpse of a lovely morning idea, the bagel with cream cheese and coffee, came to me while working at a Virginia bookstore run by a New York family. Both became my morning fixture—the chewy, fresh yeasty bread and the steaming cup of dark coffee, a highly complex melange of flavors with varying degrees of bitterness, body, and strength. That started my passionate affair with the noble bean, and it has been fueled by many detours to the roasting site of the Norfolk and San Francisco-based First Colony Coffee Company.

In San Francisco, my workday started by walking several miles to the University via the cappuccino-almond-croissants and the pain-au-chocolat route. Another favorite was the walk past the Tassajara Bread Bakery in Haight-Ashbury. There I ordered freshly baked whole grain breads from a group of bakers who passionately loved and cared for their clients. With a glass cup of coffee, I'd slip into the crowded table area with poets, who were still "reading around," medical students and residents from the University of California, leftover hippies from a time gone by, and other assorted folks glorifying the morning.

Set free at last from the breakfasts of my childhood, I opened up to the entire world of eggs, which hatched into my food consciousness with Denver omelets, Spanish sauces, eggs Benedict, coddled eggs in wine and herbs, shirred eggs, zucchini frittatas, crab and avocado omelets, and huevos rancheros. Egg cookery became a bewildering world of joy and overwhelming variety.

It is always worth getting up for breakfast.

The Morning Globetrotter

We are about to travel around the world. Don't worry about details such as passports or jet lag. We're simply going to see what's on the breakfast menu in selected places on each continent. Some breakfasts are for every day; some are for special occasions.

We'll also go grocery shopping while we're traveling in some of these fascinating venues. I like to empty my suitcase of travel-worn clothes as I wander, then fill it up again with foodstuffs, particularly spices, to bring home.

ASIA

Several of my most memorable breakfasts were in Japan. I was staying in a monastery in Kyoto, sleeping on a futon that rested on a tatami mat, in a lovely room with sliding walls that looked out to a serene winter garden.

We broke fast in the monks' eating room with steaming bowls of miso soup, the bowls gently curving to fill and warm both hands. Small individually wrapped packages of roasted seaweed, bowls of rice, and an assortment of pickles rounded out the meal. An incredible variety of vegetables are pickled in brine in Japan, many in Day-Glo colors: bright blues, deep purples, and sensual magenta. (I've often wondered if Japanese pickles are the inspiration for the Crayola crayon boxes with 250 colors.) We also drank unfermented green tea.

This was the simplest of Japanese breakfasts, yet a special meal. More elaborate breakfasts include steamed salmon and rice, with condiments of tofu, chopped spring onions, seaweed, and other pickles to sprinkle in the delicious bowls of miso soup. Because the Japanese are very active in international business, these breakfasts can now

be found in many hotels worldwide, such as the Marriott Marquis in New York, the St. Francis in San Francisco, the Hyde Park Hotel in London, the InterContinental in Vienna, the Radisson SAS Royal Viking in Stockholm, and the George Hotel in Auckland, New Zealand.

A hot trend in some Japanese cities is Kohi houses, or coffeehouses. Generally Japanese restaurants do not serve coffee. But in Kohi houses, large cups of strong coffee are served, and in the mornings, they're accompanied by Texas toast. I've never actually seen this toast in Texas, but true to the image of the state, Texas toast is big. Soft white bread is cut into huge, two-inch thick slices, toasted, and served with butter. At no extra cost is the thick layer of cigarette smoke—Kohi houses are the refuge of smokers.

Breakfast is often a hurried affair in the People's Republic of China. In Taiwan, scores of small restaurants crowd into tiny spaces between residential and commercial buildings and shops. Some have only four or five tables, with a propane heat source and a cooking pot serving as the kitchen. The people spill out into the street as do the cooks. Often a

deep fryer or a charcoal grill might be directly in the pedestrian path. Other restaurants are more elaborate, with a storefront, waiters, more cooking surfaces, and menus on the wall. Little cooking is done in ovens, as is the case in most homes, where there are no ovens. Fuel has always been scarce, and cooking is done quickly after the food is cut into small pieces, using methods such as stir-frying. Nonetheless, these food stalls are not to be underestimated. They produce some of the most delectable meals imaginable.

The traditional breakfast in areas such as the Canton province is *congee,* a thin rice gruel. It is a soothing dish, but it can be jazzed up with fish cakes or the hot pepper sauce that is always on the table. In other areas, dried soy beans are soaked overnight and made into soy milk. Served warm in a bowl, the milk can be either sweet or salty. Additions to the warm soy milk range from vinegar, hot chili, and soy sauce to chopped preserved vegetables, dried shrimp, and scallions. Another popular topping is a deep-fried, and often very greasy, foot-long cruller, cut into slices.

My favorite breakfast is a sesame pancake cooked over a grill and served with an egg if you wish. The batter is fairly thick and loaded with the delicious crunch of white sesame seeds. To drink, there is either red or green tea. (Red tea is the black fermented tea leaves more familiar to Americans.) Both China and the People's Republic of China have many excellent tea plantations.

Dim sum is a Chinese tradition that usually starts midmorning in Hong Kong. The dim sum is such a complicated affair, with hundreds of possible dishes, that it is rarely done at home and is usually held in a restaurant. In a dim sum (which means "delight your heart") restaurant, a menu is unnecessary. Instead, a huge trolley loaded with bamboo steamer baskets becomes the ultimate point-and-eat breakfast adventure. You can also order special items if the waiter can hear you over the noise and bustling activities.

Billing is easy. You just count the number of little plates on the table. There may be some unusual dishes such as braised chicken feet (which are really quite a delicacy), but even the more common steamed or fried ones are guaranteed to be exotically delicious. Look for flaky pastries filled with spicy curried meats and

vegetables, handmade pastas, crispy spring rolls, crisp scallion cakes, and steamed barbecue buns made with a yeast dough.

In Korea, foods are not usually distinguished as belonging to a certain time of the day. Whatever is available makes a good meal. Soups and rice are popular, especially when enhanced with bits of meat, vegetables, and seaweed. The potent, pickled *kimchi* (spicy, fermented cabbage or turnips) makes an appearance at every meal. Teas made of barley or rice as well as tea leaves are consumed.

In the Philippines fried rice takes center stage and is delicious when made with chopped scrambled eggs, green onion, and garlic. Matched with bread, a bit of dried fish and a cup of tea, it makes a hearty breakfast.

In Vietnam, rice appears with fresh fish and greens. A country morning meal might be sweet potatoes and squash blossoms. In the city where there is little time, many stop at a noodle shop for a bowl of the national soup, *pho*, served with hot peppers or hoisin sauce, Vietnamese mint, or basil. Plain water is consumed, or tea, preferably made from freshly picked older tea leaves boiled in water.

Rice is the center of all meals in Thailand. A fast meal is a bowl of steamed rice topped with a little meat served with a clear soup—the Buddhist's conscience keeps the quantity of meat small.

A more elaborate meal is rice with several side dishes of meat, vegetables, and soup, or a curry dish. *Khao tom* is the basic clear rice soup, but it may be made with pork, chicken, shrimp, or fish, and seasoned with fish sauce, vinegar, or hot chilies. A typical topping is fried garlic with a cilantro garnish. Pickled vegetables and salted eggs might be served on the side. In northern and northeastern Thailand, glutinous sticky rice is served with *nam phrik,* a spicy sauce. The soup has acclaimed hangover-healing properties.

Along Bangkok's canals, on soup boats, and in food alleys, vendors cooking over charcoal burners sell meals-to-go, in small plastic bags. For junk-food lovers, doughnuts are a major part of the street-food scene. Western breakfast buffets are popular in the large hotels in this capital city.

Malaysia and Singapore have integrated the cuisines of the natives along with Chinese and many other immigrants, explorers, and conquerors to make these places a breakfast-lover's paradise. Islam is the predominant religion in Malaysia, and Muslims eat no pork. Instead there is a wide variety of breakfast meats made of poultry. People of Chinese descent eat lots of pork in the morning.

At the Marina Mandarin Hotel in Singapore, the breakfast menu provides an excellent introduction to this cuisine, with soups and porridges dominated by an Oriental note, using techniques and ingredients (particularly hot spicy ones) from the Malay Peninsula. Soups include congee with chicken, pork, ginger, spring onions, and egg; pork sparerib soup with Chinese herbs and plain rice; Chinese dough fritters; bouillon with fresh fish and rice; and the famous Bee hoon soup of rice vermicelli with pork, shrimp, liver, and vegetables in bouillon.

The porridges contain mixtures such as chicken with egg; minced pork with liver and egg; and Teochew-style porridge with rice, salted fish, eggs, vegetables, Chinese sausage, and peanuts. Two traditional rice dishes are *Nasi Lemak* with rice, coconut milk, pandan leaves with curry chicken, fried egg, cucumber, peanuts, sambal, and dried anchovies; and the Indonesian favorite, *Nasi Goreng*, a fried rice with fried egg, garnished with prawn crackers.

In the cities, street food is abundant, particularly the giant *rotis*: dough that is twirled in the air like tossing a pizza crust, then grilled and folded into layers and served with a searing, mouth-burning *sambal*. Singapore has different street areas specializing in exciting cuisines: Indian (both southern and northern), Chinese, Indonesian, and Baba Nonya. And to get a proper English breakfast instead, you only need to enter the splendid Raffles Hotel.

In marked contrast to the cities, in rural Malaysia the natives subsist on food they must struggle to find from the land and the seas. One journey deep into the jungles of Borneo revealed another look at breakfast with a former head-hunting tribe, the Ibans of Sarawak, where freshly netted fish was generously offered.

AUSTRALIA AND SOUTH PACIFIC

Traveling down the globe brings us to Australia and New Zealand, followers of the traditional English breakfast school. These countries have branched out, however, using the fertile imagination of their chefs who love local ingredients. Residents still cherish the classic British breakfast with its variations of eggs, sausage, bacon, baked beans on toast, mushrooms and tomatoes, *Vegemite* and *Marmite* (dark salty spreads made of yeast and vegetable extracts), and cereals, but they also go crazy for more exotic items.

For example, Mark Halliday, the executive chef of the Hotel du Vin near Auckland, New Zealand, serves an upscale breakfast of freshly made spicy venison sausage, black field mushrooms, eggs, hash browns, a selection of lightly poached local fruits, and croissants. The Kimberly Lodge in the Bay of Islands serves oyster flan on *kumara* (similar to sweet potato) hash browns, and the Huka Lodge serves noodles with venison sausage and fresh mango chutney.

Just north of Australia is Papua New Guinea, an exotic country that shares an island with Indonesia. Rich with tribal customs and beautiful mountains, plains, and waterfront, Papua New Guinea provides a

glimpse into a special lifestyle. Traveling through the winding Sepik River on the *Sepik Spirit,* a hotel boat, you can experience breakfast with the natives who harvest sago palm trees. They make a basic pancake that is accompanied by edible tree leaves and tropical fruits in season.

Bob Bates, the owner of Trans Niugini Tours, the *Sepik Spirit,* and the three finest resorts in the country, writes "You might say that a traditional Highland breakfast simply consists of a piece of *Kau Kau* [sweet potato] plucked from the hot coals of a fire. I have even seen school children walking to school in the morning with a piece of cooked Kau Kau wedged on the end of a stick and carried over the shoulder."

EUROPE AND
THE UNITED KINGDOM

With more than thirty countries, Europe has a great variety of breakfast styles. The English claim to have the supreme answer to the first meal of the day, while over on the Continent, the French disdain gauche ingestion of large quantities of food before the "proper" lunch hours, preferring a simple meal usually consisting of bread and coffee. In Italy, Portugal, and Spain, the classic breakfast is of this same Continental variety, but serious eating takes place between this sparse meal and their late and substantial lunches.

The Germanic, Dutch and Swiss countries seek a happy medium between the two with the Continental breakfast augmented with meats, cheeses, and boiled eggs. The Swiss feature yogurt with muesli or cereals, and they like to drop a rich square of chocolate into their coffee. Traveling north, the seas play a major role in defining the breakfast of the Danish and Scandinavian countries. There thin slices of robust breads are partnered with smoked fish, meats, cheeses, vegetables, and fruits.

Gripsholm's Värdshus and Hotel in Mariefred is the oldest inn in Sweden, dating from 1609. It is the ultimate getaway from Stockholm for a romantic weekend breakfast. On the second floor the dining room, with its walls of windows and airy curtains, looks over the blue of the bay to Gripsholm's Castle, the former summer palace of Swedish royalty. Today the castle is open to the public and contains an exhaustive collection of portraits of Swedish notables.

In the enormous dining room is a table laden with freshly baked loaves of whole grain breads, rolls, and crisp bread, all serving as bases for building the breakfast sandwich of ham, cheese, turkey, salami, tomatoes, and cucumber. Other temptations are caviar paste, liver pate, pickled herring, soft and hard-boiled eggs, and pastries. For cereal eaters, there is Sweden's most popular flaked cereal—Kellogg's Cornflakes—and muesli, to be eaten with sour milk, low-fat plain yogurt with honey, or rich yogurt with pureed fruits. For drinks, there are orange and apple juices, tea, coffee, and milk.

No alcoholic beverages are offered. Most of the guests will be returning home after their romantic weekends, and the driving laws are quite strict with 0 percent alcohol limits.

Farther north in Iceland, heavy breads such as rye or pumpernickel are served with cheeses, buttermilk, and fresh fruit and vegetables such as cucumbers and tomatoes.

The French are the masters of the Continental breakfast. Coffee is always served au lait (with milk), and the baguettes, rolls, and pastries are impeccably fresh. Since bakeries and pastry shops are abundant, no one needs to spend time baking at home. In Paris, the Hotel Raphael, on Kléber near the Arc de Triomphe, creates the feeling of dining in your own elegant mansion with quiet, unobtrusive service. One enters into the hotel's Gallery, a long marble floor with oriental carpets and rare antiques.

Breakfast can be taken in the Salle à Manger. There are thirteen tables under the chef de cuisine, Philip Delahaye. Catering to the sweet tooth, the chef includes many classic Parisian pastries in a basket, usually of a petite size, to encourage sampling. One of the most delightful is pain au raisin, the buttery, multilayer dough with a smear of custard pastry cream rolled into a snail shape and filled with raisins. A proper omelet can be ordered with the Parisian mushrooms, which are small, tasty, and meaty-textured, although the French would more likely have an omelet for a light supper instead of at breakfast.

On the French Riviera, the Hotel Royal Riviera, Cap Ferat, delivers the cuisine of the sun, the earth, and the water in classic opulence. Presentation is important. If it delights your eyes, it will delight your stomach.

Breakfast can be served either on the terrace overlooking the gardens or on one's private room balcony high above the Mediterranean Sea with spectacular views of the limestone cliffs falling into the sea. The hotel's pastry chefs upscale the Continental breakfast with elegant goodies. I was served petite pain that looked just like a minibaguette, pain au chocolate, and a croissant with rose confiture from the Curtelin factory, in a woven metal basket.

Every day the basket contains a new surprise: a bittersweet chocolate-covered four-inch circle with scalloped edges, filled with sliced almonds, butter, and candied fruits; chocolate-chip brioches with crystal sugar on top; or an apple puree turnover with candied orange strips and raisins.

The Royal Riviera also includes elegant fruits with its version of the Continental breakfast—a tiny pineapple,

golden yellow with bright, shiny leaves, was cut in half and used as a serving dish for its finely diced flesh. The natural fruit was immensely enhanced with a simple syrup of equal parts of sugar and water boiled for one hour with lemon and orange juice. A sugar and water reduction with a bit of pureed strawberries and lemon glazed a fanned persimmon.

The Spanish eat dinner extremely late and don't have much to eat in the early morning. Then the munching begins. Much of this takes place in the tapa bars where one can find a freshly squeezed glass of juice, coffee, and stronger beverages. The little snacks often served with cocktails are the perfect morning nibbles. The second breakfast, midmorning, is a sandwich with ham or sausage or some tapas, and perhaps even a beer.

Generally, the Spanish take their first breakfast in the traditional Continental style except on Sunday mornings when deep-fried churros dominate. Greasy churros are dipped in heavy hot chocolate while fingers are futilely wiped on mostly nonabsorbent tiny paper napkins.

The Portuguese subscribe, for the most part, to the Continental breakfast.

In Lisbon and other cities, appetites are not sufficiently satisfied with this tiny repast, so nibbling commences mid-morning. Many sweets and savories from the numerous take-aways fill these voids. In rural areas, such as in the northern part of the country, a hearty breakfast is needed before a day of hard, physical labor in the fields. Soups and breads traditionally fill the morning bill.

The Italians also start the day with a Continental breakfast but end up in a cappuccino bar for a pick-me-up and a snack before lunch. The bakeries also do a brisk business selling sandwiches and slices of pizza.

The Germans have meat or cheese with their rolls, although they eat lightly in the early hours and stop to have a bit more in midmorning. It is quite common to see men in particular quaffing down a morning brew with a cheese or sausage roll.

Austrians, like the Germans, start slowly with rolls and coffee, but get more involved with sausages and pastries as the morning progresses. In Vienna especially, the pastry shops have become wildly popular for locals and tourist alike. The morning pastries are less sweet than those served later in the day and are considerably less sweet than those served in the United States. On weekends, eggs, liver pate, fruit, and cheeses are enjoyed.

The Dutch enjoy a much more substantial breakfast, often with whole grain breads, cheeses, hard-cooked eggs, meats, fruit, cereals, and chocolate bits on buttered rusks. In the morning, this nation that loves and produces fine aged cheeses prefers younger, more mild cheeses, saving the stronger ones for later in the day.

In Geneva and the French portion of Switzerland, the Continental breakfasts reign supreme. In Swiss Germany, more cheeses and meats are added. And in most of Switzerland, chocolates are served with coffee. All over the country people do a considerable amount of bakery hopping, looking for the special *delices* of each shop.

According to Peter Gomori, the director of the North American office of the Hungarian Tourist Board, rural Hungarians still believe in the importance of the daybreak meal, and they say "Eat breakfast as a king, lunch as a citizen, and dinner as the beggar on the corner."

City folks fail to heed this wisdom since many eat breakfast "like so many Americans—none at all, just gulping down a cup of coffee before scurrying off with the kids to the kindergarten or to work."

Fruit juices are popular, typically orange, apple, apricot, and peach. In the country, the fruit palinka or schnapps "gets the juices going." Cold cuts such as ham, liver pate, headcheese, beef tongue, salami, and dried sausages are popular. A special cheese spread is made of *liptauer* (similar to farmer's cheese), mixed with paprika, butter, and chopped onions. Because Hungarians love hot food, pieces of hot peppers, chopped tomatoes, and sausages find their way into scrambled eggs.

According to Gomori, cereals are relatively unknown and "as healthy stuff, are considered suspicious to the well being of one's stomach."

In Heviz, Hungary, about four miles from the resort town of Keszhely on the largest inland warm-water lake, Lake Balaton, I enjoyed a full-body massage for less than the price of a United States movie ticket. And the lavish breakfast buffet of fresh strawberry juice, fish, cold meatballs, cheese, cold cuts, sausage, fresh fruits, granola, potato salad, breads, and butter-laden pastries made me reevaluate my ideas of a spa breakfast.

The typical Polish breakfasts are hot oatmeal or millet, bread and butter, bagels and cream cheeses, sliced meats, and mild cheese. A grain beverage made from roasted wheat or barley with chicory (a cousin of the Lithuanian beverage of roasted oats and chicory)is consumed.

Later in the morning, snacking begins on street foods such as wild mushrooms on bread or a hot soup and sandwich. A special breakfast in Poland would be a beef brisket cooked in aspic, with scrambled eggs served with horseradish sauce. Depending on the season, there might be fresh fruit or a fruit compote. Bread is usually light and served with jelly or jam. The cheese is sliced and similar to a farmer's cheese.

In the countries formerly known as the Soviet Union, breakfasts concentrate heavily on grains, particularly cereals or dark breads. In the Ukraine, breakfast on Easter morning, which follows a week of refraining from meat or dairy, is one of the highlights of the year. A rich bread, *paska,* is decorated with a cross or bird. Other items are eggs with horseradish sauce, pork sausages (fresh and smoked), ham, roast piglet, country pate, hard-cooked eggs, pickled apples, beets, cheesecake with dried fruit, and other pastries and sweets.

In Greece, the fare is light with fresh fruits, cheese, breads, and thick, strong coffee. When yogurt is served, it is supremely rich and creamy. On special occasions, rich, sweet eggy yeast breads are prepared.

ISRAEL, TURKEY, THE MIDDLE EAST, AND INDIA

The Armenians enjoy sausage, eggs, cheese, olives, melons, and grapefruits. *Katah,* a special multilayered pastry made with yeast, eggs, sesame seeds, and a plethora of butter is served. *Bastegh,* a fruit leather of grape juice and cornstarch, is fried and served with eggs. *Bishi,* or pancakes, are also served.

Israel's cultural diversities often meld in breakfast. The standard breakfast for most everyone is bread, cheese (particularly the yogurt variety), olives, and tea or coffee. Often fresh salads and fruits augment the basics.

The traditional Turkish breakfasts in rural areas include soups made of grains and vegetables, hot milk blended with honey or sugar, fresh yogurt with honey, or cream with syrup. In urban areas, the classic morning start is tea, bread, feta or kasar cheese, honey and jam, and olives. In the central Anatolian province of Kayseri, *pastirma* (sun-dried beef) might also be served along with fruits and vegetables. Seasonally, garden produce comes to the table in salads of cucumbers, tomatoes, and tons of fruits, particularly cherries, quinces, pears, peaches, apricots, and figs. Thick, sweet Turkish coffee is always available, even though tea is the breakfast beverage of choice.

Throughout the Middle East, flat breads, cheese, and olives are eaten. Often the bread is dipped in a fruity olive oil and then in the zatar spice mix. The Lebanese enjoy sliced onions with this. In Jordan, a peasant breakfast might be a bowl of lentil soup or *humus* (the chickpea and tahini spread) with bread, accompanied by thick coffee.

In Persia fresh bread is bought every morning. Mainly, it is a flat bread. When consumed with butter, fig or quince jam,

and special tea, it is a delicious start. The color and aroma of Persian tea can be made by using half Earl Grey and half Darjeeling. And it is served sweet, with three sugar cubes.

Flat breads reign supreme in Uzbekistan, where nan is served with a sharp creamy cheese and tea in the morning. In Afghanistan giant chapatis are baked first thing and served with tea. Often many branches of the same family will live together in a large enclave and have a cook who stokes the fires predawn to make sure the morning sustenance is properly prepared.

In Northern India rice made with spices is popular for breakfast as are fresh breads such as *puris*, a deep-fried wheat flour bread with a diameter of about four inches. It is served with vegetables cooked in water and oil with a blend of cardamom, turmeric, cloves, coriander, and other spices. Spiced tea is served.

In the southern part of the country small rice cakes called *idils* are served with hot sauce called a *sambal*. Thin griddle cakes are made from fermented rice and lentils and served with curried vegetables, sambals, and chutney. Other items

included may be buttermilk or milk curds, tropical fruits, and *lassi*, a yogurt drink.

AFRICA, MOROCCO, AND EGYPT

Shashouskas, or skillet mixes of vegetables, eggs, and sometimes meats, are popular around the Mediterranean countries. In Tunisia green peppers, tomatoes, onions, shredded meat or corned beef, garlic, and eggs are quickly cooked together over high heat and served piping hot.

In Morocco many special breads are available in the early morning. As I checked into El Minzah Hotel, the conversation with Mahamed El Assili, the chief concierge, quickly advanced my research. He started detailing the richness of local breads, drawing pictures, explaining ingredients. Then everyone, guests and employees alike, got into the act, telling of their mother's, grandmother's, or neighbor's versions. People such as the famous guide, Momo Bouziane, were called in for more details, and it was arranged for me to visit the *souk*, or marketplace. The chefs came out from the kitchen, and the librarian came from the American lega-tion. It was great fun, but it took three hours to check into my room.

Called a black bread, *koubz zrah* is a yeast loaf made of bran and whole wheat flour. The Berbers, the original inhabi-tants of Morocco, eat eggs cooked in olive oil served with dark bread. *Harcha* is a 6-inch round griddle cake made with fine semolina. Another griddle cake is *rghaif,* a huge whole wheat pancake made of stiff dough pulled very thin and folded into layers. Also popular are *sfenj,* or deep-fried dough rings, served hot and sweet-ened with sugar or honey. Sweet butter or a meat fat spread, *khleh,* are traditional.

In Egypt the giant pots of fava beans, *fool,* cook for hours. Households can send out for this, take a dish at a local stand, or make it at home. The soupy beans are enhanced with condiments. Often eggs, in their shells, are cooked directly in the beans and take on a brown color. Falafels made of spiced ground chickpeas are another tasty, hearty breakfast.

The Ethiopians eat a large pancake-like flat bread, *injera,* made of the local grain called *teff. Wat,* a stew made of vegetables and lentils, is quite traditional.

Mealie-meal, a corn meal made into a mush, is popular in many African coun-tries. It is quite thin and often served with cream and sugar in the tonier areas of Johannesburg, although it's usually eaten unadorned in poorer areas. Other por-ridges are made of cassava flour or millet flour. Sweet potatoes mashed with ground chilies make the base for baked eggs on the Ivory Coast. Homemade drinks, such as ginger beer, are quite refreshing and usually highly sweetened.

NORTH AMERICA

The majority of Canadian breakfasts are based on either the English clas-sic or the French Continental. Canada can certainly boast of their supreme breakfast pork product: Canadian bacon, the lean cured pork slice. The maritime provinces, particularly Nova Scotia, lead in using seafood for breakfast. Tra-ditionally, fish cakes were made with mashed potatoes and salt cod, but in Nova Scotia, fish cakes are going upmar-ket with fresh, high-quality seafood such as lobster, shrimp, scallops, and salmon.

The original English breakfast laid the basis for breakfast in the United

States. But as soon as the Revolution ended, our experimentation started. With all the ethnic influences, regional differences, and let's-try-it-all attitude of the American public, today's breakfast scene has exploded into a Disneyesque, bigger-than-life morning opportunity. Cereals, instant breakfast, bagels, muffins, muffin tops, burritos, juices, gourmet coffees and teas, cholesterol-free egg substitutes, Hollandaise and cheese on eggs, turkey sausage—our variations know no bounds. And we still have our traditional eggs, bacon, toast, and coffee. Items that have originated in one region usually migrate around the country with the possible exception of the maligned grits, whose following outside the South is minimal.

CARIBBEAN AND MEXICO

The Caribbean areas again base their food ways on natives and settlers. Many of the English-established countries still have the English breakfast. But more predominant are eggs with hot sauces, sautéed plantains and breadfruit, steamed *callaloo* (similar to spinach), fish, soups, pastries and bread, banana porridge, johnnycakes, teas and coffees. Fresh fruits are also abundant.

Although the Mexicans have a simple sweet roll and coffee with milk or hot chocolate at their crack-of-dawn breakfast, there are no constraints on the second one, which is usually spicy enough to keep one awake for the rest of the day. Soups, eggs with hot salsas, *chilaquiles,* beans, and juices are possibilities. Tortillas or simple rolls are the major bread stuff.

SOUTH AMERICA

Moving down into South America, particularly in the major cities, the European Continental breakfasts are most common with ubiquitous white-bread rolls. Venezuela is an important exception with a much more substantial start for some; others enjoy a deep-fried corn *arepa,* a sort of mild cheese-filled pancake, and a bracing cup of coffee. The Brazilians eat quite lightly, with bread and butter and coffee with milk sustaining them until a big lunch. In São Paulo a special bread is made with cheese baked directly into the roll. Another option is a hot ham and cheese sandwich and a blended fruit juice, with combinations such as orange and banana.

ANTARCTICA

The inhabitants on this icy, desolate spot are mostly scientists conducting experiments. My breakfast information source was a chef on one of the base ships. She said they ate everything for breakfast, from the traditional bacon, eggs, and cereals, with particular cravings for heavy pancakes, to cookies.

For those not planning a scientific expedition to the South Pole, visit the marvelous Antarctica Museum just minutes from the Christchurch Airport in New Zealand. Coffee and tea, scones, and freshly baked morning pastries are served.

Which Has Precedence— the Chicken or the Egg?

THE DIGNIFIED, GRACIOUS KNIGHTSBRIDGE

The English, whose colonization efforts spread breakfast patterns to many corners of the world, claim the ultimate level of morning dining refinements. This august achievement is no better exemplified than by the "Knightsbridge" breakfast, named after the Hyde Park Hotel's fashionable London location.

Despite being in the heart of London, I felt as if I were dining resplendently in the serene countryside. Outside a window copiously framed with flowers and trees, I watched Hyde Park's joggers, bicyclists, and hard-hatted equestrians, whose casual pursuits contrasted markedly with the dignified and gracious feel of the dining room.

Intricate touches like gold leaf-edged wall panels, luminous crystal chandeliers, and soft blue-patterned carpets blend harmoniously with crisp linens and fresh flowers, to create an unequaled ambiance for celebrating the day's first eating adventure.

Massimo Celegato, the food and beverage manager, strives to fill even the most unusual dining whim and to ensure that all modifications receive the utmost attention. Manuo Paz, elegantly dressed in black suit and tie and starched white shirt, oversees the stately service. The pacing of breakfast is reminiscent of the leisurely Edwardian breakfasts (the same period as the hotel's original structure).

Crisp, dry Tattinger champagne in chilled flutes starts the event, to be sipped alone or with fresh orange or grapefruit juices. The hotel's beautifully appointed Continental breakfast table boasts a breathtaking array of fresh fruits, cereals, including muesli, yogurts in silver salvers, and tempting pastries. I opted for an elegantly cut melon, a light lemon sorbet, and fresh raspberries.

Responding to an increase in Asian guests, the chef includes a series of artfully created Japanese rice balls with fresh tuna and prawns and an elegant selection of oriental pickles.

Next comes the pièce de résistance— the delicately smoked ethereal Scottish salmon and perfect scrambled eggs, for which I would row across the Atlantic. More toast, both white and whole wheat, arrived in a silver caddie. Steak lovers can enjoy another variation of the Knightsbridge with the finest beef cooked to one's specification.

The hotel's specially blended coffee in a large pressed coffeemaker is refreshed as needed; however, English breakfast tea is more popular with the British. A silver server of airy croissants, crisp-crusted Italian rolls, and sweet pastries grace the table with fresh butter and a selection of jams.

While few today have the stamina to ingest the prodigious Edwardian quantities, many revere the quality and variety of the current English culinary achievements. And having partaken without reserve, I was well-fueled to undertake rigorous shopping in the Knightsbridge neighborhood. Harvey Nichols is directly across Sloan Street, and Harrod's is only a few blocks away. I found that a stroll in the park was in order before I set out to sample some breakfast comestibles in both department stores' revered food emporiums.

Perfect Hyde Park Scrambled Eggs with Smoked Salmon

*P*ERFECTION *is the only way to describe these scrambled eggs treated with royal dignity. Slices of creamy Scottish smoked salmon are layered generously about a full-sized dinner plate, to create a frame for the scrambled eggs. The eggs, enriched by heavy cream, are gently cooked in a bain marie and served on white toast. The chef often forms the salmon into lovely rosettes and adds four or five freshly sautéed mushrooms.*

SERVES 2

4 eggs

2 tablespoons heavy cream

¼ teaspoon salt

pinch of white pepper

2 teaspoons butter

¼ pound smoked Scottish salmon, sliced thin

2 slices white toast, crust removed

10 small mushrooms, sautéed in butter

In a small bowl, whisk together eggs and cream until completely blended. Whisk in salt and pepper.

In a small skillet heat the butter over medium heat until a water drop sizzles. Add eggs and cook over low heat until set. Do not overcook.

Arrange salmon in overlapping slices around the edges of two serving plates. Place one slice of toast at center of each plate. Cover with scrambled eggs and place five mushrooms at edge of each mound of eggs. Serve immediately.

Note: The egg yolk is high in fat and protein whereas the white is primarily albumin protein. When mixed, they coagulate at about 156°F. The addition of cream increases this temperature. The eggs may also be cooked slowly and held in a double boiler.

New Mexican Green Chile and Cheese Eggs

MOST food writers can only imagine a haven as wonderful as the Hacienda Antigua Bed and Breakfast, Albuquerque, New Mexico. The reverence that Melinda Moffitt and her partner, Anne Dunlap, have for the structural integrity of this house shows in every detail, from the original door jambs to the flooring. Outside, in the once-parched earth, there is now a garden, a paean to the loving control of good agricultural practices over native obstinacy.

Trying to see and do everything in the immediate area in less than three days for the sake of journalistic completeness left scant time for relaxing in this peaceful enclave, and the comfort of the rooms made it difficult to shuffle out of bed early. But the promise of their New Mexican breakfast, after a bath in the deep four-footed tub, was enough to get me moving.

Moffitt finds that this dish holds up well, making it perfect for guests who just aren't ready to get up yet. Serve with fresh fruit and just-heated flour tortillas.

SERVES 6

4 eggs, beaten

¼ cup flour

½ teaspoon baking powder

½ teaspoon dry mustard

1 cup grated Monterey jack cheese

1 cup grated cheddar cheese

1 cup cottage cheese

14 ounces green New Mexican (Hatch) or Anaheim chilies, roasted, peeled, and chopped (substitute chopped, canned green chilies)

In a medium-size bowl, whisk eggs with flour, baking powder, and mustard. Stir in cheeses and chilies. Pour into soufflé dish or 9 × 9-inch glass dish. Bake at 350°F approximately 40 minutes or until set. Cut into squares or wedges.

Mexican Chicken Chilaquiles

*T*HE *solution to leftover tortillas used by many Mexicans is chilaquiles. Like nachos, the ingredients can vary widely, but the texture of this dish is soft and chewy, despite the deep-fried tortilla strips.*

Soft, crumbly, tangy Mexican white cheeses are available in many markets. Mild feta and chevre, while not authentic, make suitable substitutes. The mild flavor of the corn tortillas balance the heat of the serrano chilies—as every chili-head knows, tortillas or a bit of bread, not water, temper that beloved mouth-burning sensation.

Two breakfasts are traditional in Mexico. Desayuno, usually a hard roll with coffee, *is an early morning wakeup, and almuerzo,* the more substantial repast, follows in midmorning. Chilaquiles, *for almuerzo,* might be served with refried or ranchero-style pinto beans, fresh fruits, and extra salsa or hot peppers.

S E R V E S   6

20 corn tortillas (or a 10-ounce bag corn chips)

oil for frying

1 tablespoon vegetable oil

8 serrano chilies, roasted and peeled

1 tomato, peeled and diced

2 cloves garlic, minced

1 cup water

2 chicken breasts, cooked and shredded

1 onion, sliced into thin rings

¾ cup (6 ounces) white Mexican cheese, crumbled

1 cup (8 ounces) sour cream

Cut tortillas into ½-inch strips and quickly deep fry in batches in at least ½ inch of oil until golden brown. Drain well on paper towels and set aside.

In a large frying pan, heat oil over high heat and sauté tomato and garlic until soft, about 3 minutes. Mix in water. Stir in fried tortilla strips. Cook until the liquid is absorbed, approximately 5 minutes. Transfer to large serving dish. Garnish with chicken, onion rings, cheese, and sour cream. Serve warm.

Note: To make a lower-fat version of chilaquiles, corn tortilla strips can be sprayed with vegetable spray and toasted in a 350°F oven for 10 minutes. Cover a nonstick pan with vegetable spray for preparing vegetables. Use a nonfat sour cream.

Huevos Rancheros

EGGS with onion and tomatoes in spicy sauce is a traditional day-starter in Mexico and the Hispanic southwest. Its similarity to Shashuka is amazing. The only major difference is the corn tortilla. Not so surprising is the presence of this same treatment in Egypt, with eggs cooked in Fool Midammis (page 188).

SERVES 3

1 tablespoon vegetable oil

1 medium onion, roughly chopped

2 cloves garlic, minced

2 medium tomatoes, roughly chopped

2 jalapeño peppers, seeded and minced

1 teaspoon salt

1 tablespoon freshly chopped cilantro

6 fried eggs

6 corn flour tortillas, heated

In a medium-size skillet over medium heat bring oil to a high temperature and cook onion, garlic, tomatoes, and peppers until wilted or for about 4 minutes. Stir in salt and cilantro. Place 2 tortillas on each plate. Top each with an egg and cover with sauce. *Olé!*

Shashuka 1

*S*HASHUKA *means "to shake," and that is precisely the action needed to prepare this rapidly prepared skillet dish found in the southern and eastern Mediterranean countries. Ahmed Awdallah, food and beverage director at the Radisson Moriah, Dead Sea, Israel, shared this recipe. It is the perfect return-to-earth meal after a relaxing treatment at the resort's spa.*

After a peaceful morning float high in the salty, mineral-filled Dead Sea, I indulged in a mud bath. The local black mud is mixed, heated (up to two tons per month for the resort), and smeared over the body. As it dries, it draws out impurities before it is rinsed and rubbed off. Another float, this time in the heated indoor mineral pool, followed by a brisker swim in the freshwater outdoor pool, piqued my appetite for this simple and easy-to-prepare one-skillet dish.

SERVES 1

1 teaspoon olive oil

1 small clove garlic, peeled and minced

1 small hot, jalapeño pepper, minced (ribs and seeds removed)

½ cup tomato concasse, from 2 medium tomatoes (see Note)

2 eggs

Fresh parsley

Salt and white pepper

pita bread

Preheat oven to 350°F. In a small oven-proof skillet, heat olive oil over medium heat and sauté garlic and pepper for 2 minutes. Add tomato concasse and heat until warm, about 3 minutes. Crack eggs on top. Place in oven for 5 minutes or until the eggs are baked. Garnish with parsley. Serve with pita bread.

Note: To make concasse, drop tomatoes into boiling water for 1 minute. Then remove, run quickly under cold water, and peel off skins. Cut tomatoes into quarters and remove seeds with a spoon. Finely chop the flesh.

Shashuka 2

THIS is the signature dish at the popular Tel Avivian restaurant, Dr. Shashuka, where three generations of the family, originally from Libya, are serving up fast, inexpensive food. So many short-cuts have been developed to process eaters and turn the tables that the waiter dispenses salt and pepper together with one hand to speed seasoning. The "Dr." in the name is to suggest that this is an expert place for this dish, but true to the healthy implication, I have reduced the normally high fat content.

SERVES 1

1 teaspoon olive oil

1 clove garlic, diced

1 medium tomato, chopped

1 tablespoon green pepper, chopped

2 eggs

Sprinkle paprika

Salt and pepper, to taste

Place olive oil in a small nonstick skillet over high heat. Sauté garlic, tomato, and green pepper for 3 minutes, shaking the pan back and forth to keep the contents in motion. Break eggs on top. Reduce heat to medium. Cook to desired doneness. Sprinkle with paprika and salt and pepper. Serve immediately.

New Orleans Healthful Eggs Sardou

COMMANDER'S PALACE, *New Orleans,* has the finest jazz brunch in the country. It is an experience especially enhanced by sitting in the open courtyard and indulging in Eggs Sardou, poached eggs on creamed spinach and fresh artichoke hearts, anointed with a butter and egg-rich hollandaise sauce. Eggs Sardou was created in 1908 at Antoine's Restaurant when he hosted a meal for Victorien Sardou, the French playwright.

The traditional jazz brunch menu, according to Dick Brennan, the co-owner of Commander's Palace, starts with sherried turtle soup, moves on to Eggs Sardou and roasted quail with a Creole seafood stuffing, and finishes with a whiskey-sauced bread pudding soufflé. De rigueur *beverages include Kir Royale, Absinthe Suissesse, Milk Punch, Gin Fizz, Mimosa, or Mint Julep.*

The major change here is the use of a lower-fat hollandaise sauce. Not as sinful as the restaurant's version, you can now repeat the experience many, many times and still maintain a handle on a healthful lifestyle.

SERVES 4

LOW-FAT HOLLANDAISE SAUCE

1 cup low-fat ricotta

2 egg yolks

2 tablespoons butter

juice of 1 lemon

½ teaspoon salt

cayenne pepper, to taste

EGGS SARDOU

2 pounds fresh spinach, thoroughly cleaned, stems removed (or 2 packages frozen)

1 cup water

1 tablespoon butter

2 scallions, minced

Louisiana hot sauce, salt, black pepper, and cayenne, to taste

8 cooked artichoke bottoms, kept warm

8 poached eggs, kept warm

For Hollandaise: Place ricotta in a small saucepan over medium-low heat, and blend in the two egg yolks. When warm, after about 3 minutes, stir in butter until completely incorporated, about 1 minute. Stir in lemon juice, salt, and cayenne pepper. Reserve 1½ cups for spinach. Keep remainder warm until ready for use.

For Eggs Sardou: In a medium-size pan, add spinach and water. Cover and steam until the spinach is just beginning to wilt, about 4 minutes. Drain completely in a colander, pushing out any excess water with the back of a large spoon.

In a large skillet melt butter and sauté scallions over medium-high heat for 2 minutes. Stir in spinach with ½ cup hollandaise, and add salt, black pepper, hot sauce, and cayenne to taste. On each of four warmed plates, place one-fourth of the spinach mixture. Top with 2 artichoke bottoms, and place a poached egg on each artichoke. Place 2 tablespoons of hollandaise sauce on each egg. Serve immediately.

25

Shirred Eggs with Roasted Peppers, Asparagus, and Parmesan Cream

DEREK DAVIS, the chef and proprietor of Sonoma Restaurant in Manayunk, Pennsylvania, knows that his patrons in this trendy Philadelphia suburb desire dishes way out of the ordinary. And he always delivers. Locals flock here to sample Davis's creative works.

Manayunk is one of the oldest neighborhoods in the country, and Main Street there now boasts upscale and unique shops, galleries, and fine restaurants. And after Sunday brunch, a stroll offers the chance to work off a few calories and will probably be rewarded with an unusual find.

Fresh vegetables and garlic sautéed in olive oil are the base for baked eggs that are richly topped with reduced cream and assertive Italian cheeses. The peppers can be roasted and the asparagus sautéed the night before. Just before the brunch the cream is reduced and the individual dishes assembled and baked.

SERVES 6

2 large red bell peppers

12 eggs

1 pound asparagus

2 cloves garlic, finely chopped

3 tablespoons extra-virgin olive oil

1 cup heavy cream

salt and pepper to taste

½ cup grated Reggiano-Parmigiano

2 teaspoons chopped parsley

Roast peppers under broiler until charred. Let rest in a plastic bag for 10 minutes. Peel off charred skin. Remove seeds and julienne. Break off tough ends of the asparagus and slice into 2-inch pieces.

Sauté asparagus and garlic in olive oil over medium-high heat in a 6-inch skillet until *al dente* (chewy) or for 3 minutes. Add peppers and stir until heated, about 2 minutes.

Butter 6 individual 6-ounce baking dishes. Divide vegetables among dishes.

Add cream to skillet and simmer until reduced by half. Meanwhile, crack two eggs on top of the vegetables in each dish. Season with salt and pepper and bake in 450°F oven for about 6 to 8 minutes or until eggs are close to desired doneness. Add cheese to reduced cream and spoon over eggs. Top with parsley.

Note: If the vegetables are prepared the night before, they should be either brought to room temperature or heated slightly in a microwave to maintain the same cooking time for the shirred eggs.

California Coddled Eggs with Wine, Cheese, and Dill

CODDLED eggs are the most pampered. Special porcelain cups with metal screw tops are filled and gently cooked in a water bath where every bit of flavor essence and heat stays inside until you open it. This egg has a bit of white wine, fresh dill, and sharp cheddar cheese to enhance the delicate cooking method. Serve with a demitasse spoon for a gracious breakfast.

SERVES 4

4 eggs

4 teaspoons white wine

4 teaspoons grated sharp cheddar

1 teaspoon finely chopped fresh dill

Spray the inside of each of 4 egg coddlers with nonstick spray. Fill a saucepan that will hold the coddlers with 6 inches of water. Bring to a boil. Break 1 egg into each cup. Divide wine, cheese, and dill between the 4 coddlers. Screw on tops and place into water bath. Cook for 12 to 15 minutes.

Greek Tomato and Feta Scrambled Eggs

GREEKS *in the United States have made incredible contributions to the restaurant trade. Paula and Mike Kokolis, proprietors of the Gazebo in Williamsburg, Virginia, have always tried to keep prices moderate and quality exceptionally high while feeding locals and tourists alike. Specializing in breakfast, they offer this incredible dish that transforms ordinary scrambled eggs into a creamy, colorful, and tangy dish with a definite Greek edge. The Gazebo serves this with the perfect accompaniments—a Southern biscuit (page 124) and grits.*

SERVES 2

4 eggs, beaten

1 teaspoon butter

1 tomato, chopped

2 ounces feta cheese, crumbled

1 teaspoon chopped, fresh oregano (optional)

freshly ground pepper to taste

Beat eggs. Melt butter in a medium skillet over medium heat and pour in eggs. When partially set, add tomato, feta, and oregano. Stir until set. Season with pepper.

Note: Try garlic and herb-flavored feta and omit all other seasonings.

Letter to Elaine on Fat Points and Rich Lifestyle

Dear Elaine,

My uniformed limo driver holding a sign with my name whisked me away from the Miami Airport to a different world—a world where someone else does your worrying.

I checked into my marble villa and entered the foyer into the sumptuous living room. In addition to elegant furnishings were a washed-white entertainment center, fresh flowers, soft music, and tasteful rug all in soft cool colors. A wall of windows led to the patio, beckoning toward the famous Doral golf courses. The king-size bedroom with sitting area, another entertainment center, and patio had a similarly peaceful outdoor view.

But what really knocked my socks off were the bathrooms and dressing areas. Try to imagine this. Through more double doors were two dressing areas each the size of my office, complete with large closets (with satin-padded hangers), mirrors enough for Narcissus, and two sinks on either side, loaded with amenities. I was particularly delighted to see suntan lotion included. One could not linger here too long as directly ahead the sunken Jacuzzi beckoned.

In the dining room with Kathy Casper, the public relations director, we were serenaded by a concert grand piano that anchored a three-story domed ceiling to earth. During the day, one can muse while clouds pass over this ethereal octagonal skylight surrounded by soft frescos in the style of Botticelli.

Back to the dining experience. On each table are little golf pencils and note cards for your record of your selections. The extensive and intriguing menu offers various-size portions, noting calorie counts and fat grams. A daily total is suggested by the staff nutritionist to fit into your eating goals. And naturally, attached to each menu for your convenience, is a calculator.

The meal was superb. I enjoyed a $1/4$-inch thick swordfish steak blackened (no fat, no salt, but lots of spicy herbs) and the spa's grapefruit Caesar salad.

Day 2:

"May the world hug you today with its warmth and love and whisper a joyful tune in your heart," read my morning pillow card.

"And keep me motivated with the fat point system," I thought.

Dieting at the Doral, reduced to the basics of fat grams, is a snap to follow. The midrange plan with 1,300 daily calories suggests a total of 29 fat grams per day. For breakfast that is 300 calories or 6 grams of fat.

Promptly at seven I joined twenty of the guests (mostly dressed in gray cotton shorts or warm-ups with matching shirts supplied fresh daily as part of the spa experience) for the prebreakfast walk around the grounds. Stretching and spraying for mosquitoes preceded our well-paced four miles.

Then to the dining room. The executive chef, Ron Hook, emerged from the kitchen to welcome me. "There are so many things to eat, there is no excuse not to find something healthy that is delicious," he said while standing next to the gorgeous table of fresh fruits with baskets of freshly baked spa muffins, healthful cereals, and low-fat yogurt. (There is a full menu of cooked items as well.) "You are not giving up anything, you are making intelligent choices."

Hook's goal at the spa is to show guests both fine dining and a healthful experience. The food is lighter, springing with nutritional content. "The food needs to be satisfying," Hook continued. "Anyone would prefer to have a small amount of the real product. I like to use a small quantity of a full-flavored cheese such as Gouda or Edam—$^1/_4$ ounce has only 4 fat grams. You can get enthusiastic about less, as long as it is real."

Egg white omelets can be enjoyed plain or filled with spinach, mushroom, tomato, onion, bell pepper, or cheese. One whole egg cooked any style (except fried) has 70 calories and 5 fat grams.

The menu providing tempting choices includes both calories and fat points, to be totaled with the attached calculator. If you need more help or encouragement, the nutritionist visits guests in the dining room, answering questions and supplying healthful eating information.

Returning to the outside fat world is really not a big deal after attending Chef Hook's cooking classes with easy-to-follow procedures, great ideas for substitutions, and his book, The Saturnia Collection ($25 from the Doral, 8755 NW 36th Street, Miami, FL 33178; or 800-331-7768 and 800-247-8901 inside Florida). Supermarket tours to help one make wise shopping choices can be included in the spa visit.

At the end of the interview, it was time for my full-body massage with Kathy—a women who is a knotted muscle's worst enemy. After fifty minutes I was released from her clutches and went to degrease in the shower. Then I visited the ladies' spa area with sauna, steam, and 50°F plunge pool. I was feeling very refreshed.

The number of exercise events was fabulous—water aerobics with lots of water toys in the indoor pool, bench, sculpturing, and self-inflicted events in the well-stocked exercise equipment room. Between events one is encouraged to consume vast quantities of liquids with the special house drinks being lemon water (tart without sugar) or raspberry tea (weak and very bitter).

On the luxury beauty side there are more facials, herbal body wraps, fangos, muds, cellulite treatments, scrubs, and hair and skin procedures than I even knew existed. One does, however, pay royally for the privilege.

Throwing all my stuff in my bag, I was off in the white stretch limo to the airport. So that is how the rich live. I'd like to do it again.

Much Healthier,
Martha

The Spa at Doral Frittata

*L*IVING *in the opulence of Miami's Spa at Doral guarantees the healthiest breakfasts. After an invigorating 4-mile walk and before a fun-filled water aerobics class, this frittata is destined to change eating habits. Its nutritional profile is a winner, with only 83 calories, 2 grams of fat, 248 milligrams of sodium, 48 milligrams of cholesterol and 1 gram of fiber per serving.*

SERVES 4

1 egg, medium

4 egg whites, medium

¼ teaspoon salt

pinch ground black pepper

½ cup (4 ounces) low-fat cottage cheese

1 cup (3 ounces) mushrooms, finely sliced

1 ½ teaspoons fresh thyme, minced

3 scallions, trimmed, ½-inch pieces

2 small zucchini, sliced into thin strips

1 sweet red pepper, seeded and sliced into thin strips

1 ½ tablespoons fresh lemon juice

1 tablespoon grated Parmesan cheese

In a medium-size bowl whisk egg, egg whites, salt, pepper, and cottage cheese. Coat an ovenproof skillet with vegetable spray. Sauté mushrooms, thyme, and scallions for 5 minutes. Add zucchini, red pepper, and lemon juice to mushrooms and cook until vegetables are tender and all liquid has evaporated, about 5 minutes. Remove skillet from heat.

Stir the Parmesan into the vegetable mixture. Press the vegetables into an even layer. Pour in the egg mixture. Cook over medium heat for one minute. Place skillet under the broiler and cook until the frittata browns evenly, about 3 minutes. Remove from oven.

Slide a rubber spatula around the underside of the frittata to be sure that it does not stick to the pan. Slide onto a warm serving plate. Cut into quarters. Serve immediately.

Malaysian Nasi Lemak: Fragrant Coconut-Infused Rice with Condiments

NASI LEMAK—*a coconut milk-infused rice with condiments of spicy chicken, anchovies, peanuts, cucumber, and hard-cooked eggs with a searing sambal of prawns, is Malaysia's most popular break-fast dish, eaten in the traditional Malaysian style—with the fingers.*

A serving consists of about one cup of rice surrounded by a small portion of meat (beef or chicken) or fish, with condiments and a hot spicy sambal. Street vendors often favor wrapping everything in nature's per-fect carry-out container, the banana leaf. Other restaurants serve the rice in banana leaves with side condiments family style. On the buffet table, a chafing dish of rice is sur-rounded by numerous dishes of condiments, letting everyone select their favorites.

Dabbling with the numerous hot chili pepper (often bird's eye chili) sambals revs up the morning engines faster than caf-feine. And hot foods help erase awareness of the hot climate.

While the recipe looks daunting, all parts except the rice can be made ahead.

SERVES 8

33

RICE

2 cups long-grain white rice
(Thai Jasmine recommended)

2 cups coconut milk

2 cups water

1 pandan or screw pine leaf, optional
(no substitutes)

2 teaspoons salt

CHICKEN RENDANG

8 chicken thighs, skin removed

2 shallots, peeled

2 garlic cloves, peeled

1 tablespoon ginger, peeled

2 teaspoons coriander seed

2 teaspoons fennel seed

2 teaspoons cumin seed

2 tablespoons dry red chili, medium grind

2 teaspoons curry powder

2 teaspoons turmeric, ground

2 tablespoons vegetable oil

2 teaspoons tamarind paste dissolved
 in ½ cup boiling water

4-inch piece lemon grass, bottom
 portion, sliced vertically and crushed

3 cups fresh coconut milk
 (or 14-ounce can coconut milk
 mixed with 10 ounces water)

1 teaspoon salt

SPICY PRAWN SAMBAL

1 teaspoon dried shrimp paste (belachan)

20 small, hot red chilies, topped but not
 seeded

1 tablespoon sugar

1 clove garlic, peeled

juice of 1 lime

CONDIMENTS

8 dried anchovies, heads removed,
 dry sautéed for 3 minutes

8 ounces large raw peanuts, shelled,
 dry sautéed until just browned

1 cucumber, peeled and sliced

2 eggs, hard-boiled, peeled, and
 quartered

For Rice: Wash rice and strain. Put rice, coconut milk, water, pandan leaf, and salt into rice cooker or heavy saucepan. Cover and cook over low heat for 20 minutes or until the grains have absorbed all liquid and are soft.

For Chicken Rendang: Place shallots, garlic, ginger, and seeds into small grinder. Pulse until just blended. In a large pan or wok, sauté blended and remaining ground spices in vegetable oil for about 2 minutes until fragrant aromas are released. Dissolve tamarind paste and strain. Add tamarind liquid, lemon grass, and coconut milk to seasonings. Mix. Add chicken and simmer for about 45 minutes or until chicken is tender and sauce is thick.

For Spicy Prawn Sambal: Break off piece of shrimp paste. Hold with tongs and roast several minutes over flame. Briefly pulse shrimp paste, chilies, sugar, and garlic in food processor until a coarse paste develops. Sauté for 3 minutes. Remove from heat and add lime juice. Cool.

To Assemble: Divide rice on 8 plates and serve with anchovies, peanuts, cucumber, eggs, chicken rendang, and spicy prawn sambal.

Notes:

- Coconut milk thickens while adding richness to dishes. Coconut milk is the liquid squeezed from the flesh of the coconut rather than the liquid of the coconut. For convenience try the unsweetened canned coconut milk available in many supermarkets. The first squeezing, called the rich milk, is used for intense flavoring. To make coconut milk from fresh coconut, place husked pieces of one medium-size coconut in food processor with 2¼ cups of water. Process for 2 minutes or until water turns white. Strain through fine sieve. (Throw away gratings.) One coconut yields about 2 cups of coconut milk. Store in refrigerator for no longer than 2 days.

- Tamarind juice adds a touch of astringency to further excite taste buds. Paste extracted from tamarind seed pods is sold in dark blocks. Reconstitute juice by soaking 1 ounce of paste in 1 cup boiling water for several hours. With fingers work paste until water is brown and thick. Strain and discard seeds.

- Belachan, a shrimp paste, predominately used as a flavoring base, smells like a rock at low tide. Many Malaysian chefs hold belachan (typically referred to as "Malaysian Cheese") to be one of their unique flavorings. Sun-dried local prawns are pounded into a paste and formed into blocks or circles. This keeps almost indefinitely under refrigeration. The desired quantity is broken off and roasted over a flame for several minutes before its incorporation. Belachan is also available in Oriental markets.

- Prepared hot chili paste, such as Indonesian sambal ulek, available in Oriental markets, can be substituted for fresh chilies.

This recipe was adapted from the Ramada Renaissance, Melacca, Malaysia.

The Chinese spice traders who settled in Melacca, Malaysia, took Malay wives, called *Baba Nonyas*. A special Malaysian Chinese culture intermingled the Malay language, dress, and customs with Chinese spirit and religions.

In Melacca many Baba Nonya families inhabited Jalan Tun Tan Cheng Lock, the street called millionaire's row. There, in 1896, the spice trader dynasty builder Mr. Cheng Siew Chan purchased three adjacent row houses, none wider than 15 feet, but each 180 feet long. Narrow houses made economic sense since the Dutch colonialist government assessed taxes by the facade's width.

The wealthy Chan family lived an extravagant life of luxury until the Japanese occupation during World War II. They fled, seeking safety at their rubber and palm oil plantations and leaving their home unlocked and guarded only with newspapers to shroud their priceless antique furnishings and art. In 1985 the house was converted to the private Baba Nonya Heritage Museum. It provides rare insight into the culture, dress, and dining habits of these fascinating people. Several Baba Nonya restaurants and bed and breakfast houses, complete with their own antique shops, are in the area. Still following traditions, all chefs are female.

Turkey Sausage

*I*SLAMIC *dietary laws permit no pork. Tasty breakfast sausage served in Malaysia are often cleverly made of spiced ground turkey meat. Many restaurants observe Hala, the special Muslim dietary rules. Vary the spices and generously use fresh herbs when available. Grinding meat at home permits control of the amount of fat and the ratio of dark to light meat. Before grinding and forming have meat well chilled and handle it gently so the fibers don't break down and the sausage doesn't become mushy.*

In Malaysian hotels one can check the ceiling for the arrow or Ketupaik pointing to the prayer direction. The early morning prayers are before breakfast.

MAKES 12

1 pound lean ground turkey

½ teaspoon dried thyme, crushed

½ teaspoon dried oregano, crushed

½ teaspoon salt

½ to 1 teaspoon black pepper

⅛ teaspoon cayenne pepper
  (or vary to taste)

Place all ingredients in a bowl. Mix lightly with a fork. Form into 12 patties about ¼ inch thick. Treat a large nonstick skillet lightly with cooking spray. Over medium heat cook sausage until it begins to brown or for 4 minutes. Turn over. Reduce heat and cook until completely done with no pinkness in the center or for about 4 more minutes.

Note: Turkey products must always be thoroughly cooked before eating, so cook a small piece for tasting if you desire to check the seasonings.

La Palombe, the Gascone Pigeon Hunt

In the southwestern corner of France, the autumn months of September and October bring out the famed hunt of pigeons, La Palombe. Often one goes into a small town only to find that the butcher, the baker, and others are mysteriously "ill." The illness, naturally, is the excuse for escaping into the countryside for the ancient netting of the pigeons. When the signal is given, the nets are dropped, the birds fly off, and maybe one is actually caught. One month's catch may only be ten or twelve pigeons. The techniques are not really effective.

Farther south closer to the Pyrenese, a stick is thrown that makes the sound of the palombe's enemy, the autor. Often this scares the pigeons into the hunter's direction and the bird is caught. Other hunters use guns, but still the catch is low. No problem, this tradition is more about a process than about getting birds.

At the Chateau de Lasalle Hotel, Jacqueline and Jean-Pierre Laurens provide a hunt breakfast—a serious feast supplying energy for those long hours of waiting, scheming, bonding with other males, and a general getaway from everyday life. Along with coffee, teas, and chocolate, freshly baked baguettes from the local bakery are served. Chicken Paté Gascon (page 39), rilletes, fried eggs au plat, and fried ham are also served. Even a small glass of local wine is taken as a send-off.

Chicken Paté Gascon

*K*ATE RATLIFFE, *owner and captain of the luxury canal barge,* Julia Hoyt, *obtained this recipe from her adopted French family's father, Claude Pomele. For her four-passenger cruises down the Garrone River through the rolling country-side of Gascony, she keeps this recipe on hand as a tasty, regional appetizer. This recipe is adapted from her book,* A Culinary Journey in Gascony: Recipes and Stories from My French Canal Boat *(Berkeley: Ten Speed Press, 1995). Ratliffe also operates a cooking school of Gascon regional cuisine from her ancient farmhouse on the river.*

SERVES 8

2 pounds ground chicken

½ pound bulk pork sausage

1 small onion, minced

1 shallot, minced

1 egg

2 tablespoons armagnac (or brandy)

⅛ teaspoon nutmeg

1 ½ teaspoons salt

1 teaspoon freshly ground black pepper

Mix all ingredients. Place in a large loaf pan. Cover with aluminum foil. Place in a larger pan of hot water. Bake at 375°F for 1½ hours.

Note: A speedy way to make this is to chop the onion and shallot, using the pulse control of a food processor, then add the rest of the ingredients and slightly mix.

Swimmers and Hoofers

JAMAICAN BREAKFAST, HOT AS THE MIDDAY SUN

"Mon, it is time for breakfast." The sun peers over the Jamaican Blue Mountains to start reigning over pristine beaches. Jamaican breakfast can get as hot as the midday sun in Montego Bay.

Salt cod and ackee, the national dish, matches local produce with fish introduced centuries earlier by European explorers. As the price of fish increased, the quantity used in the dish declined. Onions, tomatoes, and seasonings such as the local thyme add complex flavors. Spicy heat comes from the innocent-looking scotch bonnet peppers (*habañeros*), one of the hottest peppers known to mankind.

Bright yellow ackee pods, the size of a child's thumb, are often visually mistaken as scrambled eggs. This fruit, growing on trees and treated like a vegetable, can be poisonous if eaten before fully ripe. The red fibers adjacent to the seeds must be removed.

The executive sous chef at the Grand Lido in Negril, Jan Carmichael, originally from Canada, says "Ackee is as important to Jamaicans as rice is to Orientals." When lightly boiled, it is silky and picks up flavors of other ingredients.

Callaloo, resembling spinach, is a labor-intensive vegetable, requiring careful peeling of the stringy stalks. It is boiled then seasoned with—yes—more hot peppers.

Roger Wells, executive chef at the Half Moon Bay in Ocho Rios, serves a special

Jamaican dish every morning. His smoked, paper-thin marlin with fresh lobster alone is worth the trip to Jamaica. It is served with roasted breadfruit, avocado slices, and ackee.

Breadfruit, introduced to the island by the infamous Captain Bligh of the H.M.S. *Bounty,* hangs like lanterns from the *Artocarpus Communis* tree. Roasted over the fire or in the oven until yielding to a slight pressure of the thumb, it is peeled, revealing its pale yellow color, then served in large slices. The bland taste perfectly cools the spicy heat.

Jean Paul Lucy, former executive chef at San Souci in Ocho Rios, says there are three steps to Jamaican breakfasts "Eat, eat, eat!" On the spa's elegant patio overlooking a green lawn leading to the beach, he serves "Run Down." Coconut milk is cooked down to a custard in which pickled mackerel is simmered with chopped onions, tomatoes, more habañeros and green bananas. A more extravagant version can be created with lobster rather than with fish. He also makes an irresistible green banana porridge (page 159), made with milk, sugar, cream, and allspice.

There is enough variety in Jamaican breakfasts to have a different one every day for at least a month. Such entrees include calves liver cut in small strips and sautéed with kidneys, bacon, and ackee, and steamed fresh snapper. Skinny green boiled bananas, not yet sweet, but starchy and yummy, often appear on the plates. In the sweets department, fried or sautéed bananas reign supreme.

The favored drink for tourist is the dark, well-balanced Jamaican Blue Mountain coffee. Milk is offered to cut its strength, but espresso drinkers may prefer it straight. Due to its near-cult status among the Japanese, it has become one of the most expensive coffees, often ranging from thirty-five to fifty dollars per pound in the United States. We found one of the premier brands, Mavis Estate Coffee Roasted Beans, in an Ocho Rios supermarket for sixteen dollars per pound. Locals opt for the more affordable and gently flavored teas such as ceressaie or mint.

Jamaican Escoveitch Snapper

*T*HE Jamaican breakfast "holds a great deal of steam and can literally keep you filled all day," said Suzanne Levy, general manager of the Trident Villas and Hotel in Port Antonio, Jamaica. Levy has been savoring the cuisine at her family's hotel kitchen since it opened twenty-five years ago. The chef delights guests with breakfast entrees such as salt cod and ackee (Jamaica's national dish) or steamed fresh snapper in spicy Jamaican sauce. The generously endowed plates might keep company with boiled green bananas, roasted breadfruit, fried plantains, callaloo (cousin to spinach), and johnnycakes. Fresh fruits such as melons, papaya, bananas, pineapple, and oranges add sweetness to the morning fare.

My Trident Villas' patio stopped at the edge of huge rocks perfectly arranged by nature to create tremendous sprays and splashes by the pounding ocean surf. At the crack of dawn, eerie, blood-curdling screeching drowned the soporific sounds. Peeking through the bedroom window, I could make out large birds with long dragging feathers. Later, the peacocks strutted regally to my patio, expecting to share my breakfast. Their presence, although enjoyed, was as uninvited as their morning's cacophony. But since the kitchen had supplied enough food for my whole day, I had plenty to share.

SERVES 6

2 pounds snapper fillets

2 tablespoons flour

½ teaspoon salt

½ teaspoon black pepper

1 clove garlic

2 tablespoons vegetable oil

1 green pepper, julienned

1 habañero (scotch bonnet pepper), deseeded and deveined, minced

2 medium onions, sliced

2 scallions, sliced

2 carrots, julienned

1 cho cho (chayote squash), julienned

1 cup red wine vinegar

1 teaspoon allspice berries

2 sprigs thyme

Dredge fillets in flour, salt, and pepper. In large pan sauté garlic in oil. When soft and fragrant remove garlic. Add peppers, onions, scallions, carrots, cho cho, all-spice, and thyme and cook in vinegar until onions are soft or for about 8 to 10 minutes. Keep carrots crisp. Remove vegetables and keep warm.

Panfry fish over medium-high heat until it turns opaque, about 3 minutes on each side. Remove fish from pan and serve with the vegetables.

Notes: This recipe was inspired by Jamaican native chef Xavier Morgan at the Trident.

Allspice berries (called pimento), native to Jamaica, are picked unripe to preserve aroma, then dried for about ten days. Their exotic blend, often compared with a combination of cinnamon, nutmeg, and clove, provides the zing to the fresh fish and julienned vegetables in the Escoveitch snapper.

Black Pepper Plantation in the Jungles of Borneo

Each family of the Iban tribe, living communally in one long stilted house, cooks for themselves outside on the raised patio portion. Inside, the family has one large private room and an open area leading to the indoor communal area. Walking through any of the family's area without proper greetings is considered bad manners.

If a single man visits the family, tradition dictates that the father provides his eldest unmarried daughter for the visitor's pleasure during the night. There is no similar agreement for a visiting female—women typically do not travel. For that evening, the family sleeps in the open area, allowing the visitor and daughter the privacy of the inner room. The visitor will then be invited to breakfast.

The Ibans, who grow the prized Sarawak peppercorns, do not use any in their own cooking. Because pepper is their only cash crop, all is carried by longboats up the river for sale.

My arduous journey deep into the jungles of North Borneo in search of the piper nigrum (pepper) farms of the indigenous Ibans started with a five-hour bus trip on rough roads from Kuching, Sarawak.

Then we boarded a hand-crafted hollowed-out wooden longboat with a twenty-five-horsepower outboard motor for the several-hour trip down the river. Our progress was slowed due to a mass of logs jamming a bend. The guides, seasoned hands at this, reverted to the traditional paddles for pushing away the logs. The pace was perfect for snapping pictures of the small pepper plots growing majestically where the water lapped gently at the gradually inclining hills.

The excessive heat and humidity is the ideal climate for growing black pepper plants on the side of the river. The vinelike plants mature after three to four years and will continue to produce berries for fifteen years. A small farm has about three thousand vines trained up on poles about twelve feet tall. Yellow flowers precede the berries, which are hand-picked while still green. After being soaked in water and dried, these will be sold as white pepper. If left to mature to a reddish yellow, they are sold as black pepper. The berries are dried in the hot sun for three days, packed in burlap sacks, and paddled down the river in a longboat. They are be sent to a center for grading and export and ignominiously blended by industrial giants such as McCormick. Pepper containers rarely reveal their sources—whether from India, Indonesia, Malaysia, or Brazil.

"This is a negative-five-star facility," joked our guide, Michael Tay, warning us against false illusions of grandeur. But the facilities were quite acceptable. Each guest had a cubicle large enough for two single-bed mattresses on a raised platform, separated from their neighbors with thin wooden walls and from the hall with a flowered cloth drape. Excellent screening kept out the mosquitoes (which we appreciated since this was malaria country and even those taking Lariam wanted additional protection). The evening turned pleasantly cooler after the sunset.

Our dining and meeting facility was a covered pavilion with tables and chairs surrounded by wooden railings. Curious tribal members watched the strange white folks— the first group they had seen. The children, unabashed in their curiosity, stood for hours studying our mannerisms.

We were invited to the Batang Ai Longhouse where the chief, attired in feathered headdress, ceremonial vest, and Western clip-on necktie in basic black, warmly greeted us. As honored guests, we all shook hands with each member of the forty-one families—about 230 in all—and then sat for potent hits of rice wine.

Devoid of verbal communication, we resorted to other measures. One of our group started the sounds "Woo!" and "Wow!" and other grunts, which the Ibans repeated with glee and smiles all around. The men sat directly across from us, flanked by women and children. They stared at us. We stared at them.

A few shrunken heads hung from the wall, but that practice, a warrior's passage to manhood, was banned in 1886 by ruler Charles Brooks. Now the rites of passage are undertaken by obtaining some other valuable item— such as a radio.

More booze, more grunts, more communication, more smiles. Then the dancing began. They danced. We danced. We danced together. They drummed and played music. We sang the only song we all knew, "Happy Birthday," and danced the bunny hop. We all felt the warmth of our fellow human beings.

Borneo Longhouse Steamed River Fish in Rice Wine

FOR breakfast, freshly netted anchovy-size river fish were steamed whole in the potent rice brew, the same booze we celebrated with the previous night. No ceremony here. One just puts his or her hands right in the dish, eats the whole fish, and spits out any bones that may be too large to swallow.

SERVES 6

1 cup rice wine (or water for a plainer version)

30 small river fish, or contents of the morning's net

In a large earthenware pot (in Borneo, this was cooked over an outside cooking fire on the woven grass patio of the longhouse), bring rice brew to a boil. Add whole fish. Steam for about 3 minutes or until the flesh just begins to soften. Serve in the same pot after cooling the liquid enough to be comfortable for the hands.

Pan-Seared Mahimahi with Herb and Fruit Sauce

*T*HE Ka'anapali Beach Hotel, just north of the Lahaina Harbor in Maui, exercises a powerful commitment to sharing the native Hawaiian culture with guests. An ongoing employee training program is in place with food being an integral part. This recipe is adapted from one created by the hotel's chef, Joseph Balinbin. It is part of the native Hawaiian Wai'anae diet program. While he served this as a luncheon entree with poi, sweet potato, stewed luau (taro) leaves and an ogo (seaweed) salad, it makes a delightful breakfast.

SERVES 4

1 pound mahimahi fillets

½ teaspoon minced garlic

½ teaspoon minced ginger

1 teaspoon chopped parsley

1 teaspoon chopped mint

1 tomato, medium

1 medium Maui onion, diced
   (or substitute any mild, sweet onion)

½ teaspoon lemon juice

juice of 1 orange

Preheat oven to 375°F. Heat a large oven-proof skillet and spray with vegetable spray. Sear fish on medium-high heat until lightly browned on each side. Mix together all remaining ingredients in a medium-size bowl and spoon over fish in skillet. Cover with aluminum foil and bake for 30 minutes. Serve on warm plates, spooning herb and fruit mixture over fish.

Note: Serve this with the Taro Garden Patties (page 182) made without the corned beef.

Potlatch Salmon Hash with Smoked Fresh Tomato Sauce

SKAMANIA LODGE in Stevenson, Washington, seated on the spectacular Columbia River Gorge, is just a few miles from the salmon hatchery. The eggs are hatched and the fish released to swim downstream. Many will reappear planked on alder wood in the lodge's ovens. While much of the fish is intentionally cooked for the morning, this hash is the perfect way to use any leftovers. The flaked fish crowns browned potatoes enlivened with colorful pieces of red, green, and yellow peppers. Two healthy dollops of the awesome smoked fresh tomato sauce elevate this to a splendor of nature closely matching that of the Columbia River Gorge.

Tomatoes can be smoked in a smoker or on a rack in a covered pan with wood chips underneath. Don't use one of your best pans because the bottom may be somewhat scorched during the process. This dish is perfect for an outdoor gas or propane grill with a side burner. If prepared indoors, don't be surprised if your smoke detector goes off.

The effort, however, is well worth it because the tomato flavor is totally new. Select the ripest, red tomatoes. Depending on the season, romas may be superior to the round salad ones. After smoking the tomatoes, you can easily chunk them in a food processor and punch up the sauce with a bit of fresh lemon juice and oregano.

SERVES 4

SALMON HASH

½ pound cooked fresh salmon, roughly flaked

2 large potatoes, grated

1 onion, sliced

1 tablespoon oil

2 tablespoons each, chopped, green, red, and yellow sweet peppers

SMOKED FRESH TOMATO SAUCE

4 large tomatoes or 12 roma tomatoes

2 teaspoons fresh lemon juice

2 sprigs fresh oregano

To Smoke Tomatoes: Place a handful of wood chips (alder, hickory, or mesquite suggested) in the bottom of a pan fitted with a rack. Place tomatoes on rack. Cover with lid or foil. Place over low heat for 10 minutes. Chunk tomatoes in food processor. Add lemon juice and oregano and pulse several more times.

To Make Hash: In a large skillet over medium-high temperature cook onion in oil until it begins to soften, about 3 minutes. Add potatoes. Cook for about 10 minutes, flipping occasionally. Add peppers and continue to cook for 2 more minutes. Place salmon on top and heat for 1 minute. Divide into 4 servings and remove to plates. Serve with large dollops of the tomato sauce on the side of the plate.

British Isles Grilled Kippers

"KIPPERS," *or kippered herring, is a popular breakfast dish in the northern areas of the United Kingdom. The split fish are salt-cured, then dried and cold-smoked. The result is a very salty, mild fish treat, the perfect companion to scrambled eggs and toast.*

SERVES 4

4 kippers

On a broiling pan arrange kippers skin side up. Cook under high heat until skin begins to crisp, blister, and come away from the flesh at the edges or for about 5 minutes. Do not turn.

Note: To fry kippers, place skin-side-down in heated skillet with a tablespoon of oil. Cook over medium heat for 2 to 3 minutes, then turn and fry other side for 2 to 3 minutes.

Simpson's in-the-Strand

Even though this grand restaurant opened in 1828, as a place where fine gentlemen smoked imported cigars, drank coffee, read papers, played chess, and discussed politics, Simpson's delayed opening for breakfast until 1994. Their "Great British Breakfast," with sausage, egg, streaky bacon, black pudding, porridge, stewed fruit, mushrooms, and tomatoes might be considered heavy, but the "Ten Deadly Sins" breakfast is only for the very brave. Included are sausage, fried egg, bacon, black pudding, lamb's kidneys and livers, fried bread, bubble and squeak (a cabbage and potato hash), and baked beans, along with juices, coffee and tea, toast, pastries, cereals, porridge, and stewed fruit.

Brian Clive, the manager, has made sure that all the classics are represented, including poached haddock, kippers, grilled sole, salmon kedgeree, grilled sirloin steak, and Welsh rarebit. With the elegant high ceilings, crystal chandeliers, dark paneling and tasteful paintings, there could scarcely be a more classic place in which to indulge in the classic English breakfast.

The British have always been known to enjoy a bit of humor with breakfast, so Clive has added quite an eye-opener to the menu. It is the pig's nose, an actual pair of nostrils stewed and resting on a white cream onion sauce sprinkled with parsley. Cutting into this fatty if novel part of the pig brings to mind the truth of the old saying "tough as pig's nose." Cheerio!

Fresh Nova Scotia Maritime Fish Cakes

NOVA SCOTIA, Canada, is a seafood lover's paradise. The abundance of fin and shell fish is almost mind-boggling, particularly the lobsters, scallops, and salmon. At the Holiday Inn Halifax Centre, fish cakes are often served. The chefs take advantage of their bountiful seafood and incorporate virtually any seafood. For a crowd, the cakes can be made in advance and sautéed in butter before serving. These fresh cakes are as unlike the traditional potato and salt cod cake of Nova Scotia as fresh pasta is unlike canned spaghetti.

SERVES 6

1 pound boiling potatoes, peeled,
    cut into eighths

1 small onion, chopped

1 tablespoon oil

4 ounces fin or shell fish (e.g., salmon,
    mussels, scallops, baby shrimp,
    haddock, lobster meat)

1 egg, beaten

salt and pepper, to taste

1 tablespoon butter

red and green peppers, minced for garnish

Boil potatoes until soft. Drain and mash to a lumpy consistency using a hand masher.

Sauté onion in oil until soft. Add seafood to onion and sauté until just tender. Mix potatoes, seafood, egg, salt, and pepper. Shape into patties ½ inch thick and 3 inches in diameter. Sauté in butter until golden brown. Garnish with red and green peppers.

Note: A ¼-cup measure is ideal for forming cakes.

Bay of Islands Oyster Flan on Kumara Hash Browns

DEVELOPED by Chef Will Van Heeswyck, Kimberley Lodge, Russell, Bay of Islands, New Zealand, this is the breakfast to prepare when you want to impress your audience. The rich egg custard with fresh oysters bakes slowly in a water bath while the golden hash browns are prepared stove top. Both may be made in advance and successfully held in warming ovens.

SERVES 4

2 eggs

½ cup milk

½ cup heavy cream

1 teaspoon chopped chives

salt and pepper to taste

1 dozen large oysters, poached in water, seasoned with lemon juice

1 kumara (substitute 1 medium sweet potato), peeled and grated

1 egg white

1 tablespoon olive oil

fennel leaves, garnish

Mix eggs, milk, cream, chives, salt, and pepper. Place 3 oysters in each buttered ramekin. Pour custard over oysters. Place ramekins in a large baking pan and fill with water to come halfway up sides of ramekins. Bake 40 to 45 minutes at 350°F.

Meanwhile, mix kumara or sweet potato, egg white, salt, and pepper. Form into a thin patty the size of the ramekin. Panfry in olive oil until just cooked.

To serve, unmold oyster flan onto hash brown patty. Garnish with fennel leaves.

Traditional Virginia Hams: The Surry Way

Some Virginians say that Pocahontas saved Captain John Smith not because of love but because he was the only one who knew how to cure a ham.

In the early 1600s pigs were brought to Jamestown for food from England and Bermuda. Rubbed with salt and hickory-smoked, these were the original "country" hams, today known variously as Virginia Ham, Old Virginia Ham, Surry Ham, and Smithfield Ham. Smithfield, unfortunately, has become a generic label for traditional country Virginia ham. The Virginia Assembly created a standard of identity that designates Smithfield hams by length of curing and location within the town limits of Smithfield. Originally, hogs were peanut-fed, but a second legislative act removed that stipulation over a decade ago.

These Virginia country hams are the intense, superbly flavored, salty, deep mahogany-colored meats redolent of hickory smoking. These are not to be confused with "city" hams, those sugar-cured or spiral-cut hams that are the milder, moister, sweeter, pinker variety.

Every plantation had its smokehouse with hams hanging for special occasions and unexpected guests. Serving ham has a heritage inextricably intertwined with hospitality, happiness, and the celebration of the good life.

Surry and Smithfield hams are both products of the west bank of the James River. On Jamestown Ferry route Captain S. Wallace Edwards Sr. served sandwiches filled with his home-cured Surry Virginia hams. Response was so positive that in 1926 he retired from life on the James River to devote his energies to his smokehouse.

Today S. Wallace Edwards & Sons has perfected the traditional Virginia ham. The only change made over the years has been the breed of the hog—it is leaner and fed a diet of corn and soy beans.

"Shortcuts can be detrimental," said Sam W. Edwards III, vice president of S. Wallace Edwards & Sons, Inc., a third-generation member of the Virginia ham dynasty. "We still use the meat curing methods developed by the settlers when they first came to Virginia. We use hickory wood to smoke the product, and we duplicate the seasons by temperature control so production can progress year around.

"The longer the ham is cured, the more intense is the flavor. It is like cheese, which gets sharper with age," said Edwards. "However, it becomes too hard if aged too long.

"Moderation with country ham is important—a little bit goes a long way. I believe that is my grandmother's rule of thumb," Edwards said of his ninety-five-year-old grandmother and cofounder of the company, Mrs. Oneita J. Edwards.

Virginians say that the ham should be sliced so thin that you can read the newspaper through it. For more advanced ham preparation, David Everett, executive chef of The Dining Room at Ford's Colony, demonstrates Virginia Ham cookery as one portion of the video cookbook A Taste of Williamsburg. Produced by Metro Video Productions of Williamsburg, it is available for $19.95. Everett is well known for his unusually creative uses of Virginia products.

Edwards now provides their product line and related items via mail order (call 1-800-222-4267) and through shops in Surry and Williamsburg.

Gascon French Country Ham

GASCON *farmers in southwest France often grilled a thick slice of country ham over an open oak fire before going to work in the fields. After cooking for about 5 minutes, it was turned over and blessed with chopped shallots marinated in the local armagnac—what a flavor. Matched with thick slices of chewy country bread, this would serve as a start for the morning's activities.*

The dish is one of Kate Ratliffe's rustic meals that she serves in her farmhouse cooking school in Gascony, next to the river where she parks her barge, the Julia Hoyt.

SERVES 4

2 shallots, peeled and chopped

2 tablespoons armagnac

1 large ¾-inch slice of country ham
   (about 1 pound)

1 tablespoon oil

8 slices country French bread

Marinate shallots in armagnac for at least two hours. Grill ham over an open fire of oak wood for 5 minutes or in a large skillet with oil over medium-high heat. Turn ham over. Cover cooked side with shallots. Cook an additional 5 minutes. Cut into 4 portions. Serve with bread.

55

Pork, Posole, Polenta, and Poached Eggs

*A*T HER home in Santa Barbara overlooking the expanse of the Pacific Ocean, Shan O'Brian created one of the most superb and assertive breakfasts I have ever enjoyed. Most of the preparations can be made in advance and in larger quantities for parties. Leftovers are just as outstanding with the advantage of having the flavors of corn, fresh cilantro and ground coriander, lime, pork, garlic, and peppers meld. Shan added the last-minute touch of heating fresh flour tortillas over the gas flames and perfectly poaching eggs for crowning the substantial base. She suggests that canned hominy and tomatillo sauce works almost as well as the original dried posole and fresh tomatillos, and it is sold in ordinary supermarkets.

SERVES 8

PORK AND POSOLE

1 pound pork butt, trimmed of fat and cut in small dice

1 onion, diced

6 cloves garlic, minced

1 tablespoon oil

1 16-ounce can hominy (posole), drained and rinsed

8 tomatillos or 1 can green tomatillo sauce (Hernandez brand suggested)

2 green chilies or jalapeños, seeds and ribs removed

1 teaspoon ground coriander

1 teaspoon ground cumin

2 tablespoons chopped fresh cilantro

POLENTA

1 cup ground corn meal

4 cups water

1 teaspoon salt

ASSEMBLY

8 poached eggs

2 avocados, sliced

2 limes, cut into wedges for garnish

8 sprigs cilantro, garnish

For Pork and Posole: In a large pan, brown pork pieces with garlic and onions in oil. Add hominy, tomatillos, chilies, coriander, and cumin. Let simmer for 1 hour. Add chopped cilantro 10 minutes before serving.

For Polenta: In a 2-quart pan over high heat bring to a boil the corn meal, water, and salt. Reduce heat to a simmer. Cook, occasionally stirring, until thickened for 30 minutes. Pour on waxed paper on a baking sheet. Cool and cut into 4-inch squares.

To Assemble: Place a polenta square on each plate. Top with posole and pork mixture. Place a poached egg on top and side with avocado slices and wedges of fresh lime. Garnish with cilantro.

Note: Depending on the heat of the canned tomatillo sauce, you may want to reduce the quantity of jalapeños.

Corned Beef Hash in Filo with Poached Egg

*P*ATRICK O'CONNELL, *The Inn at Little Washington, Virginia, serves a more fashionable version of this dish. One waiter, at the end of breakfast, asked if we desired anything else. Proclaiming that we wanted nothing else, he responded, "Sometimes we find the surrender charming."*

SERVES 4

½ medium onion, chopped

1 rib celery, finely chopped

2 teaspoons vegetable oil

1 large potato, grated

1 cup corned beef, cooked and shredded

1 tablespoon chopped, fresh oregano
(or 1 teaspoon dried)

4 poached eggs

Four 14 × 17-inch filo frozen dough
sheets, thawed

1 tablespoon butter to coat back of filo
baking dishes

nonstick spray

In a medium skillet over high heat cook onion and celery in oil until softened or for about 3 minutes. Add potatoes and continue to cook over medium heat until softened. Stir in beef and oregano. Heat for 2 more minutes. Keep warm while preparing filo shells.

Cut filo dough lengthwise in half. Then cut in the other direction into 3 pieces (approximately 7 × 6 inches). Heavily butter the back of 4 individual soufflé dishes (or small bowls). Arrange 6 overlapping pieces of filo, spraying each with nonstick spray to cover the outside of the inverted bowl. Place on a baking sheet. Bake in a preheated 375°F oven until the edges begin to brown or for 10 to 12 minutes. Remove from oven and let cool for 2 minutes.

Gently remove filo shell from back of dish. Invert onto individual serving plates. Fill with hot hash and top each one with a poached egg.

Note: To prepare meat, simmer a corned beef brisket about one hour per pound or until fork tender. Let sit in cooking water for 30 minutes. Drain.

Spread, Sprinkled, or Rolled in Breads

CHICAGO BAGELS: STEAM-INJECTED, NOT BOILED

The tradition of boiling bagels before baking produces that chewy taste loved by so many. In recent years a new, controversial, technique has been developed that eliminates the boiling bath and adds a shot of steam during the baking. Bruce Goodman, coproprietor of RB Goodman's Bagel Bakery just outside Chicago, bakes from about 3:30 A.M. to 9 A.M., using the steam-injection method that produces a softer bagel. "These are good for sandwiches. The boiled ones are too tough," he says.

This cooking method extends the shelf life two or three days, a fact appreciated by many of his customers. They should be stored in a plastic bag at room temperature. Bagels can also be frozen and warmed in the microwave for 20 seconds. Popular bagel flavors include rye, pumpernickel, wheat, sesame seed, garlic, salt, onion, poppy seed, cinnamon raisin, egg, eight grain, everything, and plain.

One tale of the bagel's origin claims it was invented by a Viennese Jewish baker in 1693 to celebrate the saving of Vienna from Turkish invaders by King John III Sobieski of Poland. Formed in the shape of a *beugel* (German for stirrup), it represented the king's passion for riding.

A Trio of Bagel Spreads:
Strawberry, Peanut Butter 'n' Honey, and Peach Melba

*I*N THE UNITED STATES, *the flavors of spreads run from vegetable favorites of onions, chives, scallions, horseradish, spinach, and sundried tomato to fruity items of raisins, strawberries, blueberries, peach, and apricot as well as traditional smoked salmon, lox, and whitefish.*

This strawberry one was created for a breakfast at the Wimbledon tennis matches. These spreads were inspired by the test kitchens of Philadelphia-brand Cream Cheese.

STRAWBERRY SPREAD

YIELD: 1⅓ CUPS

one 8-ounce package cream cheese, softened

2 tablespoons sugar

½ cup coarsely chopped strawberries

Blend sugar into cream cheese. Gently fold in strawberries.

PEANUT BUTTER 'N' HONEY

YIELD: 1⅓ CUPS

one 8-ounce package cream cheese, softened

¼ cup peanut butter

2 tablespoons honey

apple or banana slices

Mix until well blended. Spread on toasted bagels. Top with fruit slices.

PEACH MELBA

Spread bagels with cream cheese. Top with red raspberry preserves and fresh peach slices.

Sautéed Wild Polish Mushrooms

*T*HE *Black Madonna, an important Catholic relic in the Polish town of Czestochowa, displayed only at certain times, dates back to the beginning of Christianity. The sacred icon, a picture on a cypress plank, may have been painted by St. Luke. Today more than one million Poles annually make pilgrimages to the Jasna Góra monastery, an impressive hill-top compound, where the icon is housed along with many other relics.*

The crowd was caught up with their religious zeal just like teenagers at a punk rock concert. We were shoved and mashed as family groups with interlinked arms physically demanded their right of way for viewing the Madonna. After what seemed hours we got close to a side door and escaped without so much as a glimpse of the Black Madonna.

In the open spaces of the town, we stopped for a street-food breakfast sandwich of freshly sautéed mushrooms on chewy bread. Our pilgrimage to this famed town resulted in finding the earthiest, wildest forest mushrooms, a true product of nature.

SERVES 4

1 pound wild mushrooms (see Note), sliced

2 tablespoons butter

½ teaspoon salt

½ teaspoon black pepper

1 tablespoon vermouth

4 thick slices of chewy bread

61

In a large skillet over medium heat, cook mushrooms in butter for 7 minutes. Season with salt and pepper. Using a slotted spoon, mound mushrooms on bread. Add vermouth to skillet. Increase heat to high and reduce liquid to about ¼ cup. Spoon the reduction over the mushrooms.

Note: Any mushrooms can be used, but the wilder, the better the taste. Only use mushrooms certified by a wild mushroom expert. Or if you are hunting in a market, try readily available mushrooms such as shiitakis, portabello, or oyster mushrooms.

A Bathtub Stopper: Yugoslavia Just Before the War Began

Sophisticated travelers often brag that they carry a bathtub stopper. It seemed like a good idea, but I had not yet obtained one. Then, after driving the coast of Yugoslavia from the Italian border, I ran into a tub without a plug near Split. I called the desk clerk from my government-run resort hotel. The clerk said one would be delivered.

I was dying to have a bath, so in went the plug. I added drops of a precious bath oil carried from an Austrian hotel. The billows and steamy water were so inviting. In I slipped and luxuriated for about two full seconds—the bottom of the tub was like sandpaper!

The next morning the madness of my reckless bathing became apparent with abrasions all over the sitting area of my body. Today, no bathtub plug is included in my travel supplies—a missing plug might simply be a subtle hint that will save your bottom.

The next morning I went down to breakfast. The cavernous dining room looked just like a cafeteria at a state university. An orangish liquid in a four-ounce glass was called fruit juice, the coffee appeared to have been brewed from freshly ground burned popcorn kernels, and the toast had been sitting to the point of soggy chewiness. The cereal was stale.

The Serbian waiter spoke at some length about problems with his wife who was Croatian, "We just cannot seem to get along. The Croats and the Serbs are just too different."

My discomfort was growing, so I thanked my server and retreated to my room, tidied up my things, and checked out. Little did I anticipate that savage wars were about to begin.

I visited Diocletian's second-century palace—an intriguing complex of apartments and shops built in and onto the original palace with bits of restoration here and there. Nearby, I witnessed tiny elderly ladies viciously bent from the weight of carrying in each hand three-foot high gasoline cans. The inflation rate at 2,000 percent per annum forced every bit of income to be invested in gas, the most valuable commodity. The gas station lines were full of the elderly queuing up while their sons and daughters furtively worked trying to make a living.

Hopefully, peace will soon return to the region and with it the tourists.

The Young Turk's Healthful Cheesy Herbed Toast

*O*UR *young, movie-star-handsome tour guide for Cultural Folk Tours in Turkey shared this easy-to-make breakfast. Concerned with fat, he mixes low-fat cottage cheese with an egg and chopped parsley, and mounds it on a slice of white bread. Run under the broiler until it is puffed and brown for a fast breakfast that lightens up eggs.*

In a small mixing bowl combine egg, cheese, and parsley. Spread on bread. Toast under broiler until puffy and it begins to brown, about 3 to 4 minutes.

SERVES 2

1 egg

⅓ cup cottage cheese

1 teaspoon chopped parsley

2 slices bread

BREAD SPREADS: MARMITE, VEGEMITE, PEANUT BUTTER, AND DIBS

Marmite and Vegemite

The telltale sign of a displaced Australian or New Zealander is their extraction of a tin of Vegemite or Marmite from a pocket, to spread on their morning toast. This salty yeast extract is dark brown and is a taste perhaps best acquired in one's youth.

Peanut Butter

The two brothers John and W. K. Kellogg, who ultimately developed and brought commercial cereals to the world, also developed a more nutritious substitute for butter in the 1890s, which they called peanut butter. Since they were steaming, not roasting, the nuts, the product was not too tasty. It was not until 1904 at the St. Louis Universal Exposition that C. H. Summer introduced the product that today is a staple in 85 percent of American homes and a worldwide favorite. The standard is a minimum of 90 percent peanuts with no artificial colors or preservatives. Sweeteners and salt may be added along with a stabilizer to prevent separation.

A new Dutch twist on peanut butter is a luscious ribbon of creamy chocolate swirled right in the jar.

Dibs

In the Arab countries dibs is a popular spread made of sweetened carob bean or date syrup.

The Lebanese often mix four parts of dibs with one part tahini, which is a paste of ground sesame seeds, for a breakfast dip for pita bread.

Middle Eastern Minted Labani Balls

65

*M*Y FIRST *Middle Eastern breakfast in Tel Aviv included small tangy cheese balls in a fruity green olive oil. These were to be eaten with freshly baked pita breads (page 105). As we traveled around Israel, I found many different varieties of labani made from many different-tasting milks. At the Mizpe Hayamin Spa Resort near the Sea of Galilee, fresh yogurt cheese is derived daily from the milk of goats and cows raised on the premise.*

Modern biblical scholars suggest that the phrase referring to Israel as the "Land of Milk and Honey" should actually be translated as the "Land of Yogurt and Honey."

This recipe is quite easy using commercial yogurt that is salted and drained overnight.

YIELD: 2 CUPS

1 quart plain yogurt

1½ teaspoons salt

1 tablespoon chopped, fresh mint

2 tablespoons olive oil

Line mixing bowl with three layers of cheesecloth. Place yogurt in bowl and stir in salt. Bring up corners of cheesecloth and tie into a bag with a piece of string. Let drain at least 6 hours unrefrigerated or until it is the consistency of cream cheese with about half the liquid drained.

Remove from cheesecloth. Roll into small balls. Roll in mint and drizzle with olive oil. Store in the refrigerator.

Note: The above recipe uses 3.5% whole milk. If a nonfat yogurt is used, the yield is approximately 1½ cups. Draining of a commercial yogurt can be done by poking small holes in the bottom of the container. Another method for draining is to use a cone-shaped coffee filter.

Bittersweet Chocolate Almond Spread

*M*ANY *countries around the world have a taste for chocolate and bread: The French have made an institution of pain au chocolat; the Danish have a special chocolate bar sold in the bread section that is the same size as a loaf of commercial bread; the Dutch have chocolate sprinkles; the Israelis spread chocolate halvah on buttered toast, and the Americans have chocolate-frosted doughnuts, which, incidentally, are very close to the greasy churros that the Spanish dip into hot chocolate.*

Since cocoa is chocolate without the fat, this clever spread has the chocolatey taste for the lips and not the hips. Try thinning with a tablespoon of water for a fruit dip or drizzle on baked items.

YIELD: ¼ CUP

¼ cup low-fat ricotta

4 teaspoons cocoa powder

2 teaspoons sugar or equivalent sugar substitute

¼ teaspoon almond extract

Mix all ingredients in a food processor until smooth or for about 1 minute. Refrigerate until ready to serve.

Chocolate "Worms" on Rusks in Holland

This Dutch breakfast is made to delight children of all ages. Start with a rusk, a three-inch round of bread so light that it cries for a topping to keep it anchored on a plate. However its crisp toasted facade makes additions challenging. Fortunately the Dutch, judging by their success with land reclamation, have proved they can do the impossible and have topped the rusk admirably.

The favorite topping is tiny pieces of chocolates called hagelslag. *One could sprinkle on the bits by hand, but in Amsterdam's historic Die Port Van Cleve Hotel,* the manager demonstrated an easier technique: Turn the rusk butter-side down on a plate sprinkled with the chocolates. After one try and one bite of the sweet chocolate, creamy butter, and crunchy light rusk, I was a convert.

On a visit to Pat Wall, the Amsterdam-based food maven and owner of the Cuisine Francaise situated in restored sixteenth-century canal houses, I learned that locals call the chocolate bits "worms" or "spaghetti." She also told me that a new mother often serves rusks with pink and white anise-flavored hagelslag, called "mice," to her baby's first visitors. Hagelslag is not readily available in America, but it's definitely worth asking for at gourmet shops.

Andalusian Garlic, Olive Oil, and Fresh Tomato Slices on Crusty Bread

I OPENED the patio door from my hotel apartment suite in the delightfully restored sixteenth-century Palacio de Santa Inés in Granada and looked up at the splendor of the Alhambra, the most magnificent Moorish palace and series of gardens in Spain. Back in the fully equipped kitchen I whipped up one of the popular local breakfasts by rubbing crusty slices of bread with a cut clove of garlic, sprinkled on olive oil, and finished it with a juicy tomato slice. Then I walked the several blocks down the Carrera del Darro into Plaza Nueva and set off for the climb to the Alhambra, where I could witness its treasures from closer range.

SERVES 6

6 slices fresh, crusty bread

2 cloves garlic

2 tablespoons extra-virgin olive oil

2 ripe tomatoes, sliced

Rub bread with garlic. Drizzle with olive oil and top with tomatoes.

Notes: Thin slices of serrano ham are often added.

Another version of this is the "miller's breakfast" of olive oil smothering hot bread topped with tomato, garlic, and cod. This is served at Spain's oldest olive oil producer, the two-hundred-year-old Nuñez de Prado, located in Baena, between Cordoba and Granada. The seventh generation of this family still produces their oils by using an eighteenth-century press.

The English Breakfast Trains

My sole purpose for boarding the train from London to Edinburgh was breakfast. The ultimate power breakfast is on the InterCity's 225 Pullman first-class dining car, or so the well-founded rumor goes. The train travels at 225 kilometers (140 miles) per hour, arriving in Edinburgh in under four hours.

The popularity of the English train breakfast is legendary. When the Pullman breakfast service started in the late 1800s on the Leeds to London route, a second train had to be added to accommodate the passengers who loved dining on board. The original Pullman, designed by George Pullman in Chicago, was adapted by BritRail with its Prince of Wales car and made cooking on board possible.

Arriving early, I checked out the newly refurbished Kings Cross train station and discovered some nice quickie breakfasts. Fresh croissants in trendy flavors and steaming espressos were ready to take away. An inexpensive eatery featured the traditional English breakfast, including the downsmarket option of "tinned" baked beans in tomato sauce on the steam table.

I enjoyed a French pressed coffee under the huge station dome with a schoolteacher from the western part of England. "This station has been completely done up for the tourists," said the teacher. "It is in not such a good area of London. They've gotten all the bums out and made it a proper place to be."

Train marketers, enticing passengers to avoid the train station food, claim "It's better on board." The self-service buffet, adjacent to the Pullman kitchen, supplies quite a satisfactory meal. The jumbo lean bacon and tomato roll on a toasted sesame bun has a loyal following, especially by many of the conductors in the BritRail system.

Pullman chefs perform their skills in petite kitchens designed for efficiency and safety. The four-burner electric stove has a protective front guard to prevent spills, but chefs still prefer the safer back burners.

Every breakfast is cooked to order. The fried or scrambled eggs are cracked and perfectly prepared. Potatoes, sliced on terra firma, are sautéed, the bacon fried, porridge (oatmeal) cooked, tomatoes, mushrooms, sausages, and black pudding grilled. The steward warned that the black pudding is not for the faint-hearted since its primary ingredient is pig's blood. Creamy smoked Scotch salmon with scrambled eggs or grilled kippers offer lovely alternatives.

At such speeds teamwork is required to make this operation run smoothly. The impeccably trained waiters dressed in dark

suits, shirts, and ties, deftly balance large trays of items and attentively serve tableside.

I asked one veteran waiter how he learned to pour hot tea and coffee on a train and he replied "it is just something you have a knack for." He was trained by InterCity.

Given the tight spaces, only the barest ingredient needs are supplied from the central warehouses, thus the kitchen might run out of eggs, but not for long. A quick onboard phone call places a supply order to an intermediate station. The food supply master will deliver everything by truck as the train pulls into the station.

Having finished my Pullman breakfast, I got off in York to wait for the next train back to London. What perfect timing—I was able to get a seat on the first-class dining car for lunch. But alas, after a Pullman breakfast, how can anyone have room for lunch?

Green Chile Breakfast Burrito

JEFF PUFAL, executive chef of the Rancho Encantado near Santa Fe, New Mexico, created this generous bundle of items wrapped in a soft, griddled flour tortilla. For nutrition watchers, please note this melange includes all four basic food groups.

Another travel writer in town during this research was the witty George Ridge of Tucson, Arizona. He could not resist greeting me one morning, saying, "Speaking of New Mexico, everything revolves around food here. Even the weatherman says chili today, hotter tamale."

S E R V E S 4

1 tablespoon butter

2 red new potatoes, cooked, diced

2 green chilies roasted, peeled, and chopped

4 pieces bacon, cooked

8 eggs, lightly beaten

4 ounces cheddar cheese, shredded

½ cup salsa, fresh

2 scallions, chopped

4 flour tortillas, warmed lightly on griddle

½ cup shredded lettuce, iceberg

1 tomato, chopped

¼ cup sour cream

In a medium skillet over medium heat, melt butter. Add potatoes, chilies, and bacon. Stir briefly, then pour beaten eggs over all and stir until lightly set and heated through, about 5 minutes. Divide into 4 portions on tortillas. Top each with cheese, salsa, and scallions. Roll up, tucking both ends under. Garnish with shredded lettuce, tomatoes, and a dollop of sour cream.

Note: You may substitute pork sausage, turkey sausage (page 37), or chorizo for the bacon.

Ham and Tortilla Rollups

To MEET grab-and-go needs, Robin Kline, a registered dietitian with the National Pork Producers Council, suggests creating healthful convenience breakfast foods at home. She designed this rollup to be prepared the night before, so everyone can grab one in the morning and be on their way. Add a serving of fresh fruit and a glass of milk for a more complete meal.

Kline advises to "Ignore food stereotypes that say certain foods are only for eating at certain times of the day." According to a random sampling of five hundred Americans in a study underwritten by the Pork Council, folks are eating all kinds of things in the name of breakfast—including cakes, soft drinks, popcorn, cold pizza, and leftovers.

Virtually every scientific study concludes that breakfast is the most important meal of the day for helping to control weight and improving learning and on-the-job performance. After the nightly fast the body needs something to keep the blood sugar from falling too low, to keep the brain alert, and to prevent fatigue. The American Dietetic Association's advice is to eat something—anything—in the morning.

SERVES 1

one 8-inch flour tortilla (whole grain suggested)

1 tablespoon low-fat cream cheese, softened

2 ounces ham, wafer-thin slices

sprouts, chopped lettuce for garnish

On flour tortilla spread cheese. Top with ham and sprouts and lettuce. Roll and wrap.

Do Romans Have Cappuccino and Pizzas for Breakfast?

Romans contend that they eat a Continental breakfast, a hard roll with perhaps jam and a steaming cup of nerve-shattering cappuccino. And they do. This same breakfast is often served with a buttery croissant in some of the finest luxury hotels in Rome.

But do not be misled. This is only the start of the morning's eating.

Friends of mine in Chicago had two tickets to Europe that they could not use. Before the day was over, I had settled plans with another friend to slip over to Rome. Never have I prepared for breakfast under such serendipitous circumstances.

Flashes from The First Man in Rome by Colleen McCollough and my old Latin books kept emerging as we climbed through the ruins of the Forum, building by building. In the Vestal Virgins' digs, we both expressed delight that at the age of ten we were not relegated to a similar life. I wondered what these ancient people had for breakfast as I ascended to the Palatine area, the elite residences of the wealthy and powerful.

More touring revealed that the skimpy Continental start to the day in this city of seven hills requires serious and frequent calorie augmentations. Everyone seemed to be pouring in and out of the cappuccino bars, but not for a typical American coffee break. "American coffee" is deemed an insipid, washed-out liquid. The Roman brew is forced with heavy steam through the earthy darkly roasted beans ground almost to a fine powder. Steam froths up the milk, adding a smoothness to the brew.

The plethora of cappuccino bars, each with sandwiches (cheese, sausage, tomato), sweets (cookies, cakes), and savory pastries (stuffed with aged ham, cheese, olives), became comprehensible.

For nonsmokers, the cappuccino bars can be a challenge. Many, many Romans enjoy tobacco with their morning breaks. Sometimes the air is cleaner by the door. In good weather, simply move outside.

My favorite early morning venue quickly became the ubiquitous bakeries, many with their specialty Roman pizzas. These paper-thin, rectangular bases, often up to ten feet long, sported toppings as simple as golden olive oil with salt, or thinly sliced potatoes with rosemary, or eggplant slices spiked with sweet red peppers. Each local bakery seems to

have its own specialty. But all are thin and crispy with fresh, fragrant toppings.

The dough is rolled, placed in the oven for several minutes, then removed and stretched. Back into the fiercely hot oven it goes until done. With tantalizing aromas the giant pizzas sit on a long counter waiting for eager buyers. Then the clerk makes an eight-inch rectangular cut with large scissors. The toppings are folded inside and the outside wrapped in a paper napkin. It's the perfect grab-and-go pick-me-up.

So the solution to the Continental break-fast is to keep adding a bit more fuel to make it to lunch. Clearly these morning items are not intended for lunch. Italians treat the luncheon meal as sanctimoniously as do the French. A mere pizza or sandwich for lunch, never!

Pita Bread with Zatar and Olive Oil

THE dark maroon spice mix known as zatar has a very special, citrusy taste. It is made from the small red berries from the sumac tree, dried and powdered, then mixed with powdered thyme or marjoram, salt, and white sesame seeds. Note that it is a different variety from the North American sumac tree, which has poisonous berries. Zatar is sometimes sprinkled on sliced, mild white onions and served with pita bread.

In the scenic mountaintop town of Zichron-Yavoc, the first wine grapes were planted in Israel by Baron Edmond Rothschild in 1882. At the Baron Winery, Sufa, the family cook for more than two decades for owners Michael and Malka Tishbi, prepared pita in a small outdoor metal wood-burning oven during our visit. She was seated on the ground in the winery's arbor while Pa'amei Zichron, an energetic, local dance troop of young folks, performed Israeli dances showing the strong bond to agriculture.

In a small room behind Sufa were the round, white domes of soft dough that had risen under cotton cloths. She placed a mound of dough on her paddle, and with the flick of a practiced professional, she popped the mound in the oven. She did this until all the mounds were in the oven. When almost baked, Sufa brushed the tops with a local, delicious, green olive oil then sprinkled them with zatar. They were returned to the oven to finish baking then served fragrantly hot. With the olive oil on top and a lower cooking temperature, the inner pocket does not form.

The Bedouins also use bread, olive oil, and zatar, but their construction slightly differs. Dining is done in their large gathering tent where only the man and his sons of age sleep. A small pottery plate is issued to each person for breakfast. A small piece of pita bread (hot when possible) is dipped into the olive oil and then into the zatar.

75

YIELD: 12

2 tablespoons olive oil

2 tablespoons zatar

1 recipe pita (page 105)

After rolling the pita rounds brush each with a mixture of the olive oil. Sprinkle with zatar. Permit to rise for 30 minutes, then bake at 400°F for 12 minutes.

> Notes: Do not confuse zatar with the herb za'atar (*Origannum cyriacum*), the Moroccan herb that is a cross between marjoram, thyme, and oregano, which is used in Tagines.

Zatar can be mail-ordered from the following companies:

1. Penzey's, Ltd., P.O. Box 1448, Waukesha, WI 53187; phone: (414) 574–0277; fax: (414) 574–0278. Made with thyme.

2. Greater Galilee Gourmet, Inc., 2118 Wilshire Blvd., Suite 829, Santa Monica, CA 90403; phone: (310) 459–9120 or (800) 290–1291; fax: (310) 459–1276. Made with wild marjoram.

In U.S. gourmet shops, an Israeli-based company, Spices by Elana, sells Arabic zatar made from hyssop, thyme, sumac, sesame seeds, olive oil, and salt. According to the *Von Welanetz Guide to Ethnic Ingredients*, by Diane Von Welanetz, (Los Angeles: J. P. Tarcher, Inc., 1982), the American version of sumac with white berries is poisonous. The red, elm leaf or Sicilian sumac with ripe, hairy red berries are acceptable.

CHAPTER FIVE

Breads and Cakes Puffed with Yeast

THE WAYFARER'S BREAKFASTS: HIKING CORNWALL

It was a place I had not been before but had somehow known. The lush green landscape, precipitously dropping to the seeming calm of the sea, meandered gently but offered abrupt challenges to even the best hikers.

Love of the outdoors and a sense of adventure were prerequisites for the Wayfarer's Cornwall walk, not one's fitness level. Our group of fifteen walkers ranged in age from thirty to seventy.

These Canadians and Americans came to England for an adventure with six days of "perfect English weather," which included sun, downpours, and magical mists. Armed with rainwear, waterproof boots, shorts, and suntan creams, the group adpated to the changes gracefully.

Nature delighted in adding new dimensions to the ever-changing vistas. The rains came. Torrential downpours turned dry land into soggy, mucky rivers of mud. The mud became fun to play in, to fall in, a way to become deliciously dirty. It was an adventure perhaps not enjoyed since childhood that filled one with reckless abandon.

Occasionally beach cottages, inns, and houses peeked from behind the hills. Tiny fishing villages were crammed into petite natural harbors. And in between, farmers tended the rich land still constrained by ancient hedgerows, certainly not productive to modern farming, but to the way the land was, and is, and may be again. The land has a

memory full of secrets, of ancient rites, the struggles for survival, and joys of simple living. These people, tough but gentle, lived from the seas and the land, both mining and farming.

Geoffrey Newman, our walk leader, well over six feet tall with long, long legs, gave us encouragement each evening after dinner for the next day's adventure:

There is no fear of snakes. The only poisonous one is the adder, and they are so rare that I have never encountered one. There is not poison ivy, but we do have a weed, the stinging nettle, which causes a slight irritation. But dock, another weed which usually grows nearby, is an antidote.

It will not be too tough. We will hike a nice, wooded river path with incredible views. We will cross the river on the Malpas ferry, actually a dory boat driven by the ferryman, who will be with his dog, Spot. It is not too tough a day. Janet Bolton, our tour manager, will meet us with refreshments in the morning and pick up any who chooses not to continue.

And sure enough, Janet arrived the next day with a station wagon filled with food for our break: lemon-barley water, orange juice, spring water, a giant basket of carefully selected fruits, and tons of biscuits (English cookies).

Survey maps detail the paths. Wardens tend each section, removing fallen logs and keeping the paths passable. The paths are highly preferable to the narrow winding roads, tightly squeezed between the hedgerows where cars attempt to simulate two-way traffic, leaving minimal breathing room for a hiker. Lay-bys are scarce, but good for pulling a car off the road to let another pass.

These gentle rolling hills provide some serious ups and downs on the well-tended coastal path extending five hundred miles around Cornwall. The right-of-way goes over fences, through pastures, and seemingly right next to farmhouses, manor houses dating from the sixteenth century, renovated mills, Celtic stone mysteries, churches dating from the 1200s, and through small hamlets and villages.

For my part, I came along to check out the walkers' fueling process. Our accommodations ranged from an elegant country manor house converted from a nunnery, to a bed and breakfast on the English Channel where Eisenhower drafted plans for the invasion of Normandy, to small family-run coastal hotels.

Breakfast became a celebration of each new day and catered to every taste. Bran flakes, milk or yogurt, fresh fruits, toast in silver caddies with jam and hot coffee and teas satisfied some. Others opted for the full English breakfast of fried eggs and bread, sausage, bacon, kippers, fresh-grilled tomatoes and mushrooms, and caddied toasts.

English bacon rashers are quite un-like American bacon strips (referred to as streaky bacon). English bacon is a lean slice of ham with a narrow rim of fat that can be easily removed.

Continental breakfasts, fresh juices with flaky croissants or brioches, butter and jam, and coffee or teas suited others. Available, but rarely demanded, was oat-meal. Even though not fashionable in the western portion of England, I usually opted for kippers teamed with grilled fresh mushrooms and tomatoes.

Fueled with breakfast, boots securely laced, pedometers reset, backpacks in place with extra clothing, cameras, and binoculars, we were off again.

Every day varied but special sites appealed to varied interests. World War II cement boxes, once offering soldiers protection, dotted the coastline but were overshadowed by Henry VIII's castles on the mouth of the Falmouth Harbor, where he had planned to stave off invasion.

Then we stopped at the twenty-five-acre Trebah Gardens on the Helford River. This refined English garden stood in marked contrast to the deadly rocks full of semitropical ferns and palms, one hundred-year-old rhododendrons, and other plants. Four major gardens, set at descending levels two hundred feet from the house, had been designed by Charles Fox for the original owner—one for each of his children. Plants from all over the world had been collected.

Eira and Tony Hibbert, the current residents, moved to this lovely area, unaware of the garden's existence because it had been ignored for decades. Then a man asked for a job in the gardens.

They responded "What gardens?"

"My husband was never one to sit idle, so we discovered the gardens and gave the man a job," continued Eira. Today the gardens are shared with the public.

Coming off the heights of the cliffs into Portlooe, we stopped for a lunch of

80

fresh crab sandwiches and substantial Cornish pasties (pronounced "past-tyes") at the century-old hotel and restaurant of the Lugger. The white-washed plastered ceilings, supported by rough-hewn dark beams, dated from the fourteenth century. The series of small and wavy-floored rooms held a magnificent collection of sea-related treasures.

The original pasties, designed for miners lunches, had a longer dough handle at one end. This piece would be tossed after eating the rest to the mine pixies, a safety precaution since the tin miner's hands often contained poisonous heavy metals. In addition the mythical pixies would protect miners from harm.

The flakiness of the pastry came from the plentiful lard. The semicircular pie had edges turned over and crimped to hold the rich load of freshly cut pieces of meat, turnips, and potatoes. A variation would be to have a piece near the end filled with hedgerow jam for the sweet dessert portion.

Today the pasties are still loved and readily available at the pastry shops, for morning consumption. They have undergone an increase in the number of fillings and include ham and cheese, broccoli, mushrooms, chicken, and fish. Sizes range from tiny hors d'oeuvre to dinner-plate hefties.

Later, Janet greeted us with more refreshments for the body and thoughts for life, including this good advice: "You can't change the past, but you can spoil the present by worrying about the future."

This walk was certainly a marvelous place to be here and now.

Alverton Manor Brioche with Glacé Fruits

CORNWALL in the southwestern part of England, the old stomping grounds of the intriguing author Daphne du Maurier, is full of fascinating haunts. One is the country Manor House in Truro, a cobbled cathedral city, with its magnificent stone inn, sweeping front lawn, and gardens. Formerly a nunnery of the Sisters of the Epiphany, the manor houses a lovely chapel popular for weddings. There is a gracious, high-ceiling entrance and mahogany-lined stairwells. Every bedroom is decorated in different styles.

For wedding breakfasts, the chef often features brioche, that delicate buttery and eggy bread. On other mornings, brioche may appear in a loaf instead of the elegant topknot form, under a bounty of fresh fruit slightly sweetened with an apricot glaze.

Brioche is a very rich dough. This recipe is an easier loaf than those requiring a sponge and is made quickly with a food processor.

SERVES 8

BRIOCHE

2 cups (8 ounces) bread flour

1 package dry (1 tablespoon) yeast

2 tablespoons sugar

½ teaspoon salt

2 eggs

3 tablespoons milk

6 tablespoons (3 ounces) melted butter

GLACÉ

½ cup apricot jam

¼ cup water

3 cups sliced fresh fruits (mangos, kiwi, strawberries, plums, apricots, peaches, or nectarines)

For Brioche: Using a steel blade in the work bowl, mix flour, yeast, salt, and sugar with several pulses. Add eggs and milk and process for 5 seconds. With machine on, pour melted butter through feed tube and process for 20 seconds. The batter will be

81

very sticky. Transfer to a buttered mixing bowl. Cover and permit to rise until size triples or for about 3 hours. Punch down. Turn onto a floured pastry board and form into a loaf. Let rise 2 hours or until doubled. Bake at 375°F for 30 to 35 minutes. Permit to cool before slicing.

For Glacé: In a medium saucepan stir jam into water and bring to a boil. Permit to cool slightly. Mix with fresh fruits. Serve warm, 2 slices per person, with a sprig of lemon balm mint. Dust with confectioners' sugar and decorate with fresh-picked elder flowers.

Why Are These Called Danishes?

Even though Copenhageners call them wiener-brøts, they are known elsewhere in the world as Danish pastries, or simply "Danish."

La Glacé Konditore has been serving fine pastries in the picturesque street off Stroget, the world's longest pedestrian street, since 1870. A fresh wienerbrøt is about 9 kronors, close to two dollars in La Glacé.

Their version of how the name came about goes back to a strike by the Danish pastry bakers. Management resorted to bringing in Viennese pastry chefs. After the strike, claims La Glacé, the Austrian chefs returned home and sold the pastries as Danish ones.

Another version of the story says that Viennese pastry chefs came to Denmark and made the pastries. They became so omnipresent that visitors began calling them Danish pastries.

The Radisson SAS Scandinavian hotel breakfast buffet presents their Danishes just slightly smaller than the traditional, so guests may easily sample more than one version. Two wildly popular versions are strawberry filling with royal icing and those with bittersweet chocolate icing.

The array of styles of Danishes is staggering. One of the largest is a triangle about twelve inches on the longest side. Others are made in large hearts, rings of every imaginable size, and long bars with pastry cream, cinnamon, almonds, and royal icing.

Even wedding cakes are made of this pastry dough, shaped into successively smaller rings and stacked. Given its sinful richness, only small slices are presented. Similar cakes are made to celebrate the New Year.

Many Danes eat a pastry and a bread roll for breakfast with a cup of coffee, often consuming fifteen to twenty cups a day and rarely resorting to decaffeinated. Business breakfasts may also be accompanied with a tiny stemmed glass of anise-flavored schnapps. Raw oats mixed with dried fruit, sugar, and milk is another favorite "at home" breakfast. But many Danes are becoming quite health conscious and insist on light milk, which is 0.5 percent butterfat content, on their muesli or cornflakes.

The sweet tooth starts early. Children put thin slices of chocolate on bread to make palaegchokolade. The product is sold in grocery stores with jams, honey, and other bread condiments—not in the candy section. And the Danish can afford to eat lots of these pastries—they have the world's best health care system.

Danish Pastry, Copenhagen Style

IN THE dozens of pastry shops in Copenhagen, bakers start early, making wienerbrøt, Vienna bread. Tourists may know them under the name of "Danish." At the Radisson SAS Scandinavian Hotel, they are serious about quality. If a pastry is not eaten within several hours, it has lost crispness, and it is discarded.

The technique demonstrated here creates more than three hundred layers of butter and dough, which, when baked, create the endlessly flaky layers.

YIELD: 16

DOUGH

- 1 package (1 tablespoon) dry yeast
- ¼ cup water (110°F)
- 2 tablespoons (1 ounce) butter, melted
- 2 tablespoons sugar
- ½ cup milk
- ½ teaspoon salt
- 1 egg
- 3 cups flour
- 6 ounces butter, room temperature

EGG WASH

- 1 egg yolk
- 1 tablespoon water

APRICOT FILLING

- ⅓ cup dried apricots
- ⅓ cup water

ALMOND FILLING

- 1½ ounces almond paste
- ¼ cup sugar

GLAZE

- ⅓ cup confectioners' sugar
- 2 teaspoons water

For Dough: Soften yeast in ¼ cup of 110°F water. In a large mixing bowl combine butter, sugar, milk, salt, and egg. Stir in flour and dissolved yeast. Using bread hooks or by hand, knead for 9 minutes or until the dough is elastic and smooth.

Roll on floured pastry board to ½-inch thick into a rectangle 18×6 inches. Spread butter over two-thirds of the dough, leaving ½ inch on perimeter unbuttered and the last third for folding into the center. Fold unbuttered third into center. Fold other third on top. Put thumb print into lower right hand corner. Cover with plastic wrap. Refrigerate for 30 minutes.

Roll, starting with notch in lower left-hand corner, into rectangle. Fold into thirds. Put 2 thumb prints into lower right-hand corner. Cover with plastic wrap. Refrigerate for 30 minutes.

Roll, starting with notch in lower left-hand corner into a rectangle. Fold into thirds. Put 3 thumb prints into lower right-hand corner. Cover with plastic wrap. Refrigerate for 30 minutes. Repeat a total of four times, each time turning the dough 90°. Let dough rest refrigerated for at least 2 more hours.

Divide dough into 2 pieces. Refrigerate one piece. Roll other into an 8 × 16-inch rectangle. Using a pastry cutter or very sharp knife, cut into eight 4-inch squares. Spread 1 teaspoon of desired filling in center of each. Bring in the tips of 2 opposite corners and secure in the center. Repeat with other 2 corners. Place on an ungreased baking sheet.

Repeat procedure for other half of dough. Let rise in a warm place until double in size (about 40 minutes). With a pastry brush lightly coat with egg wash. Bake at 375°F until golden brown or 15 minutes. While pastries are cooling on a rack, drizzle with glaze if desired.

For Apricot Filling: In a small pan over medium heat bring apricots and water to a boil. Continue to boil, stirring occasionally, for 5 minutes. Put contents into a food processor until smooth.

For Almond Filling: Mix ingredients together.

For Glaze: With fork mix together the sugar and water. Drizzle over pastries while cooling.

Notes:

- After the final turn and rolling, the dough can be tightly wrapped and refrigerated until morning for baking.

- Keep dough well chilled. It becomes very soft and difficult to work with as it warms. Dough can be frozen for 1 month but should rest at room temperature for 30 minutes before baking.

- When baking, do not leave the room in the last 5 minutes. They need careful watching to avoid burns.

- Other interesting fillings are bittersweet chocolate, jams, preserves, marzipan, and nuts.

Swedish St. Lucia Buns

*O*N THE *morning of December 13, which is St. Lucia Day in Sweden, a young girl wearing a long white gown, a red sash, and a crown of candles, leads a singing procession to wake her family members. The saffron golden buns shaped like cats, called* lussekatt, *are the traditional breakfast bread.*

YIELD: 1 DOZEN

1 package (1 tablespoon) dry yeast

¼ cup water (110°F)

¾ cup milk

½ cup sugar

1 stick (4 ounces) butter, melted

1 egg

½ teaspoon salt

1 pinch saffron (about 20 threads)

4 cups flour

¼ cup raisins

1 egg yolk mixed with 1 tablespoon water

Dissolve yeast in tepid water. Let stand until foamy or for about 5 minutes. In a large mixing bowl combine milk, sugar, butter, egg, salt, and ground saffron. Stir in flour and yeast mixture. Add raisins. Knead until the dough is smooth and elastic, about 10 minutes. Cover with plastic wrap. Let rise in a warm place for 1 hour.

Punch down dough. Transfer to a lightly floured cutting board. Using hand, form a 1½-inch diameter of dough roll about 12 inches long. Using a dough cutter or knife, make 12 segments. Roll each into a rope about 6 inches long. To form the traditional S shape, make a closed loop to the left with the upper 2 inches and another closed loop on the bottom to the right.

Place a raisin in the center of the loops. Place on a greased baking sheet. With pastry brush paint lightly with glaze. Let rise for 30 minutes. Bake in a preheated oven at 350°F until golden brown or about 20 minutes.

Nobel Prizewinners, St. Lucia Buns, and the Grand Hotel

The Nobel prizewinners stay from seven to ten days at the Grand Hotel in Stockholm, where they are entertained at a dizzying pace with receptions, parties, and ceremonies. Every morning the prizewinners in the five humanitarian areas breakfast on the Verandah Room overlooking the Baltic Sea with views of the palace and the Parliament in the old town.

The hotel was founded in 1874, and a re-creation of the first dinner served in the Versailles-style hall, with eighteen-carat gold-trimmed mirrors and Belgium crystal, is still available by special request. Despite the grandeur, the front porch had awnings that used to leak during rains, earning it the name "poor man's porch." Today, these Nobel prizewinners breakfast on the "poor man's porch," although it no longer leaks.

As the week proceeds, the winners, their families, and their entourages become better acquainted and start to table hop and visit over their morning coffees and teas. In the center of the long Verandah Room is the large table with built-in heating and refrigeration sections where world-famous smorgasbords are held at lunch and dinner. But at breakfast, there is an attempt to represent the best of a Swedish breakfast, while still catering to tastes from around the world to maintain a feeling of home for all visitors.

One particular Swedish specialty is the paper-thin, sliced smoked reindeer, darker than beef. Keeping it company are Italian mortadella, German salami, Bayonne-style French ham made in Sweden, cheeses, juices, anchovies, pickled herring, salad toppings (cucumber, red pepper, and tomatoes), caviar, mustard, hotel-made liver paté for topping knackerbread, crisp breads, freshly baked loaves of bread, or rolls.

Formerly, the Nobel prizewinners could have a mixed fruit salad, but this has been replaced with the more popular fruit buffet with sliced fresh fruits such as kiwis, strawberries, poached pears, or whatever is in season. Next to the cereals (bran, granola, cornflakes, and muesli) are yogurt, milks, and juices. On the far end are soft-boiled and hard-boiled eggs and cooked items such as scrambled eggs, sausage, bacon, potatoes, and porridge.

The awards are presented on December 11, and many guests stay the extra two days to celebrate Santa Lucia Day. A young lady, selected from the local music gymnasium (high school), is dressed in the traditional

costume. To protect her hair against fire damage from the lighted candles in her crown, a cloth handkerchief is placed on top of the hair. (Many a Santa Lucia has been burned in the past!)

Every year a story or two appears in the Stockholm papers about foreigners who, not knowing traditions of being awakened by Santa Lucia, claim that they either saw a ghost or they awoke in paradise. That is not the case at the Grand because they have carefully made plans with the guests, who leave the security chains off during the night. The receptionist checks with the Nobel guests to see if they wish to be awakened by Santa Lucia and her train of ten to twelve singing white-robed followers—who themselves are followed by perhaps as many as two hundred journalists. The wake-up call starts at 5:30 A.M., hours before the sun will rise at about 9:30 A.M.

Following the entourage is the breakfast offering of the St. Lucia bun, the special saffron buns with raisins, and ginger cookies. The ceremony usually lasts ten to twenty minutes, and the procession is mostly girls.

Swedish Sunflower, Carrot Rye Bread

Good health is the goal of the partici-pants in the Sturebadet Health Club in Stockholm, Sweden. The baker has developed many whole grain, healthy breads. Every day two different, freshly baked types tempt folks after they have worked out.

Sunflower seeds are covered with hot water to soak and develop an aroma. The dough for this bread is mixed, kneaded, and left overnight in the refrigerator for a cold rise that allows the flavors to develop further. The rye flour and the heavy stone-ground wheat flour make this into a dense bread, sweetened by carrots and molasses. The chewiness of the sunflower seeds adds unique texture and always tempts one to have a second slice. The sunflower seeds are also delicious without the soaking.

YIELD: 2 LOAVES

1 package (1 tablespoon) dry yeast

2 ½ cups water (110°F)

3 tablespoons unsulphured molasses

2 cups rye flour

2 cups bread flour

1 cup whole wheat flour

2 teaspoons salt

1 cup grated carrots

1 cup sunflower seeds

Soak sunflower seeds for about 8 hours.

In a mixing cup, add yeast to ½ cup of water. Let sit until mixture becomes foamy or for about 5 minutes.

In a large mixing bowl stir together yeast mixture, the remaining water, and molasses. Sir in flours and salt gradually. Mix in carrots and sunflower seeds. The dough will be quite sticky. Turn onto a floured pastry board. Knead for 6 minutes. Place in a greased mixing bowl. Cover tightly with plastic wrap. Refrigerate overnight.

The next morning punch down dough. Form into 2 loaves and bake in greased pans in an oven preheated 350°F until the loaves have a hollow sound when thumped or for 45 minutes. Cool on a baking rack.

Note: The overnight cold rise can be replaced by a single hour rise at room temperature.

The Sturebadet Breakfast Club in Stockholm

The breakfast club at the Sturebadet is the place for Swedish locals to get a healthy start on the day. These were the first baths in Stockholm. In 1885 the club opened as a bathhouse under Carl Curman, who stated "Sturebadet shall be treated as a temple of health ready to offer regeneration and refreshment in bright pleasant surroundings."

Planned for an upscale neighborhood of Stockholm, the club came under protest by the residents until King Oscar II became a sponsor of the club. At that time bathing took place, on the average, two times per year. Husky matrons would scrub and scrub away the grime of time.

In 1989 Sturebadet was completely destroyed by fire but reconstructed to its original splendor (with an update in spa technology) by carefully copying pictures. Over the swimming pool is a large wall of mosaics in white and blue. In the pool are daily classes in water aerobics, using the latest in techniques, including water weights. Surrounding the pool are small curtained-off compartments with lounge chairs for relaxing or reading the morning paper or having a manicure or pedicure. A wooden balcony and columns surround the mezzanine where stationary bikes or Stairmasters can be used. On the far end separated by a glass wall is the health-oriented restaurant.

The breakfast club members, from 6:45 A.M. to 10:00 A.M. on weekdays, are given a terry robe to wear as they select from a workout menu of exercise and weight machines, personal trainers, and a wide variety of classes. A full range of beauty treatments, such as mud baths, aroma therapy, and facials, are available as is a sauna. Swedish massages, the deep muscle massage, are not recommended until late in the day when the stress builds up. Lars Sandbery, president of the club since 1991, suggested that "after a sauna one should rest at least twenty minutes as it affects the body more than you think."

Today the private club with about two thousand members takes a holistic view of physical training, nutrition, beauty treatments, and mental relaxation using yoga. Positive-thinking classes for handling stress and organizing life's priorities are popular. Day memberships for most activities are available for hotel guests.

After a workout, many shower, don the white robes, and head to the dining room decorated with light Scandinavian woods with carved columns. There, nutritious comestibles are prepared by chef Lotta Voltaire, a former model, and her staff. She wants "to prepare food so people can be strong and live long."

In a glass of fresh-squeezed orange juice full of pulp and carrot juice, she drops eight or nine drops of echinacea to help ward off the Swedish colds that can be quite prevalent. She makes her own herbal teas of chamomile, mint, and wild strawberry leaves. Coffee, teas, and coffee substitutes are available. No croissants are served. Instead the baker makes whole grain breads in a number of varieties such as rye, sunflower seeds, carrot, muesli, and pumpkin with lingonberries and rye.

On the breakfast buffet are cottage cheese, grated carrots, butter and light margarine, Kalles Caviar (pink cod eggs, in a tube), cheese, and a jar of peanut butter. Traditional crackerbreads in addition to the freshly baked breads are available as are a number of fresh fruits, hot porridge, cereals, milk, and yogurt. It's a good, healthy start to the day.

The Sturebadet Breakfast Club in Stockholm

Dutch Currant, Raisin, Citron, Whole Grain Buns

*T*HIS *Dutch bun is in a rich butter, milk, and egg dough made with a 10-grain cereal, stone-ground whole wheat flour, and bread flour. It is a moist bun that will stay so for several days.*

YIELD: 16 BUNS

¼ cup water (110°F)

1 ½ tablespoons yeast

2 cups stone-ground whole wheat flour

2 cups bread flour

1 cup 10-grain cereal (see Note)

¼ cup sugar

2 teaspoons salt

1 cup milk

1 egg

2 ounces butter (½ stick), melted

½ pound raisins

½ pound currants

1 ounce (2 tablespoons) citron (or substitute 2 tablespoons lemon zest)

In a glass mixing cup dissolve yeast with water and a pinch of sugar. Permit to stand until bubbly or for 5 minutes. In a large mixing bowl combine flours, cereal, salt, and sugar. In a small bowl mix milk, egg, and butter. Add yeast mixture to milk mixture and stir into flour mixture. Stir in fruit. When combined, knead for 7 minutes, using a bread hook or by hand on a floured board. Permit to rise in a warm place until doubled or for 1 hour. Punch down dough.

Turn on a lightly floured board and knead for 1 minute. Cut dough in half. Roll each into a log. Cut each log into 8 pieces. Using a cupped hand, form into a ball.

Place on a greased baking pan. Permit to rise for 40 minutes. Bake 15 minutes at 375°F.

Note: Ten-grain cereal (made of rolled wheat, rye, barley, and oats; cracked wheat, wheat germ, and wheat bran; whole-grain cornmeal; quinoa; soy flour; short brown rice; whole millet and flax seed) is available from King Arthur Flour, Box 876, Norwich, VT, 05055; phone: (800)–827–6838, or fax: (800)–343–3002.

Dutch Whole Grain Rolls with Mushrooms, Red Peppers, and Cheese

*T*HE *Dutch grain-blends create dense, chewy, tummy-sticking wonders of bread in blacks, browns, speckled, and light shades. This roll, the ultimate in portable cuisine, satisfies all the breakfast nutrition needs. Fresh red peppers, mushrooms, parsley, and chives for vegetables, wheat for grains, and sunflower seeds and Gouda cheese for protein and fat. The flecks of red, green, and gold transform a whole grain roll into a colorful work of art for both the eye and the body.*

YIELD: 2 DOZEN

1 package (1 tablespoon) dry yeast

1 teaspoon sugar

2 cups water (110°F)

1 tablespoon oil

1 fresh red pepper, chopped

1 cup (3 ounces) fresh, chopped mushrooms

3 cups stone-ground whole wheat flour

2½ cups flour, plus additional for kneading

2 teaspoons salt

2 tablespoons finely chopped parsley

2 tablespoons finely chopped chives

5 ounces Gouda cheese, chopped

In a glass measuring cup stir yeast and sugar into ¼ cup of the water. Let stand until bubbly, about 5 minutes.

Heat oil in a medium-size skillet over medium heat. Add red pepper and mushrooms and cook until they begin to soften, about 5 minutes. Let cool.

In a large mixing bowl combine flours and salt. To the flour mixture, add the yeast mixture and the remaining water. Stir until incorporated. Add parsley, chives, and cheese.

Knead for 8 minutes with an electric mixer bread hook or 10 minutes by hand. Permit to rise in a warm place until doubled in size or for 1 hour.

Punch down dough and knead for 1 minute on a floured board. Form into a long log. Cut into 24 pieces. Shape each piece into a round roll.

Place on a greased baking pan and permit to rise for 30 minutes. Bake at 375°F for 20 to 25 minutes or until browned. Cool.

The Netherlands
Breads and Cheese

I became so intrigued with the Dutch breads that I visited the Bakkerij Bartels bakery in Amsterdam. Late at night the team of bakers arrived (all male, since law prohibits women from these night jobs) to create a wonder of loaves, rolls, and sweet pastries.

Krentenbollen, *large rolls studded with plump currants and raisins, were being made by the hundreds. Particularly popular were the miniversions. Mixing the dough with a muesli grain and more dried fruit, the bakers created a complete breakfast in a handy package. Also quite popular is the* sukerbrod, *bread with lumps of sugar that melt inside.*

Considerable capital investment provided the latest technology. Science dictated almost every movement of dough. Grain deliveries were pumped into large bins with connecting tubes to sites for mixing dough. Mixing, kneading, proofing, and shaping were mostly mechanical. Then trays of rolls or loaves were wheeled into large humidity- and temperature-controlled proofing boxes until ready for baking. Small room-size convection ovens set to the exact temperature baked the product to perfection.

The slotted racks, each holding more than one hundred loaves, were rolled to sections of the bakery where the bread would cool before being wrapped. Orders were grouped. In the wee predawn hours, trucks whisked the freshly baked breads and pastries to hotels, restaurants, and bakeries throughout the city. Then the bakery became an almost empty shell.

The day staff arrived to handle the administrative bookkeeping and to take the next day's orders. Several bakers did specialty work. When night fell, the bakers would return and fill the space once again with enticing smells, beautiful breads, tempting pastries, and tomorrow's breakfasts.

With breakfast breads the Dutch serve sliced young Gouda (pronounced howda) cheese. Sometimes the medium strength with a much stronger flavor appears. Rarely at breakfast does one see the well-aged cheeses that have a marvelously pungent aroma and a dry crumb.

I ventured by train to the cheese-producing town of Gouda with the oldest town hall in the Netherlands. Across the cobblestoned town center is their fifteenth-century cheese-weighing house, where the local dairy farmers have been bringing their product for centuries. Here the ancient cheese market is re-created for tourists during summer months.

Walking into the cheese shop with its pungent, delicious smells, I laughingly remembered my first Dutch cheese shop visit while still in college. "May I please have about one hundred grams of Gouda?" I had asked.

Showing her tolerance of tourist's ignorance, she patiently smiled while waving her hands to a wall of at least one hundred Gouda cheeses and said "which one?"

After sampling many different Goudas with Holland's staple whole grain breads, I still do not know the answer to that question. They are all so unique and flavorful.

Trilogy Cinnamon Buns

CALLED *"Mom's buns,"* these are made by Jeanette Coons for every Trilogy voyage; a voyage of sailing catamarans that takes guests from Lahaina, Maui, to Molokini and Lanai for snorkeling and diving expeditions. Guests consume several buns along with mugs of Kona coffee, because they will need the energy for the day's diving in the clear waters.

YIELD: 2 DOZEN

DOUGH

2 tablespoons yeast

1½ cups water (110°F)

½ cup sugar

1 teaspoon salt

2 eggs

½ cup vegetable oil

5 cups flour

FILLING

¼ cup butter, melted

1 tablespoon cinnamon

3 tablespoons brown sugar

ICING

½ cup finely chopped macadamia nuts

¼ cup butter

2 tablespoons evaporated milk

2 cups confectioners' sugar

¼ teaspoon lemon extract

¼ teaspoon almond extract

In a large mixing bowl stir yeast in water until dissolved. Let sit for 5 minutes. Stir in sugar, salt, eggs, and oil. With a wooden spoon mix in flour, stirring until incorporated. Knead on a floured board (or use dough hook on electric mixer) for 10 minutes or until elastic. Cover with plastic wrap. Let rise until the volume doubles or for about 1 hour.

Punch down. Roll on a lightly floured board into an 11×16-inch rectangle about ¼-inch thick. Spread with melted butter. Sprinkle with cinnamon and brown sugar. Roll lengthwise. Pinch edges. Cut into 1-inch pieces.

Place on a 12×18-inch greased bun pan with edges touching one another.

Let rise until doubled or for about one hour.

Preheat oven to 350°F. Bake until golden brown or for about 20 minutes. Sprinkle on nuts.

In a small bowl mix milk, confectioners' sugar, and extracts. Drizzle icing, using a spoon or pastry bag. Bake 2 more minutes.

Note: Dough is soft and will spread lengthwise while rolling. Finished roll should be 24 inches long. If a creamier icing is preferred, wait until the buns have cooled, then ice with a spatula.

Maui's Sugar and the Alexander and Baldwin Sugar Museum

While tourism today lures all nationalities to visit the Paradise that is Hawaii, something even sweeter attracted the many races and cultures to Maui—jobs on sugar plantations. In the 1800s, families came from Japan, the Philippines, Portugal, and Russia under three- and five-year contracts. Entire villages sprang up overnight, complete with schools, houses of worship, stores, and medical and recreational facilities.

The Arabs are credited with cane cultivation and learning how to produce sugar. They later introduced the product to Europeans. In 1493, Columbus is said to have brought sugar to the West Indies. There is evidence of sugarcane growing in Louisiana by 1751.

Hawaii supplies one-third of all cane sugar and one-tenth of all sugar consumed in the United States. Taking two years to reach maturity, the stalks grow eight to thirty feet. They are so heavy that they fall into tangled messes. One acre of cane makes twelve tons of raw sugar or 22,465 pounds of refined sugar.

Just across from the sugar production plant at Puuneue is the restored plantation home that is today the Alexander and Baldwin Sugar Museum. Gaylord Kubota came from the Bishop Museum in Honolulu to design and build the Maui museum. Today he is the curator and director.

Kubota has a graduate degree in history from the University of California Berkeley. Later he lived in Japan as a Fulbright scholar. But his roots are in Maui sugar. Both parents were educators near a sugar plantation in the highlands. Later they moved to Waililu, the major town.

Kubota is particularly gratified when he hears a grandparent saying to a youngster "come over here and look at this house. It is just like the one we used to live in." Youngsters understand their heritage better while learning the importance of sugar to the island's economy.

A working model of sugar processing follows the video production of sugar from cane, through harvest, to production to raw sugar. The processing of sugar has byproducts of molasses (used as cattle feed) and bigase, the fibers remaining after processing, which are burned to create electricity. The raw sugar is finally shipped to Concord, California, to be refined into the white substance purchased mostly in five-pound bags.

Sugar was and is king. And sugar is the only commodity exported; of incredible importance since all else is imported.

Mountain Sky Guest Ranch Pecan Rolls

PAM KIRCHOFF, *pastry chef, Mountain Sky Guest Ranch, Montana, has become justifiably famous for these addictively rich pecan rolls. The brown sugar, cream, and pecans that gloriously melt into ribbons of sticky topping are a perfect match for the not-too-sweet, soft dough.*

YIELD: 16

DOUGH

1 package (about 1 tablespoon) dry yeast

½ cup water (110°F)

3 cups flour

¼ cup sugar

1 teaspoon salt

½ cup milk

¼ cup butter, melted

1 egg

FILLING

½ teaspoon cinnamon

¼ cup sugar

TOPPING

1 cup heavy cream

1 cup brown sugar

½ cup pecans, chopped

101

Dissolve yeast in water. Let sit until foamy or for about 5 minutes.

Mix flour, sugar, and salt in a large bowl. In another bowl mix milk, melted butter, and egg. Add wet ingredients and yeast to dry ingredients, mixing all together. Knead on floured surface for 8 to 10 minutes. Let rise until doubled in volume or for about 1 hour. Punch down.

Roll into an 11×13-inch rectangle. Sprinkle with filling. Roll into jelly-roll shape that will spread to about 16 inches long. Pinch ends of dough to adhere to roll. Slice into 1-inch slices.

Mix topping. Pour half into each 8-inch round cake pan. Arrange 8 rolls in each pan. Let rise for 30 minutes. Bake at 350°F.

Malassadas, Hawaiian Portuguese Holeless Doughnuts

*T*HE *Portuguese arrived along with other contract workers to work on the Hawaiian sugarcane plantations. The Portuguese are credited with developing the Hawaiian sweet breads that were baked in their outdoor ovens in the sugar camps. Today these are deep-fried in vegetable oil and have a dense texture like cake doughnuts. Cinnamon is often added to the coating.*

YIELD: 3 DOZEN

1 package dry yeast

¼ cup water, 110°F

6 ½ cups flour

⅔ cup sugar

½ teaspoon salt

¼ cup vegetable oil

1 teaspoon lemon extract

1 teaspoon vanilla extract

6 eggs

1 ¾ cups milk

oil for frying

sugar for coating

Dissolve yeast in warm water. In a large mixing bowl combine flour, sugar, and salt. In a small bowl whisk vegetable oil, extracts, and eggs. With a large spoon add yeast and egg mixture to dry ingredients. Gradually stir in milk and mix until smooth, about 5 minutes. Let rise in a warm place until double in size, for about 1 hour.

Punch down with fist. Pinch off a tablespoon size and form into a ball. Deep-fry in hot oil until brown on one side. Turn over and repeat. Drain on paper towels. Roll in granulated sugar and serve while still warm.

Broa, Portuguese Corn Bread

THIS golden yellow, dense bread is one of the regional specialties that the Portuguese Pousada do Castelos, Öbidos, serves its guests who stay in the fifteenth-century medieval walled town and this restored Manueline palace.

By processing corn meal with a food processor or blender, the bread has a more refined and less gritty taste than other products made with corn meal. The addition of flour and yeast does not ameliorate the delightful texture of this bread. It will hold up to the toughest soups or sandwich fillings. And there is nothing quite so well matched for Caldo Verde (page 162), the green kale soup, for a hearty morning start.

YIELD:
ONE 9-INCH LOAF

1½ cups yellow corn meal

1½ teaspoons salt

1¼ cups boiling water

1 tablespoon olive oil

1 package dry yeast

2 cups all-purpose flour

Process corn meal for 2 minutes in a blender or food processor until it is quite fine. Add salt, boiling water, and olive oil. Mix. Let cool to about 110°F.

Mix in dry yeast and 1 cup flour. Let mixture sit for 30 minutes or until double in size. Knead for 5 minutes incorporating 1 more cup of flour. Let rise again for 30 minutes or double in size.

Form into a round loaf. Place on a greased baking sheet. Bake at 350°F until golden brown or for 40 minutes.

Simit, the Turkish Sesame Rings

*F*RESHLY *baked sesame rings are the national snack food of Turkey. They are available from street vendors in bakeries and in restaurants. Some are made with olive oil and some are coated with chicken fat for extra flavor.*

This recipe was shared by the Divan Hotel in Istanbul, where smaller versions of the sesame-covered breads grace the breakfast buffet. Simit should be eaten the same day that it is baked.

YIELD: 16 RINGS

1 package (1 tablespoon) dry yeast

2¼ cups water (110°F)

3½ cups flour

2 teaspoons salt

2 tablespoons sugar

1 cup sesame seeds

Dissolve yeast in ¼ cup of the water .

In a large mixing bowl combine flour, salt, 1 cup water, and dissolved yeast. Turn onto a lightly floured board and knead for 5 minutes. Let rest covered in a warm place for 30 minutes.

In a small pan over high heat bring 1 cup of the water and the sugar to a boil, stirring occasionally. Boil for 3 minutes. Let cool. Divide dough into 2 portions. Using the hands, make 1 portion into a long rope about ½ inch in diameter. Cut into 8-inch long sections. Form each section into a ring, twisting dough once. Press ends together. Dip into sugar syrup then into sesame seeds. Place on an ungreased baking sheet with the sesame-seed-side upward. Repeat with remaining dough.

Permit rings to rise for 15 minutes. Bake in a preheated 375°F oven until browned or for about 18 minutes.

Pita, Middle Eastern Flat Breads

PITA breads are ubiquitous in the Middle East. The Bedouins, traveling around the deserts, developed these yeast breads to fit their wandering lifestyle. The yeast breads rise once and, being flat, bake fast. Cooking at very high temperatures, usually over 500°F, a pocket of steam forms in the interior, creating that famed space that can be used for just about any filling. Called pide *in Turkey,* kemaj *in Lebanon,* khubiz *in Syria and Morocco,* kjesra *in Algeria, it may be baked in an adobe oven, inside a metal oven over a fire, on top of a convex round metal griddle, or simply on a stone. Not all pitas are destined to have a pocket. In Greece they are just flat. In Israel, when the bread is coated with a mixture of olive oil and zatar spice mix, it is much like a chewy pizza.*

YIELD: 12

1 cup water (110°F)

1 package (1 tablespoon) dry yeast

1 teaspoon sugar

1 teaspoon salt

2½ cups flour

In a large bowl add warm water. Completely dissolve yeast and sugar. Stir in salt and flour.

Knead on a lightly floured board for 6 minutes until elastic. Divide into 12 pieces. Shape into round balls. Cover with plastic wrap to prevent drying.

Roll each into a flat disk with a 5-inch diameter, about ¼-inch thick. Permit to rise for 30 minutes. Bake in a 500°F oven for about 4 minutes.

Notes: Using only the bottom shelf of the oven will produce better results. Try placing directly on baking stones that have been preheated.

If rolled too thin, the pita will not make a pocket.

French Baguettes

*B*READ *shops in France, by law, have posted the basic weight of the white-bread baguette. Its price is fixed, with 250 g costing about four French francs. One of the issues leading to the French Revolution was the price of bread, and even today, the French government makes sure that baguettes remain within reach of all.*

YIELD: 2 BAGUETTES

1 package (1 tablespoon) dry yeast

1 teaspoon sugar

½ cup water (110°F)

1 cup water

3⅓ cups bread flour

⅔ cup stone-ground whole wheat flour

1 teaspoon salt

1 egg mixed with ½ teaspoon salt for glaze

Dissolve yeast and sugar in ½ cup water. Let sit until bubbly or for about 5 minutes.

In a large mixing bowl mix yeast with remaining water. Stir in flours and salt until incorporated. Knead with the dough hook of an electric mixer for 5 minutes, by hand on a floured board for about 7 minutes. Cover and place in a warm place and permit to rise until double in volume or for about 1 hour. Punch dough down.

Divide in half. Roll out 1 piece on a lightly floured board into a rectangle. Roll up tightly, pinching ends securely together. Roll out again into a rectangle and roll up tightly pinching ends and tucking under. Finished loaf should be almost as long as baking sheet. Place on a baking sheet. Repeat procedure with other half of dough.

Let rise in a warm place until about doubled or for about 45 minutes. Slash a series of diagonally angled cuts down the loaf with a sharp knife. Using a pastry brush gently coat with egg glaze. Bake in a 425°F oven until golden brown or for 25 to 30 minutes.

Notes: This recipe is adapted from breads I have enjoyed made by my Francophile sister-in-law, Elizabeth Shank Hollis. The addition of stone-ground whole wheat gives it a more country taste.

Toss ice cubes into the oven floor at the beginning of baking and again after about 5 minutes to provide steam, which produces a very crisp crust.

Fast Breads and Cakes from the Oven

PORTUGUESE TAKE-AWAYS

Many folks in Lisbon, Portugal, do not eat breakfast at home, instead they stop on the way to work or take a break after getting to work. There coffee reigns supreme, with a bit of a nosh that could be sweet, such as the local delicacies of Belém, *pasteis de Belém*. These are a paper-thin crisp crust filled with a delicate sweet egg custard, with uncut cinnamon on top sprinkled with a bit of sugar. They are small, about 2 inches in diameter, but pack a sweet rich punch. The Pastelaria, Rosa D'ouro, on Rua de Belém, 116, 1300 Lisboa, serves these along with espressos starting from 7 A.M.

Then there are heavier savories, which a younger lady warned me are not healthy. Despite that, her mother and many others daily ingest these fried croquettes of rice, pork, or cod, which are deep-fried in a variety of shapes and readily available in the cafeterias and snack bars.

Bolo Real, the Portuguese Royal Pumpkin Cake

AT THE *Loios Pousada, a former monastery in Évora, Portugal, I was sharing the monks' former dining room with my fellow tourists. I imagined a priest ascending the stone stairs to the lectern for the morning sermon. I glanced at the lectern immediately above my head, but seeing no activity, I poured an orange juice. Judging from the orange trees in the center patio of the cloisters, I determined that in one month's time they would be ready for squeezing.*

From the rich breakfast buffet table I had selected a golden, dense, sweet, moist cake studded with bits of almonds with another taste that was baffling. The waiter explained that it was pumpkin. Pumpkin!

Most Portuguese sweets and cakes came from convents because the nuns had time to cook. This particular cake is credited to Convento do Paraiso in Portugal, and once used egg yolks left over from nearby monasteries who used the whites for clarifying their wines. Today the recipe solves that problem of what to do with extra yolks—yes, those golden gems often thrown away by the cholesterol fastidious. This cake uses 7 whole eggs and 5 extra egg yolks. This is not excessive considering that it makes 12 servings—just 1 egg per person. Plus there is the added advantage of this being a butterless cake—which is not to suggest that it is low calorie.

Pumpkins are also abundant in that region of Portugal just east of Lisbon. These are cleverly made into a marmalade in which the sugar coats each strand of the vegetable, preserving its integrity. After the pumpkin pieces are boiled the meat is removed from the rind with a wooden spoon. It is matched with an equivalent amount of sugar and boiled. Cooled and refrigerated until ready to use in baking, pumpkin is the ingredient that adds such an unusual dimension to this golden, egg-rich cake.

The method of preparation is also a total surprise. How can you not be completely disarmed by a chef whose first suggestions is to throw the pumpkin on the floor? No, this was not the how-to-turn-a-pumpkin-into-a-squash joke. It was a practical kitchen technique. It may be advisable to check local sanitation rules and throw on dishtowels or plastic wrap, but it works well. Unless you have the strength of Samson, you know that cutting a pumpkin with a chef's knife can be an excellent upper-body workout.

SERVES 10 OR 12

5 eggs

7 yolks

1 cup (7 ounces) sugar

1 pound almonds, skinned, coarsely ground

1 cup Pumpkin Marmalade (see right)

½ teaspoon cinnamon, ground

zest of 1 lemon

butter, for greasing pan

In a large mixing bowl use an electric beater to beat all eggs and yolks for at least 5 minutes, to incorporate copious amounts of air. Gradually beat in sugar. Continue until mixture is very creamy and pale yellow. Fold in almonds, marmalade, cinnamon, and zest. Butter a 10-inch round cake pan. Pour in ingredients. Bake in a preheated 325°F oven until a tester comes out clean or for about 25 to 30 minutes.

For Pumpkin Marmalade: Throw a ripe pumpkin on the floor, smashing it into pieces. Remove seeds. In a large pan cover pieces with water and boil until they begin to soften, about 15 minutes. Drain. With a wooden spoon pull pumpkin flesh into strands. Measure the same weight of sugar as pumpkin. In a large pan over high heat, stir sugar into a small amount of water. Add cinnamon stick and lemon zest and bring to the soft boil stage. Stir in the pumpkin strands coating each piece. Cool.

Notes:

- This cake stays fresh for 5 or 6 days.

- The marmalade can be made in large batches and preserved in glass jars. Spaghetti squash can be substituted and is very similar to the Portuguese pumpkin variety. The marmalade can be used in a number of sauces or on bread. Try as a condiment with cranberry sauce for turkey.

- Do not grind the almonds too finely. Leave a bit of crunch for additional texture.

- A royal icing can be made with decorations of candied fruit for additional eye appeal.

Viennese Marzipan Breakfast Cake with Chocolate Chips and Ginger

*P*LAYING *Johann Strauss's "Tales of the Vienna Woods," I waltz gloriously about the kitchen, swirling and laughing while preparing* schokerl kuchen, *a delicate Viennese breakfast cake with surprising chocolate chips and crystallized ginger. I turn up the stereo's volume to drown out the electric mixer while enjoying wonderful memories of the pedestrian shopping streets crowded with customers perched around tiny tables, sipping coffee and nibbling delicacies.*

I imagine my guests will enjoy this taste of Vienna with my rendition from one of Vienna's most famous master pastry chefs and owner of three konditoren, *Karl Schumacher. While not as sweet as many American breakfast items, this cake is sinfully rich. Make thin slices and serve with strong coffee or espresso. Do not be surprised when everyone accepts your offer for another piece.*

One of the secrets to elegant pastries is to have all the ingredients at room temperature to ease the combination process. The egg whites, in particular, need to be about 70°F to incorporate sufficient air to leaven the cake. Without baking powder or soda, which often causes a product to taste bitter, the folding-in process must be gentle, to preserve the effect of the airlike ladies' skirts gently swirling to the waltz.

YIELD:
TWO 8-INCH CAKES

½ cup sliced almonds

4 ounces almond paste

2 tablespoons (1 ounce) sugar

1 stick (4 ounces) butter, room temperature

1 teaspoon lemon juice

4 (2 ounces) egg yolks

2 teaspoons almond extract

4 (4 ounces) egg whites

½ cup (3 ounces) sugar

1 tablespoon cornstarch

1 cup (4 ounces) cake flour

1 tablespoon minisemisweet
chocolate chips

1 tablespoon finely chopped, crystallized
ginger pieces

Preheat oven to 350°F. Spray 2 nonstick 8-inch cake pans with vegetable spray or line traditional pans with silicon paper. Sprinkle almonds in pans.

Using an electric mixer, cream almond paste, butter, 2 tablespoons sugar, and lemon juice until light and fluffy, about 5 minutes. In a slow, steady stream, beat in yolks and almond extract. In a separate bowl, whip egg whites with ½ cup sugar for about 3 minutes or until a soft peak forms. Stir cornstarch into cake flour. Using a large spatula, gently stir flour mixture into butter mixture. Stir in chocolate chips and ginger pieces. Gently fold in egg whites. Divide batter into prepared pans.

Bake for 20 to 25 minutes or until a knife inserted in the cake's center is clean. Let cool for 10 minutes in the pan. Remove from pan and finish cooling on a cake rack. Cut into wedges and serve. Store the cake covered at room temperature for up to 5 days and keep away from those overly concerned with cholesterol and calories.

Note: Eggs can be brought to room temperature in about 5 minutes if they are placed in a bowl of hot tap water. Butter can be softened in a microwave. In the place of marzipan, use ⅔ cup whole almonds, ¼ cup sugar and 2 tablespoons water ground to a fine paste in a food processor.

Ricotta and Bittersweet Chocolate Chunk Tort

*T*HE *Hassler Hotel's rooftop restaurant, Rome's first, is certainly the eternal city's foremost venue for breakfast, known as* piccolo colazione. *There I became entranced by the view that is so often the subject of a painting that only when a person moved was I reminded to return to reality. St. Peter's Basilica loomed largest, but it was majestically kept company by scores of other domes, towers, and rooftop gardens complete with trees living high above ground level. To the right was the Villa Medici, surrounded by the soft green of its trees, grass, and open spaces, in which children romp and enjoy life.*

The colors of Hassler's interior—the gold and green striped chairs, the ochre, burnt umber, and sienna reds of the carpet and ceilings—blended harmoniously with the colors on the other side of the windows. I was also fascinated by how impeccably clean the windows were, and I inquired about the difficulties of washing so high up. The maitre d' bragged that these panoramic windows completely reverse for interior cleaning.

The Hassler Hotel has raised attention to detail to a new level. More impressive than the window cleaning was the cleaning of the brass stair guards. Daily, each guard holding the staircase carpeting to the staircase is removed, polished, and replaced. Its grandeur and gentle flow, under ancient tapestries and around priceless antiques, is much more exquisite for a walker than succumbing to the elevator.

Just below the windows are the famed Spanish steps, the radiating couture houses of Valentino, the shopping Mecca with famous Italian names like Ferragamo and Gucci, along with mass-market foreign competitors such as Reebok.

Lest one forget the real reason for being there, the waiters in crisply starched whites supply one's breakfast desires. Central in the room, on the large tiered table, the morning's offerings are in a display even more harmonious, colorful, and graceful than the domes outside. The colors were fresher than the newly cleaned Sistine Chapel ceiling, the tastes sweeter than ascension to the heavens, and the variety as tempting as the virtues of man on earth.

A serious attention stopper was the torta ricotta cioceolato tricota, *made with fresh ricotta cheese, sugar, eggs, and bittersweet chocolate in a delicate shell. Along with a steaming cup of cappuccino, a glass of the finest Italian sparkling water, San Pelegrino, and the magic of the eternal city, this is clearly the most sensible way to serve eggs, cheese, and chocolate.*

S E R V E S   8

TORT SHELL

    1 cup (4 ounces) pastry flour

    ⅓ cup sugar

    pinch salt

    1 egg

    1 teaspoon vanilla

    ¾ stick (3 ounces) sweet butter, cold

FILLING

    15-ounce container of full-milk ricotta

    1 cup (7 ounces) sugar

    4 eggs

    6 ounces bittersweet chocolate squares

For Tort Shell: Butter a 10-inch tort pan. Place flour, sugar, salt, egg, and vanilla in food-processor bowl fitted with metal blade. Pulse several minutes until ingredients are incorporated. Cut cold butter into about 8 pieces. Add to work bowl. Pulse several times until the dough is the size of large peas.

Remove to a lightly floured pastry board. Knead several times. Roll about ¼-inch thick. Placing rolling pin on the center of the dough, roll half the dough over top of pin. Pick up pin and transfer dough to tort pan. Spread out dough patting into bottom. Use pin to roll dough over the sharp top edges to cut off any excess dough.

For Filling: In a small mixing bowl, whisk together ricotta, sugar, and eggs until creamy. With a large, sharp chef's knife, roughly chop chocolate into ⅛-inch chunks. Sprinkle chocolate over bottom of dough. Pour in ricotta mix. Bake in a 350°F oven for 50 to 55 minutes or until a toothpick inserted in the center comes out clean. Let cool at room temperature for at least 1 hour.

King David's Warm Cheesecake

BREAKFAST at the elegant, high-ceilinged King David Hotel looking over rocky gardens to the ancient walls of Jerusalem, is a sumptuous affair with roots in many cultures and cuisines. Dairy products, particularly hard and cream cheeses and yogurt, ranging from nonfat to rich, grace the buffet tables. To balance this, one might select salads, including grated carrots, cucumbers, and tomatoes, from the lavish display. The warm cheesecake, held in a warming pan, is an excellent winter dish, rich and creamy—especially festive for a buffet breakfast. This is not available on the Sabbath because cooking and any other work is not done by the religious Jews.

An Israeli breakfast promises to fuel pilgrims for following the stations of the cross on the Via Delarosa, or for visiting the Church of the Rock where Mohammed left on his divine trip to heaven. Religious fervor may be witnessed at the wailing wall, where men and women pray separately.

Shoppers can have their own religious experience by meandering in the covered bazaars, bargaining for artifacts, jewelry, leathers, and any other type of goods desired.

SERVES 6

1 stick (4 ounces) butter, room
   temperature

⅔ cup (4 ounces) sugar

1 teaspoon vanilla extract

2 eggs

½ pound cream cheese, room
   temperature

½ cup (2 ounces) flour

In a large bowl, with an electric mixer at low speed, cream the butter, sugar, and vanilla extract until it is a fine, uniform mixture, about 5 minutes. Add eggs one at a time, mixing until fully incorporated. After the last egg, mix for 2 more minutes. Add cream cheese and mix lightly on slow speed for 2 minutes. Add flour and mix thoroughly for about 2 minutes. Bake in a large, greased casserole dish at 350°F for 30 minutes or until a tester comes out clean. Serve with a spoon while hot.

Notes: Fresh fruits are an excellent accompaniment.

Tester, Bertha Scaggs, found this to be supremely excellent when served either cold or at room temperature, declaring it even better than most cheesecakes.

New York Fresh Apple Cake with Maple Syrup

A PORTION *of the culinary legend of Alice Fargo Brown Spalding (1882 to 1976) were the ethereal cakes, cookies, and pies she developed, perfected, and shared generously with friends and family. The love she felt while baking, a necessary ingredient in every recipe, was dearly enjoyed by every one blessed with her delectable gifts. One of my favorites was this apple cake made from crisp fall apples carefully arranged on a thin cinnamon cake base and topped with pure, heavenly maple syrup. Every slice came with an adoring smile and more love. The apples are quartered and sliced and the half-moon shapes are stacked closely on their edges in the stiff batter. Share this with those you love.*

SERVES 8

1 egg

⅔ cup milk

¼ cup melted butter

1 teaspoon vanilla

2 cups flour

⅓ cup sugar

1 teaspoon baking powder

½ teaspoon salt

4 apples, peeled, cored, ⅛-inch sliced

2 teaspoons cinnamon with
    2 tablespoons sugar

maple syrup, warmed

Mix egg, milk, butter, and vanilla in a small bowl. Combine all dry ingredients. Pour egg mixture into flour mixture and mix with a few strokes until just combined.

Pour into a buttered 9-inch glass pie pan with at least a 2 inch side. Arrange apple slices on top. Sprinkle with cinnamon sugar. Bake in a preheated 375°F oven until a tester inserted into the center comes out clean or for 25 to 30 minutes. Cut into wedges and bathe in maple syrup.

New Zealand Whole Orange and Apricot Muffin

ARROWWOOD JUNCTION *is a wisp of a town just outside Queenstown, New Zealand, wrapped in the beauty of Alpine mountains and lakes. At a lovely bed and breakfast called Taranga, Suzy Wood shares her piece of paradise with an alpaca, several sheep, pigs, and another few special friends. Wood, a renowned New Zealand weaver, also cleans, cards, and spins the wool, and creates her own design.*

Breakfast is huge, with fresh fruit compote (page 201), cereals, muffins, tea, and coffee. These orange and apricot muffins appeared hot from the oven on the morning we were scheduled to fly in a small plane over Mount Cook to the Milford Sound. While cruising the breathtaking fjords of the Southern Alps, we were enthralled with the penguins and sea lions frolicking and the waterfalls cascading down from glaciers into the deep and mirror-perfect lake.

The muffin is a no-fuss New Zealander's approach to healthful practicality. Using even the bitter orange pith produces a subtle taste of marmalade while adding extra dietary fiber.

Y I E L D : 1 D O Z E N

2 whole oranges, quartered, seeded

¼ cup vegetable oil

1 tablespoon unsulphured molasses

1 egg

1½ cups (6 ounces) whole wheat flour

½ cup bran

½ cup brown sugar

1 teaspoon baking powder

1 teaspoon baking soda

½ cup chopped dried apricots

Place oranges, skin and all, into a food processor. Whirl until pieces are fine, the size of uncooked barley grains. Add the oil, molasses, and egg. Pulse until combined. Add remaining ingredients and pulse until just mixed.

Scoop into greased muffin tins. Bake at 400°F for 15 to 20 minutes. Let cool in pan for 2 minutes before removal to cooling rack.

Doral Spa's Blueberry Bran Muffin

EVERY day a different muffin graces the breakfast table at the Doral Spa in Miami, Florida, always with substantial nutritional content and flavor. Each 2-ounce muffin has just under 100 calories and not quite 1 fat gram. Its moisture content is quite high and the taste is superb.

YIELD: 1 DOZEN

½ cup low-fat buttermilk

½ cup unfiltered apple juice

½ medium egg

1 medium egg white

⅓ cup (3 ounces) brown sugar, packed

1½ teaspoons vanilla

⅔ cup (2.5 ounces) all-purpose flour

⅓ cup (1.5 ounces) whole wheat flour

⅔ cup (2 ounces) wheat bran

1½ teaspoons baking powder

½ teaspoon baking soda

1 teaspoon cinnamon

1 cup frozen blueberries

In a medium-size bowl, mix milk, juice, egg, egg white, sugar, and vanilla. In another bowl combine all dry ingredients. Fold wet and dry ingredients together, until dry has dissolved. Do not overmix. Fold in frozen blueberries.

Fill muffin tins coated with vegetable spray ⅔ full. Bake in a preheated 375°F oven for about 20 minutes.

Note: The convenient powdered buttermilk can be used by substituting 2 tablespoons powder mix in ½ cup of water.

Cape Breton Gaelic Oatcakes

MADAINN MHATH (*pronounced madeen va*) is the Gaelic *"Good morning"* greeting, proudly spoken by many Cape Breton folks living on Nova Scotia, Canada's northern island. There the Gaelic College of Celtic Arts and Crafts teaches the ancient language with the eighteen-letter alphabet.

To preserve their heritage, students can take classes in bagpipe, Highland dances, Cape Breton step dance, Celtic harp, Scottish violin, and weaving. Summer school is the most popular when scores of young students dressed in their various clans' tartans parade and pipe their very complicated instruments.

One serious student piper told me that a bagpipe must be played every day. "It is not like a guitar which can be shoved in the closet. Pipes are sensitive to humidity and temperature. Plus your fingers and hands need daily exercise."

And when a piper says "Tha'n t-acras orm" (*pronounced Hahn tach cruss orrum*), meaning "I'm hungry," it is a good time to munch on an oatcake. The Scottish and Irish love oats, which they have been milling for centuries

YIELD: 2 DOZEN

1 cup flour

1 cup old-fashioned rolled oats, not quick oats

3 tablespoons sugar

3 tablespoons brown sugar

1 teaspoon salt

½ teaspoon baking soda

⅓ cup canola oil

½ cup cold water

granulated sugar for sprinkling after baking

Mix dry ingredients. Stir in oil and water. Refrigerate overnight. Divide into 24 balls. On a lightly floured board, roll each ball out to ¼-inch thick for 2-inch rounds.

Bake on a greased cookie sheet at 350°F until edges are just beginning to lightly brown, 12 to 15 minutes. Sprinkle tops with granulated sugar. Cool on a rack. Store in an airtight container.

Note: The original oatcakes are made with solid shortening and/or butter. All granulated sugar can be used, but add ½ teaspoon molasses.

Oatmeal and Chickpea Cookies for Ethiopian Children

WHEN people migrate from their homelands, there can be dramatic dietary changes if native foodstuffs are not readily available. Dr. Naomi Throstler of the Hebrew University of Jerusalem's faculty of Agriculture, studies the diets of immigrants in Israel. "Every group clings to eating habits," Throstler said. "The Ethiopians convert approximately 80 percent of food to energy, as opposed to the Western rate of only 40 percent conversion." Once immigrants settle in a new land, she said, "It is impossible to change their metabolic makeup. Russians immigrating to Israel have difficulty in adjusting to the hotter climate. Caloric requirements are less because not as much energy needs to be converted to body heat."

The Ethiopians in Israel no longer have their staple grain, teff, used to make their bread, injera. Becoming city dwellers requires less than half their former physical workload. Being exposed to a more Western diet of sugars and fats leads to weight gain, high blood pressure, and an epidemic of diabetes.

Throstler, who earned her doctorate at the University of California, Berkeley, developed the following recipe for a healthful, lower-fat breakfast cookie for Ethiopian children to whom the chickpea is a familiar item and taste.

YIELD: 5 DOZEN

½ cup butter or margarine, room temperature

½ cup sugar

1 egg

⅓ cup cultured buttermilk

¼ cup milk

1 tablespoon honey

1 teaspoon vanilla

1 cup whole wheat flour

¾ cup chickpea flour

2 cups rolled oats

1 teaspoon baking powder

½ teaspoon baking soda

½ teaspoon cinnamon

½ teaspoon cloves

½ cup chopped walnuts or pecans

½ cup raisins

In a large bowl cream margarine, sugar, egg, buttermilk, milk, honey, and vanilla with an electric mixer for about 3 minutes.

On slow speed incorporate flours, oats, baking powder and soda, and spices. Stir in nuts and raisins.

Shape into walnut-size balls. Flatten on greased cookie sheet, using a slightly moistened hand. Bake at 350°F until edges begin to brown or for about 15 minutes.

Note: Chickpea flour is available in ethnic markets or by mail order from King Arthur Flour Company.

Personal Trainer's *Whole Grain Date Scones*

A T THE *President's Health Club in Dallas, one of the personal trainers asked me to develop a low-fat, healthful scone for his breakfast. After several experiments ("reps"), these were deemed to be perfect. The dough is extremely soft. Do not be tempted to add additional flour, just be gentle. As with most low-fat baked goods, this has a one-day shelf life but can be successfully frozen and reheated.*

YIELD: 1 DOZEN

3 tablespoons apple juice concentrate

1 cup buttermilk

1 tablespoon safflower oil

1 ⅔ cups whole wheat flour

⅔ cup rolled oats

2 teaspoons baking powder

½ teaspoon baking soda

¼ teaspoon salt

½ teaspoon cinnamon

¼ teaspoon nutmeg

pinch of ground cloves

½ cup dates, chopped

1 tablespoon buttermilk for glaze

In a large mixing bowl whisk thawed apple juice concentrate, buttermilk, and oil. In another bowl combine all remaining ingredients except glaze. Stir well. Add liquid ingredients to dry and quickly stir until just combined. Do not overmix or the scones will be tough. Place dough on lightly floured board. Press to ¾-inch thick. Cut into rounds with biscuit cutter or in wedges with a knife. Transfer with a spatula to a cookie sheet treated with vegetable spray. Lightly brush tops with buttermilk. Bake at 425°F for 10 to 12 minutes or until golden brown.

Note: Try with other dried fruits such as cherries, cranberries, blueberries, and combinations of fruits cut into small pieces.

English Cheddar Cheese Scones

JANET BOLTON, the English Wayfarers's hiking manager (page 78), often entertains her family and friends with freshly baked scones—cheese, fruit, or plain. She rubs the softened butter and finely chopped cheese into a mixture of flour, sugar, baking powder, salt, and dry mustard. Then with a few quick strokes the egg and milk mixture is incorporated. The dough hits a floured board and is gently patted down, cut into rounds or triangles, and baked into a delectable breakfast treat. The blandness of the dough is delightfully accentuated by the strongest cheddar, preferably English, cheese available.

YIELD: 15 SCONES

2 cups flour

1 tablespoon baking powder

1 tablespoon sugar

½ teaspoon salt

½ teaspoon dry mustard

3 tablespoons butter, softened and cut into small pieces

3 ounces sharp English cheddar cheese, at room temperature, finely chopped

1 egg

½ cup milk

In a large mixing bowl combine flour, baking powder, sugar, salt, and dry mustard. Cut or rub in butter, then cheese. Quickly stir in egg beaten with milk. Transfer to a lightly floured board. Pat down to about 1½-inch thick. Cut with a 2-inch round cutter or into triangles. Bake on a baking sheet at 425°F for 13 to 15 minutes or until golden brown.

Note: Fruit scones can be made by eliminating the dry mustard and cheese and adding ⅓ cup of raisins that have been floured before adding to the dough. These are especially tasty with Hot Pepper Jelly (page 212).

The South Is Rising Again Biscuits

THE only item we learned to cook in seventh-grade home economics was biscuits. Since the school had no ovens for students to use, we had to make these, measuring at least 1-inch high, at home (as proven by a signed affidavit from a parent). The finished biscuit should be light, flaky, and not suitable for hitting with a baseball bat. It amazed me that this single item received as much attention as geography and the solar system combined. Could the school board and curriculum planners all have been good ol' southern folks who had freshly baked biscuits every morning? Did they lament that the only practical way for the South to rise again was with baking powder and soft flour?

Lard was the traditional fat of choice, but today, according to Vanessa Johnson, Southern Living Magazine, "Crisco is the way to make biscuits."

YIELD: 16 BISCUITS

1½ cups flour

1 tablespoon baking powder

2 teaspoons sugar

½ teaspoon salt

4 tablespoons shortening

⅔ cup milk

In a small bowl mix flour, baking powder, sugar, and salt. Using a pastry cutter or fork, cut in shortening until it is the size of peas. Make a well in the center and stir in milk.

Turn on a lightly floured pastry board and knead quickly. Roll or pat to ½-inch thickness. Cut into 1½-inch biscuits and place on an ungreased baking pan. Brush the top of each biscuit with a little milk. Bake at 450°F until the tops are lightly browned or for about 10 minutes.

Grand Teton Lodge Oven-Baked French Toast

*R*OBERT WALTON, *executive chef, Grand Teton Lodge Company, serves this rich French toast with maple syrup, butter, honey butter, and fresh fruit. In total it requires a half pound of bread. This French toast puffs up almost as tall the Grand Tetons, which can be viewed from the dining room, with its panoramic view of the mountains just over from Moose Flats. Those with particularly good eyes can spot these magnificent animals.*

SERVES 6

18 slices French bread loaf, 1 inch each
   (or use 8 slices of white bread)

6 eggs

1½ cups milk

1½ cups half and half

1 teaspoon vanilla

⅛ teaspoon nutmeg

½ teaspoon cinnamon

½ cup butter, softened

TOPPING

1 cup brown sugar

2 tablespoons corn syrup

1 cup pecans, chopped

Butter a 9-inch baking dish. Fill with sliced bread. Mix eggs, milk, half and half, vanilla, and spices. Pour mixture over bread slices and cover. Refrigerate overnight.

In the morning, mix topping and spread evenly over egg and bread mixture. Bake in a preheated 350°F oven for approximately 50 minutes, until puffed and golden.

CHAPTER SEVEN

Stove-Top Pancakes, Toasts, and Waffles

WYOMING BREAKFAST WITH BINOCULARS, OR DRIVING WITH THE CATTLE TO BREAKFAST

On a crisp, sunny morning we headed out to Big Horn from Sheridan, Wyoming, to Ron Spahn's Bed and Breakfast. Progress was delightfully delayed by a cattle drive—several hundred head were moving from the valley to mountainside grazing slopes for the summer months. Four wranglers on horseback moved to the shoulder of the road and looked back at our jeep, expecting us to take some action. The herd of cattle filled the road for at least a mile as far as I could see, so I shouted "I am a city slicker. What do we do here?"

One cowboy responded, "Just work your way through."

So we did. Most of the cattle politely parted to the sides, but several obstinate ones stood their ground solidly. One frisky calf scampered alongside as a mascot.

Spahn had invited us for breakfast with our binoculars, to take advantage of the chance to see wildlife from high atop his paradise. On some occasions, a moose might stroll so close that binoculars aren't needed. We sat on the porch happily eating buttermilk pancakes in the sweet, fresh air, feeling as if we were in the midst of more animals than we had ever imagined.

Buttermilk Pancakes

*B*Y FIRST *measuring the buttermilk in a 1 or 2-cup glass measuring cup and whisking in the egg and melted butter, these can efficiently be poured into the dry ingredients. Mixing each separately and completely allows a nifty, quick combination to prevent the flour gluten from toughening the pancakes. Experiments with butter and vegetable oil show each gives excellent results, but the butter does depart its characteristic taste. When adding fruit or extracts, you don't taste the butter, so oil might be the healthier alternative.*

YIELD: 8 CAKES

¾ cup buttermilk

1 egg

1 tablespoon melted butter

1 cup all-purpose flour

1 tablespoon sugar

½ teaspoon salt

½ teaspoon baking powder

½ teaspoon baking soda

In a glass measuring cup mix buttermilk, egg, and butter. In a small mixing bowl combine flour, sugar, salt, baking powder, and baking soda. Pour liquid into bowl, stirring with swift strokes until just moistened. Do not be concerned with lumps. Use a ¼-cup measure to pour batter on medium-heat griddle that has been treated with vegetable spray. Cook until bubbles appear, for about 3 minutes. Flip and continue cooking for another minute.

Notes:

- Beat whites separately for lighter pancakes.

- Cakes should be served immediately as they toughen when held.

- For whole grain pancakes, use half whole wheat and half white flour.

- If no syrup is to be used on the finished pancake, double the sugar in recipe.

- Add 1 tablespoon fresh fruit per pancake.

- If plain milk is used instead of buttermilk, use 1 teaspoon baking powder and eliminate all the baking soda.

- Mix with sparkling water for a bit of different texture.

Jackson Lake Lodge
Buckwheat Blueberry Pancakes

*R*OBERT WALTON, *the executive chef of the Grand Teton Lodge Company, for years directed all the food programs and restaurants in this Wyoming National Park. It is a daunting job making sure that all the summer visitors are well-fed and that he has sufficient staff to meet the seasonal demands.*

Two out-of-doors breakfasts require advance reservations. One is a boat trip to an island in the middle of Jackson Lake, where chefs cook while deer and other animals watch their human visitors. Another is a horseback ride (or horse-pulled wagon for nonriders) to an outdoor cowboy breakfast.

YIELD: 16

1 cup buckwheat flour

1 cup all-purpose flour

2 tablespoons sugar

1 teaspoon baking powder

1 teaspoon salt

¼ teaspoon cinnamon

2 cups milk

¼ cup vegetable oil

1 egg

½ lemon, juiced

⅛ teaspoon vanilla

½ cup blueberries, fresh, frozen, or canned and drained

In a large mixing bowl combine flours, sugar, baking powder, salt, and cinnamon. In a small bowl combine milk, oil, egg, lemon juice, and vanilla. Stir wet ingredients into dry and quickly mix. Fold in blueberries.

Pour ¼ cup for each pancake onto a medium-hot griddle. Cook until air bubbles start to burst on surface, about 2 minutes. Flip and cook 1 to 2 minutes more until golden brown.

Native American Wild Rice

On the shores of Kitche Gummi (Ojibway name for Lake Superior meaning "great water"), wild rice is still the domain of the Native Americans. Manoomin, as the Indians call the rice, grows best in clear, shallow lakes with depths from three to seven feet. The American Indians still have exclusive rights for harvesting wild rice on the reservations, which accounts for approximately 10 percent of the annual harvest. Commercially grown products, paddy wild rice, is said by the hand-harvesters to be inferior because it has a lighter color and milder taste. The harvesting method of cutting from a canoe has changed little over the centuries. After cutting, hulls are removed by sun drying, then are processed in a steel drum with heat to pop off the hulls. Sieves are used to separate the hull from the grain and for grading.

A simple breakfast is a bowl of cooked wild rice seasoned with butter, salt, and cinnamon, then garnished with raisins. A practical technique is to make the rice the night before, then reheat in the morning.

The Grand Portage Hotel, at the northeastern tip of Minnesota, owned and operated by the Native Americans, serves wild rice pancakes. Typically, 1 cup cooked wild rice is mixed with 2 cups buttermilk pancake batter. An alternative is to grind wild rice into flour and use 1/2 cup of it with 2 cups of all-purpose flour in a pancake recipe. The pancake becomes a carbo-loaders dream, full of chewy grains. The pancakes are somewhat heavy, not for those who are fussy about light cakes.

The wild rice theme is also carried through with turkey and wild rice sausage and wild rice breads. For breads the rice grains should be soaked in water for ten minutes then cooked for twenty to maintain a firm, chewy texture similar to that of wheat berries.

The Unicorn's Souffléd Pancake
with Strawberry-Honey Sauce

DAVID NOBEL let his creativity go wild—he needed a solution to the dispirited feeling that his wife, Arlan, was suffering from just before giving birth to their daughter. It was the first week after opening their Unicorn Inn in South Gillies, Ontario, about fifteen miles south of Kakabeka Falls Provincial Park. The old farmhouse, tucked into 440 acres of country serenity framed by the rugged cliffs of the Canadian Shield, was eventually to become the highest rated restaurant in the Lake Superior region of Canada.

Downstairs in the kitchen Chef Nobel began to beat egg whites in a manner similar to an old German recipe, but finished with the panache of an experienced baker and expectant father. Knowing that this breakfast would cheer up the most reluctant morning-greeter—and Arlan—he lovingly seasoned his soufflé with Grand Marnier and fresh orange zest. Then ever so gently he folded the ingredients and placed them in a well-seasoned cast-iron skillet. After a brief cooking on top of the stove it went into the oven while he made the strawberry-honey topping.

A large wedge of the pancake with the strawberry sauce was then delivered to Arlan, who devoured his gift, felt much better, and later delivered their daughter, Sarah. Sarah, now 12, adores the same German pancake.

And from that day on, this has been the Unicorn Inn's morning specialty. Guests select their breakfast hour the night before so that the soufflé can be at the point of perfection. The fresh juice is squeezed, the rich scones are made with heavy cream and served with sweet butter and homemade preserves, and freshly ground gourmet coffees are steaming hot. By the way, this soufflé does not loose its puff; it proudly sits up until the last bite.

SERVES 3

SOUFFLÉ

4 large eggs

¼ teaspoon cream of tartar (use if not whipping whites in a copper bowl)

2 tablespoons cornstarch

¼ teaspoon fine sea salt

1 tablespoon sugar

¼ cup milk

3 tablespoons hot water

1 tablespoon Grand Marnier

zest of 1 orange, made in long fine shreds

2 tablespoons unsalted butter

STRAWBERRY-HONEY SAUCE

2 cups frozen strawberries, thawed

¼ cup light honey

For Soufflé: Separate whites and yolks. Place yolks into a medium-size mixing bowl. In a small bowl combine cornstarch, salt, and sugar. Whisk starch mixture into yolks, combining well. Add milk, water, Grand Marnier, and zest. Preheat a 10-inch cast-iron skillet over low heat. In a large bowl with an electric mixer beat egg whites until foamy. Add cream of tartar (omit if using a copper bowl) and continue beating until the whites are very stiff.

Melt butter in skillet. Warm yolk mixture slightly by whisking over a hot-water bath. Scrape whites into yolk mixture. Fold in well by hand. Pour batter into pan. Cook over low heat for 3 minutes. Transfer to a preheated 400°F oven. Cook for 10 minutes or until set and well browned. Cut soufflé into wedges and transfer to warm plates. Serve immediately with warm Strawberry-Honey Sauce.

For Strawberry-Honey Sauce: Heat honey in a double boiler over simmering water. Add the strawberries and stir well. Cover and heat for 7 to 10 minutes or until hot and still brightly colored.

Note: At the Unicorn, fresh farm eggs make this a more flavorful dish. Frozen strawberries are preferred to fresh since the berries' structure when thawed easily releases the juices. Fresh berries can be used by cooking longer to release juices.

Bay of Islands Kerikeri Orange and Macadamia Nut Piklets with Fresh Orange and Maple Syrup

WILLIAM VAN HEESWYCK and Debbie Armatage, manage the deluxe Kimberely Lodge, Russell, in Bay of Islands, New Zealand. For breakfast, this small, thick pancake made from local oranges from Kerikeri and the first harvest of nuts brought us back inside from gazing at the magnificent harbor.

YIELD: 1 DOZEN
2½-INCH PANCAKES

1 cup all-purpose flour

2 tablespoons macadamia nuts, chopped

1 tablespoon sugar

1 teaspoon baking powder

½ teaspoon salt

½ cup milk

1 egg

1 tablespoon butter, melted

1 tablespoon grated orange zest

½ cup maple syrup

¼ cup fresh Kerikeri orange juice

Mix flour, nuts, sugar, baking powder, and salt in a small mixing bowl. Stir together milk, egg, butter, and zest in another small mixing bowl. Pour wet ingredients into dry and quickly mix.

Pour batter 1 tablespoon at a time on a greased flat-bottomed pan over medium heat, making 2-inch diameter cakes. Cook until air bubbles start to burst or for 2 minutes. Flip and cook 1 minute more. Mix together maple syrup and orange juice in a small saucepan. Bring just to the boiling point. Serve warm.

Pancakes with Aloha

ONCE I heard the famous Hilo, Hawaii, photographer and professor John Penisten brag about how much his daughters, aged 8 and 11, loved his weekend breakfast pancakes. So I challenged him for his recipe.

Of these dad breakfasts, Penisten says, "My girls enjoy trying things like banana slices, pineapple, strawberries, and kiwifruit, just to name a few. Just before turning over the pancakes, I add the fruit pieces, and I have an assortment of syrups available, like guava, passion fruit, pineapple, and genuine maple syrup. Powdered sugar can be used to dust pancakes, too.

"Serve the pancakes with a cheery warm smile and hugs for the youngsters," said Penisten. "Remember neither the pancakes nor the diners stay young forever."

YIELD: 14 TO 16
SMALL PANCAKES

1¼ cups buttermilk pancake flour

1 cup milk

1 egg

1 tablespoon vegetable oil

Mix ingredients in a large bowl. Hand-stir with fork until ingredients are just blended. Preheat griddle to medium or until drops of water dance on the pan. Avoid high heat, which burns pancakes while leaving soggy middles. Swab pan with small amount of oil on paper towel, to prevent sticking and aid in browning.

Place small amounts of batter no larger than palm of your hand on griddle. Turn over when air bubbles almost cover the surface and edges are dry. Remove from pan when other side is golden brown. Do not burn.

Note: A Quaker Oats survey in 1994 found that the number of dads fixing breakfast on weekends in America only jumped to 21 percent from the weekday 15 percent. Moms fix 61 percent of weekday breakfasts for children. Perhaps the most significant finding was that breakfast is a great time for the family to talk and visit.

Roti Jala, Lacy Coconut Pancakes with Tropical Fruits

*R*OTI JALA *is a splendid action-cooking item for special breakfasts or brunch in Malaysia and Singapore. Similar to a lacy pancake, these can also be served as a dessert with a fruit sauce. The mold is about the size of a half cup with a handle and a series of tiny funnels in the bottom. The batter is swirled onto a hot griddle, permitted to set, then folded into quarters forming a triangle.*

Local fresh fruits add a pleasant counterpoint. Popular tropical fruits include mango, papaya, rambutan (hairy reddish pink with spines), guava, coconut, banana, pineapple, carambola, or mixtures. At home one could use durian. The durian, *a giant yellow green fruit with dangerously sharp pyramidal spikes, is one of the mysteries of the food world. How can the durian be nirvana to some and immediately nauseating to others? Without an answer to that perplexing dilemma, hotels request that the smelly durian be left outside.*

S E R V E S   8

2 eggs

2 cups coconut milk, strained

½ teaspoon salt

12 drops yellow food color

2 cups (8 ounces) flour

½ cup (4 ounces) clarified butter or ghee

fresh tropical fruits

Beat eggs till fluffy. Whisk in milk, salt, and food coloring. Add flour, stirring constantly until smooth. Let batter sit for 15 minutes.

Brush medium-heat griddle with butter. For each serving, place ⅓ cup batter in roti jala mold (see Notes). With a gentle circular swirling motion, drop batter in lacy strands on an 8-inch diameter portion of the griddle. Cook for about 15 seconds until batter is set. With a spatula, flip over and finish cooking. Fold over into quarters to form a triangle. Serve immediately with a generous selection of fresh tropical fruits.

Notes: A roti jala mold can be made by drilling 5 holes with a ³⁄₁₆-inch drill bit in a ½-cup plastic measuring cup with a handle. If batter is too thin, individual drops will form instead of lacy lines, so add up to ½ cup flour. If batter is too thick and won't pour easily through the mold, add up to ½ cup water.

This recipe is adapted from the Pan Pacific Hotel, Kuala Lumpur, Malaysia.

101 Waffle Whimsies

*A*N ALL-AMERICAN *tradition is pan-cakes in a million flavors, but waffles have not received as much attention, although they're ripe for additions. After determining how much batter your waffle iron uses (an 8-inch diameter circular one uses ⅔ cup), place the fruit or nuts in the measuring cup before filling it with batter. Lightly stir in the measuring cup, then pour into the iron. If the iron is lightly sprayed with vegetable spray just before cooking, sticking is a thing of the past.*

S E R V E S   4

2 eggs, separated

1 cup low-fat milk

1 tablespoon vegetable oil

½ teaspoon vanilla

½ cup all-purpose flour

½ cup whole wheat flour

1 tablespoon sugar

1 teaspoon baking powder

½ teaspoon salt

With an electric beater beat egg whites until stiff. In a medium-size bowl whisk egg yolks, milk, oil, and vanilla. With a spoon quickly mix in flours, baking powder, sugar, and salt until just slightly lumpy. With a spatula gently fold in egg whites.

Heat waffle iron, following manufacturer's directions. On most machines the light will go out when it is ready for batter. Pour measured amount in sprayed waffle iron, spreading to cover about three-quarters of the surface. The light will go out again when a light waffle is cooked. Allow several more minutes if crispness is desired. Subsequent batter should be added immediately after reheating the waffle iron.

Waffle Variations

Fold into measuring cup with batter 1 tablespoon of any of the following or any combination of these items, chopped, for one waffle:

- *fresh strawberries, peaches, apples, plums, pears, banana*

- *banana chips, candied ginger, chocolate chips*

- *raisins, sun-dried cranberries or cherries, prunes*

- *pecans, walnuts, peanuts, sunflower seeds, poppy seeds, sesame seeds*

Notes: Fruit juice can be substituted for the milk and the flavors made more prominent by using 1 teaspoon of the zest.

In place of sugar, try 1 tablespoon of jam or preserves. Then experiment with extracts other than vanilla such as maple, lemon, and peppermint. Include up to ½ teaspoon of spices such as cinnamon, ginger, allspice, and nutmeg.

Fruit-Stuffed Brioche French Toast

STEPHEN PEDALINO, *executive chef of the Mountain Sky Guest Ranch, lives by his philosophy—use top-quality, fresh ingredients and prepare with a variety of cuisine styles. It must be the food that his guests want and the food that makes them happy. It is obvious that he enjoys pleasing folks because the buffet variety is as enormous as Montana's outdoors, with wild berries, potatoes, noodle kugel, fresh mountain trout in brown butter, lamb or venison sausage, pastries, French toasts, buckwheat pancakes, omelets to order, and an amazing variety of prepared egg dishes. His egg dishes also run the gamut from shirred eggs with fresh chilies, tomatoes, spinach, and asadero queso to poached eggs with Parma ham on brioche with hollandaise, to scrambled eggs with peppers, cheeses, and fresh herbs. A spicy shredded beef with onions is another offering.*

SERVES 6

1 cup strawberries, sliced (use more if desired)

2 bananas, sliced

½ lemon, juiced

12 slices brioche loaf, cut deep pocket inside of 1½-inch thick slices

8 eggs

1¼ cups heavy cream

pinch salt

½ cup sugar

¼ teaspoon cinnamon

pinch nutmeg

1 teaspoon vanilla

1 mango, sliced

1 nectarine, sliced

½ cup chopped pecans

confectioners' sugar

Soak strawberries and bananas in lemon juice. Stuff fruit into brioche pockets. Dip each brioche side into the mixture of eggs, cream, salt, sugar, cinnamon, nutmeg, and vanilla. Cook each side on a hot griddle until golden brown. Combine mango, nectarine, and pecans. To serve, dust toast with confectioners' sugar and top with sliced fruit and nuts.

Colonial Williamsburg's White Corn Hoe Cakes

ACCORDING to Patricia Gibbs, a food historian in Colonial Williamsburg, the eighteenth-century Virginia inhabitants were early risers off to mind their business—such as George Washington's overseeing his fields or William Byrd's doing paperwork—for several hours before breakfast.

In the kitchens, it took about 1 hour to get a good fire going from coals baked the previous night. Often bread was rising overnight (baking powder had not yet been invented), then freshly baked in the morning to be served with slices of yesterday's roast, a hash, or paper-thin slices of cured Virginia hams. Both coffee and tea were enjoyed.

A broken, metal-headed 10 × 7-inch hoe could be recycled in the kitchen—an ideal implement for cooking white corn cakes over the open hearth—which is how they became known as hoe cakes. These corn cakes were also cooked on griddles or buried in the ashes. The cake could be eaten dipped in melted butter with a drizzle of sweet, earthy molasses.

YIELD: 6 CAKES

1 cup white corn meal, stone-ground
½ cup water
½ teaspoon salt
1 tablespoon cooking oil
2 tablespoons sorghum molasses
butter, melted for dipping

Mix meal with water and salt. Stir until completely incorporated. Take about ¼ cup in the hands and pat into a roundish ½-inch patty. Brush cooking oil on griddle and bring to a medium heat. Cook each hoe cake until browning begins or for about 3 minute and turn over. Cook until golden brown or for 2 more minutes. Serve with a drizzle of dark sorghum molasses. Dip morsels into melted butter.

Note: Depending on the dryness of the corn meal, another tablespoon or so of water may be needed to bind the cake.

Singapore's Little Indian Roti Canai, Paper-Thin Griddle Bread

*I*N SINGAPORE *one can hop from the elegance of Raffles Hotel's newly renovated splendor and the international buffets at modern high-rise Marina Mandarin Hotel restaurants to hawker food stands. In these immaculate outdoor cooking facilities, hungry breakfasters watch the action of swirling dough to create roti canai. One hand revolves while the other anchors the huge thin platter of wheat-based dough, stretching it thinner than the thinnest paper. Then the giant disk is popped on a griddle, flipped with a spatula, folded into papery layers and cut with a Chinese cleaver into finger-size strips. The heat-brave opt for a fiery sambal topping and a cup of thick local coffee.*

Competitions for roti dough swirling are great culinary sport—an enchanting, mesmerizing dough expansion that stretches highly developed gluten strands (benefiting from an overnight rest) well beyond believable limits.

When I started playing with this dough, my swirling ended up more like a shredding operation. I found that the dough can be placed on a lightly floured board and rolled, pulled, and coaxed into a huge, thin sheet with little effort. They were never perfectly round, but what difference does that make when the cooked versions are folded over and sliced?

SERVES 8

5 cups all-purpose flour

1½ cups water, warm

1 tablespoon sugar

1 teaspoon salt

1 egg

3 tablespoons ghee or clarified butter

Mix all ingredients except ghee. Knead with bread hook for 10 minutes. Divide into 8 balls. Let rest a minimum of 8 hours covered in refrigerator.

Spread ghee or butter on balls and flatten. Similar to pizza dough tossing action, spin dough until paper thin. Place on 18-inch diameter hot griddle brushed with ghee, and cook until browning begins. Flip and finish cooking.

Fold in sides to form 9-inch diameter circle. On cutting board, score with cleaver or sharp kitchen knife so that slices can be pulled off and eaten by hand. Serve with hot sambal or dahl.

Note: Roti Pratas are made by adding 1 beaten egg on top of the almost-cooked roti canai before folding. Other popular fillings are fish and onions.

Venezuelan Corn Arepas

*C*ORN *arepas, or "Venezuelan bread," are worth the trip to Venezuela. Typically round and slightly flattened, they are sold all over the country in special shops.*

Made of harina pan, *a precooked white corn flour, they have no resemblance to the coarse corn bread that uses meal not previously cooked. To make arepas, harina pan is essential. Before leaving the country, my trip to a supermarket ensured that I had sufficient quantities to start experimentation back home until I could find a local or mail-order source. Much to my delight the harina pan is readily available in the United States.*

Typically round and slightly flattened, these are ubiquitous. Plain, they are served with a meal, filled they can be the whole meal. The heap of fillings ranges from soft cheeses similar to crème fraiche to shredded meats with tomatoes and onions. Rather than frying arepas, they can be flattened a bit, browned on each side on a stove-top grill, then finished in the oven.

On the resort island of Margarita I looked for a cookbook with arepa recipes.

The lady in the bookstore, quite accustomed to tourist's requests, said no recipe is needed because "they are too easy to make."

At the Hotel Melia, Caracas, Venezuela, Executive Chef Alejandro Sarabia makes a smaller version, called arepitas, which fit on the plate along with other foods.

YIELD: 8 TO 10

2 cups harina pan, precooked white
   corn flour

1 teaspoon salt

2 cups water

Mix flour with salt. Stir in water to make stiff dough. Let stand 5 minutes. Form into balls 3 × ½ inch. Cook on greased griddle over moderate heat 5 minutes a side. Bake at 350°F for 20 to 30 minutes, turning 2 or 3 times during cooking.

Note: To make cheese arepas, add
1 cup *queso fresco* or *queso blanco.*

Father's Day at the Hotel Melia Caribe, Caracas, Venezuela

The Hotel Melia Caribe's director of food and beverage, Dr. Jose Luis Viaduretta, had specifically featured criolo foods, those of the progeny of the Spanish settlers, for this Father's Day morning repast. Families on this Sunday morning studied the buffet table and went back to their seats with heaping plates.

In perfect English (having earned a Ph.D. in Dairy Science at Louisiana State University), Viaduretta created an indescribable hunger for this cuisine. Viaduretta is a professor of food science at Caracas's Simon Bolivar University. Much of the food had substance, such as the caraotas negros, black beans, and the deep-fried arepas.

Seafood is abundant off the shores of La Guaira, the major port town just north of Caracas. But the locals do not like to eat too much fish. Taking advantage of the local supply, we had sweet-sour baby shark that had been cooked with fresh tomatoes. For red meat lovers, there was carne machada (beef cooked and shredded), sausages, and sliced hams. Five different fruit juices included watermelon, cantaloupe, pineapple, papaya, and orange on that particular day.

Cheeses are popular for breakfast. Several fresh cheeses, such as the tangy queso blanco or the queso palmita, are quite popular. One of the country's specialties is a seven-month aged white cheese, queso de ano, which is wrapped in coffee grounds for the aging process. Another popular selection is yellow, round, and wrapped in red wax in the style of a Gouda.

The Venezuelan coffee, "far superior to the Colombian-grown beans," said Viaduretta, is strong, hot, and thick, often cut with milk and sugar. Served "American" style, it comes with a bottle of hot milk so you can cut your own.

One very special treat was the hallaquita, a corn meal dough with bits of meat wrapped and tied in corn husk and simmered in chicken stock. Similar to a tamale, it was smooth, dense, delicious, and difficult to unwrap.

Fresh fruit marmalades are popular. Similar are the guava shells, peeled with seeds removed, cooked in sugar spiked with cinnamon. This same treatment is done with passion fruit peels.

Giant doughnuts dipped in chocolate with silver nonpareils the size of BB's, copious pastries, and other sweets were popular items.

Homestyle Papaya Johnnycakes

*J*OHNNYCAKES, *a deep-fried golf-ball-size dense dumpling, are a substantial offering. Chef Xavier Morgan, at the Trident Villas and Hotel in Port Antonio, Jamaica, adds new twists to Johnnycakes with pureed papaya and seasonings of nutmeg and cinnamon. After frying he adds a sprinkle of sugar.*

YIELD: 12

Mix flour, milk, papaya, salt, baking powder, nutmeg, cinnamon, butter, and egg in bowl. Knead until a thick dough is formed.

Pinch off pieces. Form into large balls by pulling dough over and tucking in with thumbs. Fry in 1 inch of vegetable oil until golden brown. Drain, sprinkle with sugar, and serve hot.

2 cups (8 ounces) all-purpose flour

¼ cup (2 ounces) milk

½ cup pureed papaya

¼ teaspoon salt

2 teaspoons baking powder

¼ teaspoon nutmeg

¼ teaspoon cinnamon

2 tablespoons (1 ounce) butter, room temperature

1 egg

vegetable oil for frying

2 tablespoons sugar

Tortillas de Harina, Flour Tortillas

JANE BUTEL, in her Albuquerque studio, taught me how to make these staple tortillas. Trying both lard and solid shortening, we agreed that the lard taste was superior. Oh well, all things in moderation. This recipe is adapted from her Tex-Mex Cookbook *(New York: Crown, 1980).*

YIELD: 8 TO 10

4 cups all-purpose flour

2 teaspoons salt

2 teaspoons baking powder

½ teaspoon sugar

4 tablespoons lard, solid vegetable shortening or butter

1 ½ cups water, warm

Combine dry ingredients. Cut in shortening with a pastry blender or fingers. Add warm water, a few drops at a time, and work dough with hands until manageable. Knead dough 15 times. Let stand covered for 10 minutes.

Form egg-size balls. Roll with a bollito or small rolling pin on a lightly floured board to ⅛-inch thick and about 6-inches in diameter. Cook on an ungreased preheated griddle until light brown flecks form on each side.

The Cereal Granary
and Soup Pot

KELLOGG'S, THE GIANT FILLING BOXES

The original cornflake, invented in 1898 by Will Keith Kellogg, was prescribed in the Battle Creek, Michigan, sanitarium owned by his brother, Dr. John Kellogg. Cold cereal, an important part of the sanitarium's health program, quickly was copied by scores of manufacturer's rolling wheat, then corn, into flakes. A bit of a family squabble precipitated W. K.'s leaving his job with the sanitarium and creating the W. K. Kellogg Company in 1906. Other superstar cereals followed: Bran Flakes (1916), Rice Krispies (1928), Raisin Bran (1942), Frosted Flakes (1952), and Fruit Loops (1963).

The snap, crackle, pop and the family feud could be heard around the world as W. K. Kellogg sued his competitors. This was just the start of the fiercely competitive dry-cereal market. Today in the United States, Kellogg's has 35 percent of the market; General Mills is close behind with 29 percent; and Post has only 12 percent.

Kellogg's is big business in the global market, reaching more than 800 million consumers worldwide. The first plant outside Battle Creek, Michigan, opened in 1914 in Ontario, Canada, followed by its 1924 plant in Sydney (where Rice Krispies are called rice bubbles). The first plant in Great Britain opened in 1938. Now plants are in operation worldwide, including Latvia, Hong Kong, and India.

The most recent analysis of ready-to-eat cereals lists Ireland with the highest consumption at seventeen pounds per person per annum. Other power cereal eaters are the

United Kingdom at fourteen pounds, Australia at thirteen pounds, Canada and the United States at ten pounds. From there it dramatically falls off with Denmark at five pounds, Germany and France at three pounds, Mexico at two pounds, South Africa and Spain at one pound, and Venezuela at 0.5 pounds. Poor markets are South Korea with six ounces, Japan, Colombia, and Argentina with four ounces, and Brazil with less than one ounce.

Cold cereal production is a series of violent incidents in which materials are mixed, formed, flaked, steamed, toasted, roasted, sprayed, exploded, and cut. It's a song of praise to modern food technologist. To make flakes, corn grits, milled rice, brans of corn, wheat, or oat, and flours are cooked under steam pressure with added flavorings, vitamins, and minerals. Flaking mills exert tons of pressure to flatten the dried mix into thin flakes. Toasting brings out colors, flavors, and crispness. More vitamins are added by spraying. Flakes can be frosted by being sprayed with hot syrup in a rotating drum, then quickly dried.

Puffed cereals come from dried pellets subjected to extreme pressure and temperature, causing them to expand to several times the original size. Other cereals are extruded from cooked dough into long ropes that are cut with high-speed knives.

The heat-sealed colorful cartons with moisture-proof liners ultimately find their way to the supermarkets where aggressive distributors have found shelf space. Savvy consumers or anyone shopping with a child knows that cereals are usually stocked by manufacturer, with healthful cereals on higher shelves and flashy, sweet, cereals with plastic toys and premiums just at the little ones' eye levels.

But all this technology and marketing are not without a cost. Consider the price of raw ingredients going into the products. Why not eat fortified whole grain bread with jams and drink a glass of milk at a fraction of the price? Cold cereal advocates might answer "It is so convenient, can be eaten right out of the box, needs no special storage, can easily travel, and tastes good."

Muesli, New Zealand Style

NATIVE *New Zealand chef Mick Dryden of the Panama Brasserie in Parkroyal, Wellington, serves this rich version of muesli. It is one of the few cereals of which I have witnessed folks having second helpings. Dr. Max Bircher-Benner, the doctor who invented the cereal, would certainly have protested having his name on this recipe under the guise of a healthful food. Quickly he would substitute all the cream and whole milk with slimming, fat-free skim milk.*

SERVES 4

4 ounces rolled oats

2 ounces sliced almonds

2 ounces raisins

2 ounces whole hazelnuts

3 ounces honey

⅔ cup (5 ounces) light cream

⅔ cup (5 ounces) milk

1 diced apple

1 diced banana

Mix all ingredients together. Refrigerate 12 hours. Serve with seasonal fruit.

Muesli for Health

Dr. Max Bircher-Benner, the Swiss physician who died in 1939, advocated a healthy living regime, including raw foods—quite a radical approach in an era when uncooked foodstuffs were considered unhealthy.

His recipe for muesli used ten grams of rolled oats soaked in three tablespoons water for twelve hours. The oats were enriched with one tablespoon of sweetened condensed milk or yogurt, honey, and the juice of half a lemon, and he added one large unpeeled, grated apple, seeds, core, and all, sprinkled with one tablespoon grated walnuts, hazelnuts, or almonds. Another of his creations he called "raw fruit porridge." Fruits such as plums, cherries, strawberries, apricots, and peaches, were suitable.

Muesli appears around the world today in many guises. Those made with heavy cream certainly transcend the healthy bounds established by Dr. Bircher-Benner, but the taste is a richly sensational way to start the day.

Granola, unlike the uncooked muesli, is toasted grains sweetened and mixed with fruit and nuts. Touted in the early seventies as the healthy breakfast, it has suffered some disrepute from the use of coconut oils and fats in its preparation. Still, many health food stores and co-ops are stocked with bins of granola in as many flavor combinations as a chain ice-cream store, and today, granolas' loyal followers have a multitude of choices, including the delicious nonfat versions.

Montana Breakfast Nuts

*O*N MY *first horseback outing at the incredibly luxurious Mountain Sky Guest Ranch in Emigrant, Montana, I was the only person on the Adult Beginners ride. What a treat to have wrangler Jascon Newton for my private lesson, which was followed by a glorious ride across bubbling streams, through the mountains, woods, and pastures blooming with summer wildflowers. Eclipsing this natural beauty were the fascinating tales Jascon related of his 7 months as the sole cowboy managing a giant herd for a large commercial venture.*

"Seven months alone makes one rethink quite a number of priorities in life," *he quipped.*

Never social affairs, his meals were built on fundamentals. For breakfast he often made his own cereals. Below is a variation of one of his staples, quite inexpensive when compared with those technological wonders in the brightly colored boxes.

YIELD: 4 CUPS

1½ cups stone-ground whole wheat flour

½ cup sugar

½ teaspoon salt

½ teaspoon baking soda

½ teaspoon cinnamon

1 cup buttermilk

1 teaspoon almond extract

¼ cup slivered almonds (optional)

Mix dry ingredients in a large bowl. Completely mix in wet ingredients. Pour into a baking sheet that has been treated with vegetable spray. Bake at 350°F until the edges are light brown or for 15 to 18 minutes. Remove to a cake rack and permit to cool for at least 2 hours. Break into large pieces and pulse in a food processor until pieces are the size of buckshot. Stir in almonds (optional). Bake at 275°F until mostly dry or for about 35 minutes, stirring halfway through baking time. Cool. Store in an airtight container.

Variations: Substitute ¼ cup bran for an equivalent amount of flour. Substitute 1 cup oats for ½ cup flour. Use other extracts and ground spices. Add dried fruits.

Mountain Sky Cowboy Breakfast

A special event at Mountain Sky Guest Ranch is the early morning ride under the giant, never-ending sky, across the mountains, through the forests and streams in the freshest of air. A backup wagon is possible, and walking will also pump up appetites.

Ranch manager Shirley Arsenault gets to the breakfast site early and has the fire blazing and the food near completion. She fries the bacon, scrambles eggs, and brews up a big blue tin pot of cowboy coffee, according to Chef Pendalino's rules. Efficiently, she only has to warm the biscuits, gravy, hash brown potatoes and blueberry muffins that were prepared in the ranch's kitchen. Copious quantities of fresh fruit are ready when the riders dismount from their ride.

The picnic tables near the stream are covered with red-and-white-checkered cloths and are complete with real china, cutlery, and blue enamel tin cups. The tins will soon be filled with hot coffee or hot cocoa. Shirley has even tucked in a few marshmallows for the younger ones to roast after breakfast.

Pop, Pop, Popcorn Cereal

*P*OPCORN, *believed by Native Americans to have a demon in each kernel who became angry near the heat and finally exploded, makes a superb breakfast cereal. Actually, the heated moisture sealed inside each kernel turns to steam to create the explosion. Orville Redenbacher, the Indiana agronomist, spent 40 years crossbreeding more than 30,000 hybrids to create his kernels that consistently popped up light and fluffy, earning him the title "Popcorn King."*

Redenbacher's breakfast cereal is based on an early American settler's recipe. While over 50 percent of the American market for popcorn is in microwave bags, it is much less expensive to pop your own. The newer gadgets for microwave ovens (such as Presto popper) make this an easy recipe.

YIELD: 4 CUPS

1 quart popped corn

1 teaspoon sugar or more to taste

1 teaspoon salt

¼ teaspoon cinnamon

pinch nutmeg

2 cups puffed cereal (rice, wheat, or both)

¼ cup raisins or dates

2 tablespoons chopped peanuts

Place popped corn in a large bowl. Mix together sugar, salt, and spices. Sprinkle over popcorn. Toss with remaining ingredients. Store in airtight container. Serve with milk.

Note: Our kid testers also enjoyed this as a snack item.

Battle Creek Cereal Festival and the San Antonio Livestock Show Breakfast

No doubt the original founder of the Battle Creek Sanitarium, which developed wheat flakes, Dr. Kellogg, would be horrified that Poptarts, Donut Holes, and Tang accompany today's lines of Kellogg, Post, and Ralston Foods, and of course, bananas and milk, at what is claimed to be the world's longest breakfast table. (Don't confuse this with the largest pancake breakfast held annually in Springfield, Massachusetts).

More important than the food is the community focus "Where one big family (of fifty thousand) eats breakfast together . . . and shares a special breakfast and multitude of friendship." Held on the second Saturday of June in downtown Battle Creek, more than three hundred tables are manned by four hundred volunteers serving a free breakfast. During the three-day festival, Miss Cereal City is crowned, and costumed bigger-than-life Tony the Tiger, Toucan Sam, and Snap, Crackle, and Pop cheerfully mingle with the crowd.

Held in conjunction with the San Antonio, Texas, Livestock Show and Rodeo, the north San Antonio Chamber of Commerce with five hundred volunteers serves a free breakfast to more than thirty-five thousand rodeo enthusiasts. From 5:45 A.M. to 9:00 A.M., on the menu are biscuits with beef gravy, sausage and bacon, sausage tacos, egg tacos, hash brown, juice, and coffee. And of course, 32,500 one-ounce packets of picante sauce.

Night-Before Grains

*B*OB'S RED MILL *(grains available by mail from 5209 SE International Way, Milwaukie, OR 97222) suggests preparing whole grains—wheat, rye, oat, millet, or blends the night before. It is also a terrific way to travel with your breakfast on a boat or a car trip.*

SERVES 6

1 cup wheat flakes

4 cups water

1 teaspoon salt

In a pan bring water, grains, and salt to a boil. Stir. Pour into a preheated thermos. Screw on cap. Turn on side until breakfast.

Note: Use a wide-mouth thermos for easy access to cooked cereals and for more efficient cleaning.

Hot Whole Grain Porridges

*B*RAN, *germ, and endosperm make up whole grains—the natural, basic complex carbohydrates boasting maximum fiber. Eating whole grains is a throwback to the way cereals were consumed before this era of high-processing. These wonderful cooked cereals leave you feeling full and supplied with brain fuel. Buckwheat groats are the fastest, cooking in only 15 minutes, whereas barley pokes along for about 85 minutes. Millet, popular with Lithuanians, is a tiny round grain that cooks up to be quite fluffy. It needs to be started 25 minutes in advance as do cracked wheat and amaranth. Brown rice or oats requires approximately 45 minutes. The prices of these cereals are remarkably modest.*

This chart suggests timing for 1 cup of whole grains that will yield from 2½ to 4 cups cooked.

155

GRAIN	WATER	TIME (minutes)
amaranth	3 cups	22
barley	3 cups	85
brown rice	2 cups	45
buckwheat groats	3 cups	15
bulgar	2 cups	18
cracked wheat	2 cups	25
millet	3 cups	25
oats	3 cups	40
wild rice	3 cups	60

Notes: For a nuttier taste, toast millet in heavy skillet for 5 minutes.

Since whole grains contain fat, it is best to store them in airtight containers, preferably refrigerated.

Scottish Oatmeal

*P*ERHAPS *no morning cereal comes with more tradition than Scottish porridge. When water has come to a boil, the oats are added in a steady stream with the left hand while the right hand stirs in a clockwise direction. The stirrer is a straight wooden stick also known as the spurtle or theevil. After simmering ¼ cup medium-size flakes of oatmeal in 1 cup of water for 10 minutes covered, a little salt is stirred in, then simmered over very low heat, covered, for another 10 minutes. Referred to as "they," it is best eaten in a wooden, birch bowl with a horn spoon. Milk or cream is served separately. Each spoonful of "they" is dipped into a separate bowl of cold milk or cream before eating. Scottish porridge is thinner than the Irish or English versions. And Scotsmen have been known to take a glass of stout or porter with their morning porridge.*

SERVES 1

1 cup water

¼ cup medium-size oat flakes,
    not quick oats

¼ teaspoon salt

cream or milk, in bowl

In a small pan bring water to a rolling boil. Stir in oats. Reduce heat to low and simmer covered for 10 minutes. Stir in salt. Continue to cook until all the water is absorbed or for about 10 minutes. Serve in a separate bowl from the cream or milk.

Note: The Scottish use oats in many forms: *Crannachan,* which is whiskey and oatmeal with cream; *Bannocks,* which are oat cakes made in front of fire on a griddle, divided into sixths; and *Brose,* cold oats with hot water.

Stockholm City Hall
Hot Rye Flakes with Lingonberries

STOCKHOLM'S city hall, a busy center well known for its Nobel prize banquets, hosts many other occasions, including breakfast. In the modern kitchen on the top floor, one of the chefs revealed his favorite hot cooked cereals—rye flakes. To the flakes cooked in water until just chewy, he adds fresh or frozen lingonberries and sugar.

SERVES 4

2 cups water

1 cup rolled rye flakes

1 teaspoon salt

¼ cup lingonberries

2 tablespoons sugar

In a medium-size pan over medium heat, bring water, rye, and salt to a boil. Stir and reduce heat to low. Cover. Cook until the water is absorbed by the grains or for about 20 minutes. Add berries and sugar before serving.

Note: Also try with oats, wheat, and triticale (a hybrid of wheat and rye with a rich protein content) or with fruits such as blueberries or cranberries, either fresh or sundried.

157

Bondi Beach Couscous with Figs and Honey

*A*T THE *beachside eatery at Bondi Beach in Sydney, Australia, I finally found couscous on a breakfast menu. Again the Australians should be lauded for their open-mindedness of cuisine. In the North African countries of Morocco, Algeria, and Tunisia, the couscous belt, it is claimed that no one ever eats the coarsely ground durum wheat in the morning. But after a busy morning on the waves, Australian surfers consume steaming bowls of the cooked grain served with figs and honey. The surfers, many of whom carry their boards in backpacks on bicycles, join morning swimmers or those out for a bit of fresh air, for a really healthy start to the day. Both Near East and Fantastic Food brands of couscous have breakfast cereal recipes printed on the box, and cookbooks suggest serving it as a porridge with milk and raisins.*

SERVES 4

1½ cups water

1 tablespoon butter

1 cup couscous, quick cooking (precooked)

½ teaspoon salt

2 dried figs or dates, chopped

4 teaspoons honey

Bring water to a boil in a medium-size saucepan. Stir in butter, couscous, and salt. Reduce heat and cover for 2 minutes. Remove from heat. Leave covered for 2 minutes or until most of the moisture has been absorbed. Spoon into bowls. Top with figs and drizzle with honey.

Ocho Rios Green Banana Porridge

WHEN I first tested this dish, what looked like a bad science experiment eventually turned into porridge, from a recipe by Chef Jean Paul Lucy at the elegant SuperClubs' Sans Souci Hotel and Spa in Ocho Rios, Jamaica. Never did I imagine that this much liquid would be thickened by four medium-size bananas. Also surprising is the taste. Many tasters could not even guess that it was made with bananas. The trick is to start with unripe, green bananas. Ask your grocer to let you know precisely when a new shipment is to arrive. Get the bananas and go.

SERVES 6

4 green bananas, medium, or 1 large plantain, peeled

4 cups milk

2 cups water

1 bay leaf

2 tablespoons sugar

½ teaspoon vanilla

½ teaspoon allspice

½ cup light cream

Place bananas in a blender with 2 cups milk and 1 cup water. Blend for about 2 minutes. In a medium-size saucepan bring to a boil. Add remaining milk, water, and bay leaf. Cook over medium heat until thickened for approximately 20 minutes. Stir in sugar, vanilla, and allspice. Drizzle with cream. Serve hot.

159

Mexican Two-Squash Soup with Avocado and Lime

*V*EGETABLES *are not usually a morning feature. The Mexican chefs and kitchen help often make versions of this colorful soup for a simple and healthful breakfast.* Chayote, *an indigenous Mexican pale green fruit with mild white flesh, has a single seed. Sometimes it is called* mirliton *in markets. If chayote is unavailable, use 2 zucchini.*

Chef Kathi Long gave me this miracle-of-the-morning vegetable soup while I was working on a magazine story in Santa Fe. Chef Long has cooked in many Mexican restaurants in the United States and traveled extensively through Mexico. Currently she teaches at the Santa Fe School of Cooking, where she specializes in healthful cuisine. Her salubrious touch can be seen in her book, Mexican Light Cooking *(New York: Perigee Books, 1992).*

SERVES 4

1 tablespoon vegetable or olive oil

1 onion, chopped

2 cloves garlic, minced

1 chayote, diced

1 zucchini, medium, diced

1 ear of corn, cut into ½-inch slices

2 cups water

1 bunch fresh cilantro, stems removed, chopped

3 roma tomatoes, diced

1 teaspoon salt

4 serrano chilies, finely chopped

1 avocado, diced

4 lime wedges, to garnish

cilantro sprigs, to garnish

In a large soup pan cook in oil, stirring over high heat, the onion, garlic, chayote, and zucchini until just soft for about 5 minutes. Add corn, cilantro, and water to cover. Cook over medium heat until corn is soft, for about 8 minutes.

Add tomatoes and salt. Cook until tomatoes are heated for 3 minutes. Add chilies and avocado. Ladle into bowl.

Garnish with lime wedges and cilantro. Serve with corn tortillas.

Note: A squeeze of lemon juice over the cut avocado will help prevent the flesh from browning for a short time.

The Cereal Granary and Soup Pot

161

Caldo Verde: Portuguese Green Soup

*H*OSPITALITY *at the government-owned-and-operated* pousadas *(inns in historic buildings, convents, monasteries, and castles) is copious and straight from the hearts of the giving Portuguese people. The castle hotel in Óbidos sits atop the hill several hours by train north of Lisbon.*

The station is a few miles from the walled town. Just across the tracks I could see the hill and the castle wall. Off I set on foot carrying camera equipment and with my computer in a backpack. It was a delightful climb through the massive gate and around the narrow streets of charming houses.

Even though caldo verde was not on the menu that day, the chef made a special pot for my breakfast. Teamed with the substantial broa, *a corn meal bread loaf (page 103), this makes a hearty breakfast. It is quite popular in the northern parts of the country and particularly suitable for those who work in the fields, or for hiking tourists.*

The finished soup is garnished with Portuguese sausage, linguica, or chorizo slices, olive oil, and freshly ground black pepper.

SERVES 4

4 cups water

2 large potatoes, peeled and quartered

1 clove garlic, peeled, sliced

½ pound fresh kale (substitute collard greens or spinach)

1 teaspoon salt

2 tablespoons olive oil

8 slices Linguica or chorizo

freshly ground black pepper

In a 3-quart pan over high heat bring water, potatoes, and garlic to a boil. Cook until potatoes are soft or for about 15 minutes. Add kale. Cook for 5 minutes. Add salt. Transfer to a food processor and pulse several times or until coarsely blended. Ladle into bowls. Add olive oil, chorizo slices and pepper.

Note: *Linguica* is a fatty, stuffed sausage link made with pork and garlic. *Chorizo* is now available in a low-fat version from Salamanca, Spain, called *Bovilight*, made from beef, veal, and white poultry meat.

Bora Özkök's Cultural Folk Tours

Turkey, across the Bosphorous, magnificently provides the transitions from Western to the Eastern countries. It is both a geographical and a cultural bridge. Women, in this country where 99 percent of the 60 million inhabitants are Muslim, were given the option to unveil when Ataturk led the country into its Westernization phase in 1923. Bora Özkök, the dynamic force and leader of Cultural Folk Tours, said that his grandmother went so far as to even wear a bikini.

But many women, especially in the rural areas, prefer to stay with the veil. The country's dichotomous approach to tradition, particularly to marriage, finds some young people making their own liaisons and others following the tradition of arranged marriages. With the arranged ones, the only time the couple may see each other is for a visit over tea and coffee, where the potential bride serves the potential groom while being chaperoned. Later the grandmother or another older woman, looking out for the best interest of the potential groom, will invite the young lady to a Turkish bath. In the rite of soaking, scrubbing, rinsing, and massaging, according to the ancient Roman style, all body parts are visible for a discreet inspection.

Bora, a native Turk now residing in California, shares his cultural knowledge of the Turkish people with his touring groups, visiting refined places such as the Blue Mosque and Topkapi Palace in Istanbul, as well as the mysteries of the underground limestone cave cities in Cappadocia. And in the covered bazaar in Beyazit with its four thousand shops, he is an excellent guide and a big help when bargaining for the finest silk and wool rugs the country has to offer.

It is a special treat to watch him sit in with his wind instrument playing Turkish tunes with any local group. But he really is in his element when dancing, energetic and frenetic. This is a country where the men, holding hands high above their heads in lines, more than the women seem to dance in public. Women can and do join in, of course, and their grace and sensuality is traditionally exhibited in the elegant style of belly dancing.

His passion for eating often prompts Bora to stop the tour in front of a local bakery, run in, and return with freshly baked bread for all. Or he might stroll up to a street vendor to buy simits (page 104), the ringed sesame breads, to share. Because the Turkish mezes, or appetizers, are probably the country's culinary strength, he makes sure plenty of these are available at both lunch and dinner for sampling with the freshly baked pitas.

Spicy Turkish Tomato Lentil Soup

TURKISH village women prepare the morning meal, kahvalti, which mainly consists of freshly baked breads, pungent black olives, and fresh tangy cheeses, served with tea in glasses. While seated for cooking over an open-hearth fire, the cook protects her lap with a sofra, a flat-woven heavy garment. The sofra weaving patterns are passed from mother to daughter. Tradition is very important in the villages, providing a sense of stability. "It is not a rug," the villagers claim of the sofra. "It is us."

In cold weather or in the mountains, soups such as lentil or vegetable are the morning fare. Meat soups are considered too heavy for the morning.

In ancient towns, soup kitchens provided foods much the same as they do today. Between 1550 and 1555, Suleyman the Magnificent built Daruzziyafe, a public soup kitchen, to celebrate the century celebration of the conquest of Istanbul. Today, in the magnificent arched halls with its open courtyard, this same soup kitchen is back in operation as a restaurant, serving, among other classic Turkish fare, soup.

Modern Turkish chefs still trace their cooking lineage to the last chef of the Sultan, including Yusuf Isler, executive chef at the Sheraton in Istanbul. He suggests enhancements for the simple village lentil soup, such as garlic, parsley, a little bit of cream, and a gratin of mild yellow cheese, and crunchy croutons to finish.

SERVES 4

2 tablespoons tomato puree

1 cup dried lentils, picked over

1 carrot

6 cups water

salt, to taste

black pepper, to taste

Place tomato puree, lentils, carrot, and water into a medium-size pan. Cook for about 1 hour or until the lentils lose their firmness. Add salt and pepper.

Notes: The ingredients can be pushed through a sieve if a thicker soup is desired.

The Lebanese form of this soup would include 1 teaspoon of ground cumin.

Chinese Congee (Jook)

ONGEE *is the ultimate in Oriental comfort food, warm, soupy, and available not only at breakfast but all day and night. Boiling rice in lots of water until it becomes creamy and white with just the tinniest bits of discernible grains is all there is to basic congee. It is not thick or lumpy like oatmeal.*

In Taiwan's earlier days, when the economy was not so strong, sweet potatoes were added to stretch the rice. Today they are added as a tradition. Congee is usually treated like an enhanceable starch base—a canvas to paint. Late night to early morning, dozens of congee restaurants abound, each outdoing the other with bowl after bowl of meats, vegetables, and condiments to put on the basic congee. Hot spicy sauces are available.

On the deck of the Marina Mandarin Hotel overlooking Singapore Harbor, congee is served with help-yourself dishes of dried fish, red chili peppers, green chili peppers, dried anchovies, and roasted salted peanuts.

SERVES 6

1 cup rice, long grain

3 quarts chicken broth or water

1 teaspoon minced gingerroot

1 teaspoon salt

GARNISHES

strips of cooked beef, pork, fish, shrimp, duck, clams, seaweed

tofu

salted eggs

stir-fried vegetables such as broccoli, bamboo shoots, bean sprouts, Napa cabbage, eggplant

hot pepper sauce

In a 3-quart pan over high heat bring rice, liquid, and gingerroot to a boil. Reduce heat to low and simmer, uncovered, until grains are broken up and the consistency is creamy and thick, for about 1½ hours. Stir occasionally. Add salt and garnishes.

Grace Liu's Return Visit to Taiwan

Grace Liu was the "number-two daughter," a sickly child who was to be left behind with relatives when her parents fled their native Hunan province of China. At the last minute, Grace was saved by her father, a Kuomintang Air Force engineering specialist following Chiang Kai-shek in the 1949 Nationalist China relocation to Taiwan.

"If we perish, we perish together in this new land" were the sentiments bravely declared by these opponents of communism.

So Grace Liu came to Taichung, situated several hours south of Taipei in the rich mountainous area, the Republic of China's third-largest city. Today, along with her husband, Dr. Eddie Liu, she is the owner of the highly acclaimed Dynasty Chinese Restaurant in Williamsburg, Virginia.

Recently, Grace and I returned to her family's old house in Taichung (all family members have since moved). The neighbors warmly celebrated her return with feasts and animated talking in the singing cadences of Mandarin Chinese. There was a strong feeling of happiness, shared remembrances, and love for missed friends. The neighborhood, one of the few not yet replaced with the city's modern concrete high-rises, bespoke the Japanese influence with interior gardens, sliding doors, and shoes left outside. Even the tree Grace climbed as a young girl remained.

I quickly learned that each time Grace made a phone call, it resulted in more family members and friends appearing—usually followed with a food celebration—not simply a meal, but a banquet.

"Chinese people love to eat," Grace constantly reminded me. And eat we did.

Our stated mission—research on breakfasts in Taiwan—quickly became enhanced by the strength, love, and warmth of traditional Chinese families. Grace's energetic and brilliant sister, Joan Lo, with a Ph.D. in economics from SUNY, is currently designing Taiwan's controversial national health insurance plans. Joan and her dentist husband shared their spare apartment with us, the one inhabited by Joan's elderly father-in-law. Their main apartment, a flat provided by the medical school, is shared with their two children and mother-in-law. Housing space is precious in Taipei.

In this busy working family, the grandmother (age seventy-nine), prepared the meals—including Szechwan-style feasts for us—and cared for the children while the grandfather visited daily to walk the little girl to school and participate in other family matters.

We ate soy milk served in bowls, in both sweetened or salty versions. Fried cruellers were sliced and used to top many dishes as were on-the-table condiments that ranged from spicy-hot to spicy-dangerous. Over small charcoal grills pancakes were made, thin and studded with sesame seeds. A bit later in the morning we stopped in restaurants to assuage our addictive dim sum habit.

We ate many foods of salubrious value at breakfast as well as at other meals, including shark's fin soup for strength and virility, red herbs to improve eyesight, and other popular treats such as fermented tofu-cheese (more pungent than Limburger), pig's hooves soup, and thimblefuls of potent rice wine.

Most Chinese abide by universal life principles, such as the roles of yin and yang in foods. They balance hot foods, such as beef, with cool foods, such as fresh fruits. Furthermore, they espouse the inseparability of food as medicine and medicine as food.

"Most of the people practice it. It works and makes life more energetic," stated one native Chinese woman. "Men, for example, are hot (yang) and need to consume more cooling (yin) foods."

"I'd like the people in the United States to appreciate more of the Chinese tradition and culinary richness," said Grace. "Learning more helps you to better understand others while enriching your life." For the Dynasty Restaurant, Grace said "I am particularly interested in promoting quality food. We do not have to keep all traditions. In this world we need to change. I am already experimenting and serving healthier and better food."

Thai Jasmine Rice Soup with Shrimp

*T*HE sidewalks and back alleys of Bangkok are filled with street vendors selling hot soups and noodles with an amazing array of condiments. This fragrant jasmine rice soup, Khao Tom, is one of the basics. Since it is made from cooked rice, it is a natural use of leftovers for creating fast morning fare. Considered a universal healing food with powers similar to that of chicken soup, it is the cure of choice when one feels poorly, including hangovers. Virtually any seafood or meats can be used to enrich the broth. Vinegar, chilies, salted eggs, and pickled vegetables can be added for more variety. Often these are eaten from a small, plastic bag—a container requiring adroit manipulations to avoid spilling.

SERVES 4

1 clove garlic, sliced

1 teaspoon oil

2 cups water or chicken stock

1 stalk celery, minced

¼ teaspoon white pepper

1 tablespoon Thai red chili paste or 1 teaspoon preserved vegetables (*tang chi*)

1 teaspoon light soy sauce

1 tablespoon fish sauce (*nam pla*)

1 cup cooked Jasmine rice

4 ounces shrimp, shelled and deveined

cilantro, garnish

In a small skillet sauté garlic in oil until golden. In a medium-size pan add water or stock, celery, pepper, chili paste, soy sauce, and fish sauce. Bring to a boil. Add rice. Stir. Cook for 2 minutes over medium heat. Add shrimp. Continue cooking until rice is completely heated and the shrimp have just turned an opaque pinkish white or for about 3 minutes. Garnish with fresh cilantro.

Korean "New Mother" Seaweed Soup

*I*T IS *a very old custom for mothers of newborns to have seaweed soup in the morning. A large handful of dried seaweed is thought to make the blood strong while helping the mother produce good milk.*

Kyu Hargrave and Chong White of the Kyu Tailor Shop in Williamsburg, Virginia, shared many variations for this soup. Kyu suggested doubling the quantity of seaweed for a thicker soup and adding 2 more cloves of garlic. Chong said dried anchovies expand the flavor dimensions.

Chicken, beef, or pork bones can be used to make stock. Even canned broth for a quicker version makes an excellent soup.

The dried seaweed from the package looks like black threads and will bulk up into large, green pieces of seaweed. It has a pleasant taste with a wonderful slippery texture.

SERVES 4

1 chicken (2½ pounds)

6 cups water

½ cup (½ ounce) dried seaweed (*ito-wakame*), broken into ½-inch pieces, well rinsed

salt to taste

black pepper

1 clove garlic, mashed (or more to taste)

169

In a large pot bring chicken in water to a boil. Cook over low heat, never permitting a boil, until the chicken starts to fall apart or about 1 or 2 hours. Remove chicken from pot and save meat. Refrigerate stock until fat hardens. Remove fat. Bring about 4 cups of stock and seaweed to a boil, adding more water if necessary. Boil until the seaweed becomes softened or for about 5 to 7 minutes. Season with salt, pepper, and garlic. Bring back to a boil and cook 2 more minutes.

Note: The seaweed taste can be enhanced by stir-frying in one teaspoon dark sesame oil before adding to the stock. Chicken meat can be added back to the soup or saved for another purpose. For a fast soup, use canned chicken stock.

Praying for World Peace in Kyoto Monastery
Kyoto, Japan—December 31.

The loud gong awoke us from our deep sleep inside warm futons on the tatami mats in the monastery. The head priest had graciously invited us to join the monks for the chilly predawn service. It was the type of weather that made suitcases obsolete for travelers; in the futile search for warmth every piece of clothing had to be layered on your body.

Sliding open our paper-thin door, we moved through the gardens to the unheated temple. The monks were assembled, chanting and periodically hitting the gong. We sat on the floor, thankful for the layers of clothing trying to protect us from the bitter cold.

After about forty-five minutes, the serene chants and words in Japanese ceased. The priest arose and approached us with a special message. "Thank you for praying with us for world peace," he serenely said with a wishful, patient, hopeful smile. Suddenly we were very warm in our hearts and spirits. We too fervently wanted peace. We now understood our invitation to the assembly.

We walked back to the monastery, removed our shoes, and filed into the austere room simply furnished with wooden benches and tables. Then steaming, glorious bowls of miso soup appeared along with the hot, deeply appreciated bowls of rice. The arrival of hot tea convinced us this was truly heaven on earth.

Because this was the last day of the year, the monastery would be closed to visitors such as ourselves.

We were sent off to a hotel in the monastery's upscale Toyota—with its white-lace seat protectors and jar of air freshener—a cold jolt of reality after our cocooned monastic life. The entire city was furiously cleaning in preparation for new beginnings. At midnight we joined the throng taking turns hitting a large wooden pole against a metal gong, then stopped for cold sake in freshly made cedar cups.

Japanese Miso-Shiru (Miso Soup)

*T*HE simplest Japanese breakfast is miso soup, rice, and nori (dried seaweed). Additions of pickled vegetables, fermented soybeans, broiled fish, and raw egg served with tea make it much more traditional.

The miso breakfast is served very simply in South Korea. The setup is a kettle of hot water, miso paste, bowls of dried seaweed threads, tofu, and finely sliced scallions. Each person adds a teaspoon or so of miso paste to the bowl, pours on the boiling water, stirs, then selects the desired garnishes from each of the bowls. This is an incredibly delicious and low-calorie start to the day.

SERVES 4

1 piece *kombu* (dried kelp), available in Oriental markets

4 cups water

1 teaspoon *katsuo-bushi* (dried bonito shavings)

1 tablespoon miso paste

In a medium-size pan over high heat bring kombu and water to a boil. Add katsuo-bushi and boil 2 minutes. Strain stock. Mix miso with a small amount of the hot water and add to the pan. Cook just to the boiling point. Serve in small bowls.

171

Note: Miso paste will keep indefinitely in a tightly sealed refrigerated container. For a bit more zing add ¼ teaspoon cracked Korean red chili peppers.

Saimin, Hawaiian Noodle Soup

SAIMIN is eaten in Hawaii for breakfast, lunch, dinner, and snacks. At the Banyan Tree Restaurant at the Ritz-Carlton Kapalua Hotel, it is served in huge bowls, loaded with noodles, garnished with scallions, fishcake slices, and chopped cooked eggs. The restaurant and the resort were originally planned to be right on the water's edge, but with the discovery of the Honokahua Burial grounds and 900 ancient graves dating between 610 and 1800, the entire resort was moved inland.

Japanese in origin, this soup stock can be a miso, dashi no moto, or chicken. The dried noodles are made of enriched wheat flour, semolina flour, salt, and water. The fishcakes, a mixture of surimi and spices, are sold in oriental markets. Another version is a "dry noodle," which is the cooked noodles and additions without the broth, similar to a pasta dish.

Many Hawaiian natives simply use a dry package of "ramen" for a quick breakfast or pick up a serving at their local McDonalds along with a fruit punch.

SERVES 3

6 cups boiling water

⅓ ounce shrimp dashi no moto (or 3 tablespoons miso paste)

2 tablespoons soy sauce

1 teaspoon sugar

salt to taste

7-ounce package dried saimin noodles

6 slices fish cake

1 hard-cooked egg, chopped

1 scallion, sliced

In a medium saucepan bring water to a boil. Stir in shrimp dashi no moto, soy, sugar, and salt. Add noodles and cook over medium heat until tender for 3 to 5 minutes. Serve in bowls garnished with fish cake, cooked egg, and scallion.

Chilled Cantaloupe Orange Mint Soup

O RANGE *mint and orange juice con-centrate flavor this easy-to-prepare summer cantaloupe soup, a cool way to start the day. Originally I served a version of this soup for dinner. But credit must be given to my clever cousin, Gene Spalding of Warm Springs, Georgia, for elevating it to breakfast. He requested the leftovers the next morning, proclaiming, "This is a great breakfast!" And indeed it is, particularly since it is high in vitamins and low in fat. Sprinkle a bit of cereal on top for crunch if desired. It also can be made ahead and refrigerated for several days—the ultimate in liquid breakfasts.*

SERVES 1

1 large cantaloupe, peeled, deseeded,
    cut into large chunks

1 cup nonfat plain yogurt

⅓ cup frozen orange juice concentrate

2 to 4 tablespoons sugar (optional)

⅓ cup fresh orange mint leaves

mint sprigs for garnish

Place all ingredients, except garnish, in food processor. Pulse until almost smooth, but still with a bit of chunkiness. Add optional sugar if melon is not perfectly sweet. Chill. Serve in frosty soup bowls. Garnish with mint.

Note: For five-star presentation, drizzle 3 thin concentric circles of yogurt in soup bowl. Pull knife from center to edge, imitating the spokes of a wheel. Finish the soup with a splash of Grand Marnier.

173

Potatoes, Beans, Vegetables, and Other Complex Carbohydrates

THE SPANISH RAILROAD, ATOCHA STATION, MADRID

After days of traveling around on the Eurorail system in and out of the masses of humanity in the European capital-city stations, I found Spain's rail system to be a breath of fresh air. International trains arrive in the main railroad station, Chambertin. It is only a fifteen-minute escape to reach this pavilion of Atocha, certainly the cleanest train station in the world. It is a public transportation station on a par with the luxurious Singapore airline terminal—perhaps not as posh, but airy, clean, and with an indoor tropical oasis of trees reaching toward the sky in an atrium. Atocha even has a large waiting room the size of a football field with enough seats, in contrast with many other stations, to seat the crowd arriving for a major soccer game.

I had just escaped from the madness of Paris, both the Gare de Lyon and the Gare d'Austerlitz stations, with an unwanted Hollywood touch of soldiers dressed in fatigues patrolling with guns. One is not surprised since several weeks earlier, the station had been bombed.

And for the travelers in need of refreshments, espresso, in singles and doubles, and a delightful sandwich of cold potato tortilla can be had at the same stand-up bar. This was a full-size portion of the cocktail tapas, served on freshly baked crusty bread.

Even the outdoor portion of the station leading to the AVE, the superluxurious trains of Spain, bespeaks spacious comfort. You are finally away from the smoking madness that seems to be everywhere, heading toward the modern gates welcoming one to train travel in the technological age.

Outside these new high-speed trains, stewardesses, dressed in bold-colored blue capes, greet passengers entering the special compartments and the club car. The exterior of the trains are white with blue. Even the station signs carry through that same color scheme.

Small lamps gently light the tables for four. A semicircle club car is in the front of the train for the very special class of passengers. Here also are comfortable seats with tables, some gathered around tables for four, others in two, just about the size of business-class airline seats. A headset is included with each seat so passengers can select their own music pleasure as the trip proceeds.

From Madrid to Cordoba, for example, the trip takes one hour forty-four minutes and on to Seville is less than twenty minutes more. These trains are fast.

The transfer from Madrid's bustling station is an easy jaunt. Go down the escalator to track number one, which is the local track, and take any train the three stops to Atocha, about fifteen minutes. This local is also incredibly clean. There is no additional charge to use the local train because it is also included in the Eurail pass.

It is absolutely imperative to buy a reservation on the AVE. At the entrance to the train, an employee will greet you and take the ticket. Everyone boards well in advance, because at the stroke of the hour, the train glides out of the station.

The Spanish are truly setting standards for upscale railroad travel.

Spanish Potato Tortilla:
The Tapa that Came to Breakfast

*T*HE *Spanish, who dine fashionably late—well past 10 A.M.—are not particularly known for breakfast. The Continental favorites of a crisp-crusted roll, butter, jam, and coffee, or a richer version with a croissant is, understandably, quite in vogue. But like the Italians, who simply peck at a bit of breakfast and then start noshing away at morning goodies with coffee and the like, the Spanish are also morning nibblers. While tapas, or little snacks, assuage hunger and are served during cocktail hours, they are also available for morning consumption. According to Penelope Casas in* Tapas: The Little Dishes of Spain *(New York: Alfred A. Knopf, 1985), tapas were originally a slice of cured ham or chorizo placed over the mouth of a wineglass served compliments of the house. The verb "taper" means to cover. These goodies were salty, just like chips and peanuts in United States bars and helped increase beverage sales.*

Our recent trip to Spain revealed virtually no limit to what could be served as tapas. The only observed rules seemed to be that the portions are small and the tapas arrive at the table quickly, even those requiring some additional cooking. But most sit on bar counters, under glass in the better establishments, ready to eat. Sometimes they are hot, sometimes they are cold.

The tapa bars opened in the morning served the potato tortilla cold, along with bits of lamb and other meats. While coffee was offered, a number of men opted for more spirited liquids. In Madrid's Atocha Station, slices of the rich egg-and-potato tortilla are slipped into a crusty white baguette for the perfect quick breakfast. Teamed with a steaming espresso and the ever-present bowls of oranges, who could want anything more?

This multilayered tortilla is cooked slices of fresh potatoes sautéed in fragrant olive oil with onion, and bound frittata-style with eggs. Using a plate midway through cooking, the entire affair is turned over and returned to the pan to cook the other side.

SERVES 6

¼ cup olive oil plus one tablespoon, divided use

1 onion, chopped

6 (about 2 pounds) boiling potatoes, ¼-inch slices

4 eggs, well beaten

1 teaspoon salt

ground pepper, to taste

Heat oil in a 12-inch heavy skillet until hot. Add potato slices and onions, cooking for 10 minutes on each side or until they are softened and slightly browned. Reduce heat. Pour in eggs and salt. Lift potatoes so that egg mixture can seep underneath and cover the bottom of the pan. Cook for 5 minutes over medium heat or until the eggs begin to set.

With a spatula, loosen the tortilla from the bottom and sides. Place a flat dinner plate on top of the skillet. Using hot pads to hold the skillet to the plate, turn tortilla onto plate. Add 1 tablespoon of oil to the pan. Heat. Return tortilla to pan by sliding it off the plate so that the browned side is now on the top. Cook until the bottom is lightly browned, about 3 more minutes. Turn onto a serving plate. Serve wedges either hot or at room temperature.

Note: Do not confuse this Spanish tortilla with the Mexican variety that is a flat corn or wheat pancake made with flour, shortening, and salt (page 145).

Big Bear Lake Potato Pancakes
with Fresh Watermelon Salsa

*A*T THE *Wainwright Inn in Big Bear City, California, these potato pancakes are served warm and crisp with a choice of watermelon salsa or homemade applesauce. The potato pancakes may be made ahead, refrigerated, then reheated in a single layer on a baking sheet at 450°F. The watermelon salsa, an option for the adventuresome—easy to make, and a delight to eat—but best made close to service time because it will begin to weep if held too long.*

SERVES 4

POTATO PANCAKES

   3 medium potatoes (about 1¼ pounds), peeled and quartered

   ¼ medium onion, peeled and quartered

   1 egg

   1 ½ tablespoons all-purpose flour

   ½ teaspoon salt

   pinch white pepper

   vegetable oil for frying

WATERMELON SALSA

   2 cups seeded watermelon, diced

   1 clove garlic

   ½ bunch cilantro, leaves only, chopped

   ¼ red onion, thinly sliced

   1 teaspoon chili powder

   ½ teaspoon salt

   pinch cayenne pepper

   juice of 1 small lime

For Potato Pancakes: Combine potatoes, onion, egg, flour, salt, and pepper in food processor. Pulse until coarsely chopped. In large skillet over medium heat bring enough oil to cover bottom of pan to the smoking point. Pour batter into pan, using a ¼-cup measure. Fry until crisp and brown or for about 4 minutes. Flip and brown other side for about 2 minutes. Drain on paper towels.

For Watermelon Salsa: Mix ingredients together and refrigerate for at least 30 minutes to let flavors blend. Serve on warm pancakes.

New Mexican Green Chile Breakfast Potatoes

RANDY MONDRAGON *is a Native American Pueblo Indian and the former executive chef of the Hotel Santa Fe in New Mexico. He makes these earthy potatoes and enhances them with aromatic onions, garlic, and fire-roasted green chilies. He suggests using peppers with a heat range to suit your ability to tolerate spicy hot.*

SERVES 6

2 tablespoons vegetable oil

1 onion, chopped

2 garlic cloves, minced

½ cup blistered, peeled, diced green chilies

4 cooked baking potatoes, skin on, ½-inch slices

salt and pepper, to taste

In a large skillet over high heat cook in vegetable oil the onion and garlic until limp or for 10 minutes. Add chilies and potatoes. Cook over low heat, flipping occasionally until soft, for about 5 minutes. Add salt and pepper to taste.

Note: Serve with hot red salsa.

Fresh Corn Griddle Fritters

*T*HIS *recipe is so simple yet the results are mind-boggling. But the corn must be picked at its peak of perfection. Corn harvested fewer than 24 hours from its stalks is still sweet and has not yet become starchy. Fresh salsa makes a good accompaniment. Try it as an alternative to hash brown potatoes or grits with eggs.*

SERVES 4

4 ears corn, freshly husked

2 egg whites, whipped until stiff, not dry

½ teaspoon salt

Cut kernels from corn cob with a very sharp knife. Fold the corn and its liquid into egg whites. Mix in salt. On a nonstick griddle treated with vegetable spray, drop batter by the tablespoon. Cook for about 2 minutes on each side until golden brown.

Note: Credit for this recipe goes to my mother, Louise Spalding Hollis, who made thousands of these for us as kids. For a richer taste, Richard Walker, my friend and an exceptional chef, tried it first by lightly sautéing the corn kernels in butter.

Cheesy Grits with Sun-Dried Tomatoes

*Y*OU *either love grits, which are ground hominy (corn with the hull and germ removed and treated with lye), or you hate them. In the South a spoonful of grits, often lumpy and with a melting pat of butter, is* de rigueur *with a fried egg and a biscuit. When treated with respect, dignity, and some compatible ingredients, grits become delectable. They add a wonderful texture to this soufflélike casserole, rich with cheese and eggs and punctuated with flavorful hits of sun-dried tomatoes. This dish, conceived in the South, will inevitably be adopted by all persons with impeccably good taste.*

In a saucepan over medium heat bring grits, water, and salt to a boil. Stir occasionally. Cook until most of the water is absorbed or for about 8 minutes. Stir in cheese, milk, eggs, tomatoes, and pepper. Pour into a 1½-quart buttered casserole dish and bake at 350°F until puffed and golden or for about 45 to 50 minutes.

181

1 cup grits, stone-ground

3 cups water

½ teaspoon salt

1 cup grated sharp cheddar cheese

½ cup milk

3 eggs, beaten

2 tablespoons sun-dried tomatoes

¼ teaspoon cayenne pepper

Kahakuloa Valley Taro Garden Patties

A COUPLE of these carbohydrate-rich patties are just the right start for a day's hike such as those lead by the Ritz-Carlton hike masters at Kapalua, Maui, into a north shore valley. These valleys in the West Maui mountain range, formed by the now-extinct volcano, Mauna Kahalawai, wind through the waterfalls from lake Manowai, which the ancient Hawaiians called the juncture of heaven and earth.

We hiked into this private valley where Oliver Dukelow, a retired law-enforcement officer, volleyball coach, and Hawaiian teacher, demonstrated the ancient ways of growing taro in water, dating back to the 1500s. Dukelow grows taro in the terraced Kahakuloa Valley with vast water pools held in place by rectangles of lava rocks. He harvests in the same way as his forefathers—with his bare feet, and absently tossing out any centipedes, some of which grow to eight inches. Of the more than 300 varieties of taro, he grows 20.

Taro, made into poi, was an important staple in the traditional Hawaiian diet. It has been highly successful in reducing diabetic insulin dependency, reducing blood cholesterol levels, decreasing high blood pressure, and helping reduce weight.

After the tubers are steamed for 2 to 3 hours, peeled, and cubed, they are ready for other flavoring ingredients. The taro patties Dukelow makes are in the style of hamburgers, and he panfries them until golden brown on each side.

Dukelow has an unquenchable commitment to the land, land that he does not claim to "own in the western legal land terminology" but that he respects, protects, and uses for his nourishment during his lifetime "in the ancient Hawaiian tradition." This commitment is further shown by the two homes he had built a mile or so up in the valley, where no roads exist. Every board and piece of equipment was carried in on his and his family members' shoulders.

In the supermarkets it is difficult to get taro roots as "it is all sent to the poi factories," said a spokesperson for Star Markets. But it is readily available from the Hawaiian farmers and at their local roadside stands around the islands.

SERVES 4

1 pound taro (substitute potatoes)

3 ounces corned beef (Dukelow prefers New Zealand brands)

½ cup Kula onion (substitute any sweet onion)

1 scallion, sliced

2 tablespoons coconut milk

1 egg, beaten

In a medium pan over medium heat steam taro root for 2 hours or until softened. Peel skin. Cut into ½-inch cubes. Mix with remaining ingredients. Form into 4-inch patties. Grill on a lightly oiled griddle until golden brown for approximately 3 minutes. Turn over and repeat.

Indian Dosai with Curried Potatoes

*I*N SOUTHERN *India a large, lacy pancake made from pureed lentils and rice becomes a fast casing for fillings such as spicy Curried Potatoes or Masala Dosai. In Singapore's Little Indian, dosai about 16 inches in diameter are served on a banana leaf with searing hot sambals. After washing one's hands, only the right hand is used for eating (with no additional utensils).*

The quantity of water added makes a difference. More water produces a fatter, softer cake, whereas less water makes a crisper cake with a thin batter similar to that of a crepe's.

Serve with Coconut Cilantro Chutney (page 208).

SERVES 6

DOSAI

1 cup rice, soaked overnight in water

1 cup split red lentils, soaked overnight in water

1 teaspoon salt

1 tablespoon rice flour, optional to thicken after fermentation

Vegetable oil, for frying

cilantro, to garnish

CURRIED POTATOES

2 tablespoons oil

1 medium onion, chopped

1 jalapeño, minced

1 teaspoon ground cumin

1 teaspoon ground coriander

1 teaspoon turmeric

2 medium tomatoes, chopped

6 boiling potatoes, cubed, boiled for 12 minutes or until soft, drained

1 teaspoon salt

black pepper, to taste

For Dosai: Overnight, soak rice and lentils separately, covered with water. Drain. Grind rice until it is a rough paste, adding a small amount of water. Grind lentils, gradually adding water until it is smooth and frothy, about double in volume (add about ¼ cup water for each cup of lentils). In a large mixing bowl combine rice, lentils, and salt. Let ferment in a warm place, above 80°F for about 12 hours.

Heat a large griddle, iron preferred, and add 1 teaspoon oil. If batter is thinner than a crepe batter, add optional rice flour. Using ¼ cup, spin batter from center of griddle in concentric circles. Cook for 3 minutes. Add more oil around the edges and turn over. Cook for 2 more minutes. Garnish with cilantro. Makes 1 dozen 6-inch cakes. Fill two per serving.

For Curried Potatoes: In a large skillet over medium-high heat cook in oil the onion and jalapeño until softened or for 3 minutes. Add spices. Stir and cook until their fragrance is released or for 2 minutes. Add tomatoes. Cook 2 more minutes.

Add potatoes. Stir gently until potatoes are coated with the other ingredients and completely heated through or for about 3 minutes. Add salt and pepper.

Notes: Yukon golds, excellent boiling potatoes, are particularly good in this recipe. Baking potatoes are too mealy.

If time does not permit making the lentil and rice pancakes, try the curried potatoes as a stand-alone dish served with chutney or sambals.

Idils are made of the same ingredients as dosai but are made into airy, spongy round cakes.

Chef James Chang, The Noodle-Pulling Champion

Stretching dough builds the pectoral muscles of Chef James Chang of the Lai Lai Sheraton, Taipei. He is the world's noodle-pulling record holder. No slave to Nautilus machines, he warms up by mixing five kilograms of flour (about eleven pounds) with water.

Then the showmanship begins. Chang pulls the dough, coaxing it into one long, fat rope. With a high twist and twirl, he folds the dough into two ropes. Interrupting the rhythm only for a flour dusting, the dough becomes aerial with pulls, twirls, folds, and smiles. Four, eight, sixteen. More smiles accompany his skill, coordination, adroitness, great pecs, and perfect timing.

Chang's world record of 8,192 strands was established during the Taiwan Food Festival August 1991, and he has since repeated it at elegant Imperial Banquets at the Sheraton. Noodle pulling is a bonafide spectator sport—the crowd counts, cheers, oohs, and ahs after each fold and pull. They marvel at the fragile thinness of the noodles.

Because "you-got-to-see-this-to-believe-it," Chef Chang makes television appearances with his skinny noodles to prove that he can thread an ordinary sewing needle with a single strand.

"My favorite food is noodles with just a bit of seasonings," revealed Chef Chang. And the Chinese have been eating these excellent carbohydrates for centuries. Evidence of pasta exists from at least the third century B.C. in the Han Dynasty. In northern China more noodles than rice are consumed; they are an inexpensive staple and a great filler.

The Chinese like to slurp noodles. They like to be noisy and show gustatory spirit (and wear washable clothes or a big napkin). Do not break noodles, the longer the better. On birthdays, noodles are the dish of the occasion. Long noodles are a longevity symbol in China.

Huka Lodge Noodles with Venison Sausage and Fresh Mango Chutney

AT NEW ZEALAND'S *exclusive fishing retreat, Huka Lodge, each room is a separate cottage. Fabrics are draped romantically from the ceiling over the bed where one can gaze out over the rapidly flowing river coming from Huka Falls. A short walk over the manicured lawns with perfect border gardens brings one to the main lodge, where the lavish fruit and pastry buffet centers the dining room. Each entree is cooked to order by the kitchen staff. Often on Sunday mornings this pasta creation is one of the special choices.*

SERVES 4

PASTA

- 8 ounces medium-width egg noodles
- 8 venison sausage links
- 1 teaspoon extra-virgin olive oil
- 1 tablespoon fresh, chopped basil

MANGO CHUTNEY

- 1 mango, peeled and sliced into small pieces
- 1 tablespoon sugar
- 1 tablespoon rice wine vinegar
- 1 teaspoon minced ginger
- pinch cayenne pepper

For Pasta: Cook pasta noodles according to manufacturer's directions. Drain. Cook venison sausage links in a large skillet in olive oil over medium heat. When they are no longer pink inside or after about 7 minutes, toss with sliced sausage, chopped basil, and noodles. Remove from heat.

For Mango Chutney: Combine all ingredients. Permit to sit for at least 15 minutes before serving so flavors can meld.

Egyptian Fool Midammis, Fava Beans with Tomato, Eggs, Olive Oil, and Lemon

*I*N EGYPT *small purple fava beans simmer for hours with various other ingredients. Street vendors are always ready to dish up a quick breakfast to go. Often eggs with creamy yolks and tanned exteriors, cooked for up to 6 hours, accompany this heavy dish along with freshly baked pita breads. The small dried favas, found in the United States in health food stores, need to be soaked overnight and cooked before preparation. Their skins are tough, and some chefs suggest it should be removed. Our tests found that if the beans were simmered over very low heat for several hours, the skins became an edible, chewy source of fiber.*

Here is a fast version of Fool, using canned, cooked fava beans. These are giant beans with an assertive flavor. Add fresh lemon juice, parsley, and a drizzle of olive oil to finish the fool. Eggs are cooked right along with the beans and vegetables for an incredibly easy breakfast.

SERVES 4

one 19-ounce can cooked fava beans

1 large onion, chopped

1 medium tomato, chopped

1 teaspoon ground cumin

1 teaspoon red chili flakes

4 eggs

salt and pepper, to taste

2 tablespoons chopped parsley

juice of 1 lemon

2 teaspoons olive oil

pita bread (page 105)

In a medium-size saucepan over medium heat, add beans, onion, tomato, cumin, red chili, and eggs. Bring to a boil. Reduce heat and cover. Let simmer for at least 15 minutes before serving. Add salt and pepper to taste. Garnish with chopped parsley, lemon juice, and olive oil. Present with pita bread.

Caraotas Negros, Venezuelan Black Beans

THE black beans are cleaned, cooked, then sautéed with onions, bell pepper, and tomatoes. In Argentina there is a special sweet-and-sour sauce that is added. The sauce is approximated here, using sugar and vinegar. Black beans are one of the few dried beans requiring no presoaking and about 1½ to 2 hours to cook. Serve these as a side to scrambled eggs with fresh tomatoes, fried plantains with shredded white cheese, and Venezuelan Corn Arepas (page 142).

SERVES 10

- 1 pound black beans, carefully cleaned and double-washed
- 8 cups water (or more, depending on evaporation)
- 1 tablespoon oil
- 1 medium onion, chopped
- 1 green bell pepper, chopped
- 3 tomatoes, finely chopped
- 1 tablespoon sugar
- 1 tablespoon cider vinegar
- salt to taste

In a medium-size pan bring beans and water to a boil. Reduce to a simmer. Cover and cook over low heat until the beans are tender or for about 1½ to 2 hours.

In a large nonstick skillet heat oil and sauté onion, pepper, and tomatoes until tender or for about 10 minutes. Add to cooked beans with sugar, vinegar, and salt to taste.

Maui Spam Musubi, Sticky Rice Balls

OVER there," said Wesley Nohara, pointing to the undulating Ritz-Carlton Kahana's parking lot, "is where my family lived in the Japanese village." His was the fourth generation of his family who came to work the land and to fish the sea. He recalls his grandmother's making bento, the food to go to the fields, which she carried on one end of a long stick over her shoulders for herself and family. Many times the counterweight was a new infant.

"I never spoke with my grandmother. She spoke only Japanese and I only spoke English," said Nohara who today is the Honolua plantation superintendent for Maui Pineapple Company, Ltd.

With a hardy laugh Nohara recalls some of his childhood bentos—"Spam, we had lots of Spam, and Vienna sausage out of a can. Sometimes you just needed a break from fish."

He cupped his large, strong hands, showing the baseball size of short grain, white rice that formed the musubi or rice ball for the bento. These hands have worked every job in the pineapple fields as he put himself through school, culminating with a geography degree from the University of Hawaii.

A slice of Spam, or whatever desired, can be placed on top of the rice ball and the whole thing is wrapped in a sheet of roasted seaweed.

Even today, the bento tradition for breakfast lives on. Mike Kitagawa's Chevron and Food Mart in Kahaului has a complete line of minibreakfast bentos along with a 24-hour towing service for those tourists who get their rental cars stuck when driving beyond suggested roads. Their 6 types of musubis (Spam, chicken, tuna, luncheon meat and egg with spring and Maui onions, teriyaki meat, and char siu and egg), retailing for under $2, are efficiently made into rectangles for easier stacking, displaying, and eating.

Maui claims the highest per capita consumption of Spam in the world. It is *convenient, not too expensive, and since the end of World War II it has become a staple. For breakfast it is sliced and grilled in the pan, as served at the Honolua Store in Kapalua.*

YIELD: 6

one 7-ounce can Spam

3 cups steamed sticky rice, cooled to room temperature

6 sheets 4 × 8 inches nori (roasted seaweed)

1 teaspoon water for sealing

Slice Spam into six slices. Cupping water-moistened hands, form rice balls by gently pushing so rice will stick together. Place rice in center of shiny-side-down nori. Place Spam slices on top. Fold seaweed around rice and Spam, sealing like a three-fold business letter, using a small line of water on the edge of the seaweed to seal. Eat with the hands.

Note: If the musubi-size nori is unavailable, use regular-size sushi

sheets of nori cut in half. In Japan often the musubi is centered with a piece of pickled umeboshi plum, and the shape is either a cylinder or a triangle. Sushi rice with added sweetened rice vinegar is used. The hand-shaped cone with raw seafood and blanched vegetables is called temaki-sushi. For sushi, start with 1¼ cups raw rice and 1½ cups water, bring to a boil, cover, and lower heat, cooking for 25 minutes. Add 3 table-spoons rice vinegar mixed with 2 teaspoons sugar and ½ teaspoon salt to the cooked rice. Let cool before forming.

Nutritious White and Brown Rices

According to the Rice Council, 98 percent of rice sold in the United States is of the white variety. Many vitamins, minerals, and bran have been polished away to make white rice from the more nutritional brown variety with its nutty, crunchy taste.

The long-grained varieties are particularly suited for salads; the stickier short-grain is good for a side dish and mixtures. Rice bran is suspected to have many of the same cholesterol-lowering properties as oat bran and barley bran.

One cup of cooked brown rice supplies 50 grams of carbohydrates, 5 grams of protein, 1.6 grams of fat, and no cholesterol. More than half the world's population exists on rices. Orientals per capita consume more than four hundred pounds compared with the ten pounds averaged in the United States.

Brown rice is economical and easy to cook. Place 1 cup of brown rice in a three-quart saucepan. Add 2$^{1}/_{2}$ cups of water for short-grain or 2 cups for long-grain. Bring to a boil. Cover. Reduce heat to a low simmer. Cook 45 minutes or until all the liquid has been absorbed. If you like a drier, fluffier rice, let it sit another 5 or 10 minutes. Fluff with a fork. Vary rice dishes by cooking with chicken stock instead of water, by adding herbs (thyme, tarragon, or basil), vegetables (onions, celery, and carrots), spices (curry powder), or by sprinkling with soy or Worcestershire sauces.

Any leftover rice makes a quick breakfast treat. Mix about 1 cup of rice with 1 beaten egg, a pinch of salt, and a tablespoon of chopped onions. On a heated nonstick griddle with vegetable spray, make into 4 cakes. Cook for about 3 minutes on each side or until they are golden brown.

Israeli Kibbutz Morning Salad

Boker tov, *Good morning.*

*S*ALADS, *salads everywhere—from the mixed combinations to heaping bowls of freshly grated carrots, chunks of European-style cucumbers, red, ripe tomatoes, avocado and whatever else is fresh, salads deserve top billing. In hotels, there might be up to 15 different salads on the breakfast buffet. Combine that with a little fresh cheese, pungent black olives, and top with a bit of plain yogurt, lemon juice, or olive oil, and eat with fresh breads. What could be healthier?*

Many of the vegetables grown on the Kfar Blum Kibbutz's 1,225 agriculture acres, a cooperative community in reclaimed swamp area called the Huleh Valley, Israel, will appear in the communal dining room for breakfast. While just over half the adult population still works in Kibbutz's

agriculture, the electronic factories, or the 90-room tourist guest house, many still gather after several hours of work at 9:00 A.M. for breakfast. The vegetables, washed and not otherwise prepared, are stacked high. One selects several, gets some cutlery and plates, and joins fellow workers. Preparation is done right at the table, providing a longer breakfast with time to socialize and share.

SERVES 2

1 cucumber

2 tomatoes

1 avocado

1 carrot

labani (page 65) or goat cheese

black olives

Slice, dice, mix, and serve while carrying on merry conversations.

Pueblo Indian Calabacitas

*R*ANDY MONDRAGON, *the former executive chef of the Hotel Santa Fe in New Mexico, makes enormous pans of this delightful morning melange of summer vegetables from abundant green zucchini and pale yellow squash with fresh corn kernels bursting with the rich taste of the sun. Onions add aromatic notes while the mild green chilies add a tangy bite. The cheddar cheese unites all these colorful vegetables into an excellent dish. Serve with freshly made, warm flour tortillas (page 145) and salsa (page 211). After sautéing they can be held in a warm oven.*

SERVES 4

2 tablespoons vegetable oil

2 zucchinis, sliced

2 summer squash, sliced

1 cup fresh corn kernels

½ onion, chopped

½ cup green chilies, chopped

½ cup cheddar cheese, grated

In a large skillet over medium-high heat cook the vegetables in vegetable oil, stirring occasionally, until just soft for about 8 minutes. Cover with cheese.

The Crocodile People in Papua New Guinea

The crocodile is revered and feared along the Sepik River. Young boys passing through the rites of puberty are scarred with razor-blade cuts from the neck to below the knees so that the skin resembles the pattern of the crocodile.

Men daily gather in the spirit lodge, haus tambarans, carving from local woods the revered and fearsome crocodiles, fertility figures, masks, small animals, and birds while chewing beetle nuts, playing flutes and drums, and governing the tribe. Sale of such items to tourists, or to traders who take them to more populated areas, is the sole cash source for the village.

In the haus tambarans, the largest village structure, only men are permitted. To be admitted to the upper portion, men have to pass through the sacred procedure of crocodile scarring. Typically, the young man is given leaves to chew, providing a mild anesthetic, as he lies on his mother's brother. Cutting with a razor blade, about 1^1/$_2$ inches deep, is begun. The pattern, with hundreds of cuts, will be packed with dirt or oil, and after it heals, the raised scars imitate the skin of the revered, feared, and worshiped crocodile. It is symbolic that the blood flows back on his mother's side of the family.

During the healing months, the secrets of manhood and life are passed down from the elders. The interiors of the haus tambarans include carved pillars with anatomically correct male appendages. Traditionally gourds cover this body part.

Tribes such as the Bird of Paradise tribe dwell in stilted palm houses, subsisting on a diet of sago palm, river fish, and tropical fruits. Subsistence is basic, but life is joyous in this primitive setting.

At the time of my visit, the ten-year flood meant the river was at its peak. To get from one stilted house, made mostly of parts of the sago palm tree, boats were mandatory.

To get to this region was exciting in its own right and well worth my overnight flight from Perth via Sydney. In the central part of Papua New Guinea, I had requested a hiking adventure. But because I was a woman traveling solo, the trekking outfit based in Tari refused to escort me—a refusal easily understood after I met a Chicago couple who detailed the war in progress between two local tribes just outside the Tari Airport.

The war had begun over an ancient theme: a man sleeping with another man's wife. The warriors were heavily clad in war paint, feathers, and shells, bows, and arrows,

and little else. Five persons had been killed that week and several huts burned. But the tourist were safe. The Chicago couple had eight native guards on their bus along with ample photo opportunities.

To get to the Sepik River, I had come from Mount Hagen, the home of the mud men with their famous masks. During the night my bed shook uncontrollably for what seemed to be an eternity, but it was only a mild earthquake. Transport over the mountains to the river region was in a four-passenger plane. Standing on the tarmac, we were greeted with, "Hi, I'm Timothy. I'll be your pilot today." Timothy, from Minnesota, explained that MAF was missionary air fellowship, which operated planes in more than thirty countries to deliver needed supplies. Extra seats were sold to tourists.

Here was almost an untarnished civilization of people living from their lands and waters without electricity, sewers, significant clothing, and twentieth-century pressures. Their problems were much more basic—where to get dinner, how to raise their children safely in a land where infant mortality is high, how to live with their spirit gods and the Christian missionaries proselytizing?

The Sepik Spirit, a ninety-eight-foot, air-conditioned floating lodge owned and operated by Trans Niugini Tours, caters to tourists.

With nine guest cabins, an eight-person crew, and cruise ship amenities, she carries her own generator, water, and supplies for trips of three or six days.

Daily the smaller, covered pontoon jet boat takes passengers for a discovery trip into different villages for sing sings (dances), to visit village schools (average education is through third grade), or to see sago demonstrations. Often the entire village waits excitedly on the riverbank for the chance to show and sell that tribe's art craft and watch these strange tourist from afar.

The adventure intensifies with canoe trips into the blackwater region, where floating islands of dense grass require expert navigation and luck. Lawrence Domnic, our wonderful, native guide, respected, well-educated, and an excellent communicator, took us into the villages. Each evening in the ship's salon he shared stories of his people's beliefs, customs, and lives. The last evening he dressed in native costume while he served us dinner.

My trip ended at the Karawari Wilderness Lodge, high above the river's jungle. Local woods and artifacts created a spectacular dining and reception area. The generator cuts off at 11 P.M., so you can fully listen to the sounds of nature and the river.

The last morning I left with one of the natives for a walk through the wet jungle, teeming with awesome plants, birds, and wonder. We finally reached a stream, filled with huge boulders, leading up to a pristine waterfall. Using the boulders as stepping stones, I grabbed an adjacent tree for balance, and spikes of pain shot through me.

My guide screamed "Bees!" and "Run!" We escaped but not until the bees had punished us with dozens and dozens of stingers. Back in the woods, we found a native wild mustard leaf that he rubbed on my wounds. I was curious about the guide's initial refusal to let me rub the mustard leaf on his back where most of his stings were concentrated. I asked if it was taboo for a woman, not his wife, to touch him. "Yes," he said, "but that is not what I am concerned with. I have not yet become a crocodile man." To him, this was the ultimate sign of manhood. He preferred to endure the pain to removing his shirt and showing his smooth skin.

I explained that in my culture that was not the rite of passage. He finally removed his shirt. I rubbed him with the leaves, and we both did our best to endure the pain as we hiked back through the wet jungle to the lodge. I later downed antihistamines with bottled water and was flown to the closest "sick house" in Mount Hagen.

197

Papua New Guinea Sago Pancakes

*I*N THE *middle regions of the black waters of the Sepik River, the home of the crocodile people, breakfast usually consists of sago pancakes with a few leaves from the tulip trees and fresh tropical fruits. Dress for breakfast is usually quite minimal, perhaps a cotton wrap around the waist for the ladies, shorts for the men, and maybe nothing for the children.*

Over open coals from a wood fire, the pancake, made solely of pounded sago starch, water, and some ashes from a burned palm tree, is poured into the cooking dish. After setting, it is turned over, using the fingers and cooked for several minutes on the other side.

It is removed from the dish, set to cool for a few minutes on leaves, then served. Neither plates nor utensils are used, nor are they needed. This super resilient cake has quite a tough consistency and is very chewy.

The flour is the result of extensive labor, starting with felling the palm tree, cutting it into logs, and pounding the interior with primitive wooden mallets to a soft pulp. This pulp is then taken to the river and washed. The slurry water collected is strained. The collected particles are the sago starch, the staple food. This can be dried for flour or used immediately.*

My measurements for the recipe are quite rough. I trust that most readers will only try to duplicate this if in the wilds of Papua New Guinea. And then the accommodating natives will be more than willing to assist.

SERVES 4

2 cups sago starch

2 cups water

2 pinches ashes

Mix together, using hands. Pour about ¼ into cooking dish over coals. Cook until set or about 8 minutes. Turn with hands. Cook several more minutes.

Fruits of the Earth and Heavenly Condiments

SOUTH CAROLINA PEACHES

Ahead on a South Carolina highway, through the summer haze, appeared a rustic stand perched on the edge of a rough gravel pull-off. The sign, hastily sketched in dripping red paint, seductively promised PEACHES.

I wondered if it would be possible to find a piece of fruit that tasted like the ones we used to pick straight from the tree, the fuzzy ones whose juices mixed with the flesh in an earthly nirvana.

The farmer promised me that these would be the best I'd ever eaten. Taking a huge bite out of the one on top of my just-purchased sack, juice spurted forth with the force of the Trevi Fountain. It began running down my arms into small streams on the dirt. Grinning ear to ear, I took a second bite—this time pushing back my sleeves and leaning forward from the waist so that the gushes could be slurped noisily into my mouth. This was fun.

"Yup, that is the finest peach I ever had. And thanks." I shouted as I went to my car. And when I find another one of those stands, I pray for a repeat performance.

Virginia Cinnamon Apples

*W*HEN *the potentates of pork gather for breakfast, more than bacon is on the menu. One of my favorite men-of-thrift, Republican Senator Phil Gramm from my former state of Texas, stumped for a new Virginia candidate pleading "I want our America back."*

This gathering celebrated our freedoms—assembly, speech, and breakfast menus. At 7:30 A.M. we dined on a traditional American breakfast of scrambled eggs, sausage, bacon, pancakes, biscuits and jam, fresh fruits, and cooked cinnamon apples.

SERVES 6

3 large apples (Granny Smith or other tart variety)

¼ cup apple juice concentrate (thawed)

2 tablespoons brown sugar

½ teaspoon cinnamon

1 tablespoon butter, optional

Peel and core apples. Cut lengthwise into ¼-inch slices. Place ingredients in a small saucepan. Bring to a boil and stir to incorporate. Reduce heat to very low. Cover. Cook until the apples are *al dente* or for about 8 minutes. Stir in optional butter.

Note: Leave apple skins on for greater fiber and less preparation time. This compote is also delicious served on cooked grains, such as a dish of millet, or as a topping for pancakes and waffles.

New Zealand Fruit Compote

NEW ZEALANDERS *love fresh fruits combined into sweet compotes. Luxury resorts such as the Huka Lodge, Taupo, where Queen Elizabeth has fished for trout, line their kitchen walls with these and other jarred fruits poached with sugar. On a smaller scale, Suzy Woods, at Taranga Bed and Breakfast outside Queenstown, makes batches that she freezes in small quantities. This process is simple and works for just about any fruits. Let your imagination run wild with fruit combinations, such as cherries with peaches, mangos with green grapes, or peaches with plums and pears.*

SERVES 8

2 pounds selected fruit, stone or seeds removed

juice of 1 lemon

½ cup sugar (adjust to sweetness of fruit)

½ cup water

2 cloves

Remove skins if desired. Cut into big chunks. Place lemon juice, sugar, and water in a heavy 3-quart pan. Bring to a boil stirring until sugar is dissolved. Add fruit and cloves. Bring liquid back to the boil. Stir for several minutes. Cover pan. Turn off heat and let fruit sit for about 10 minutes. Place in airtight containers. Refrigerate or freeze. Serve with the syrup.

Fresh Summer Peaches with Blueberry Compote

*M*ARY DELLARATA, *a dear lady and accomplished cook, shared her quick, delicious recipe for modestly enhancing nature's abundance of blueberries and peaches. This fresh-tasting compote will keep refrigerated for at least a week.*

SERVES 4

1 pint fresh blueberries

1 tablespoon sugar, or more to taste

freshly squeezed lemon

4 large, ripe peaches, peeled and sliced

fresh mint sprigs, garnish

Wash berries. With water still clinging, place in a heavy-bottomed pan over low heat, sprinkle with sugar, and cook until the skins just begin to burst, about 2 minutes. Remove from heat. Add lemon. Refrigerate until slightly chilled or for 1 hour. Ladle over peaches. Garnish with mint.

Note: Explore the versatility of this compote on pancakes, waffles, salads, chicken.

Kapalua Pineapple Chile Compote

*T*HE *touch of chili adds a special taste,"* said Patrick Callarec, *executive chef of the Ritz-Carlton in Kapalua, Maui. Originally from the Provence area of France, he delights in matching fruits such as pineapple with flavorful peppers and herbs. Many of these he can harvest from his garden just outside his restaurant, Anuenue (Hawaiian for rainbow), which specializes in Hawaiian Provencale cuisine. This garden, growing lemongrass, numerous varieties of basils, thyme, peppers, and mints, purportedly saves more than $12,000 a month in ingredients costs. Picking an herb just when needed ensures the best tastes particularly early in the morning when the concentration of essentials oils is at its peak.*

According to Lini Nieto, garde manger chef at the Ritz-Carlton, the most efficient method of preparing fresh pineapple is to slice off the top and the bottom. Then hold it upright on the cutting board and cut off the skin. The vertical strips should follow the curvature of the fruit. Turn on its side, cut in half from top to bottom. Making a V slice on either side of the core; remove it. Finally, slice the fruit into half-moon pieces. Lani completed the entire operation in a matter of seconds with her 10-inch chef's knife.

The core, according to local wisdom, is eaten by pregnant women to promote good health.

SERVES 6

1 large ripe pineapple

1½ cups sugar

2 cups water

2 teaspoons chili flakes

1 teaspoon fresh gingerroot, minced

Peel, core, and cut pineapple into ½-inch cubes. In a medium-size pan combine sugar, water, chili flakes, and gingerroot. Over medium heat stir until the sugar dissolves or for about 5 minutes. Add pineapple and bring to a boil. Remove from heat. Place in a glass dish. Cover. Refrigerate immediately for at least 3 hours. Serve chilled.

Golden Pineapple at the Rainbows' Ends

Of the 8,000 acres on the Honolua Plantation surrounding the Ritz-Carlton, Kapalua, 3,800 are planted in pineapples, on land owned by the Maui Land and Pineapple Company. The fruits grow under the frequent rainbows—here is the true golden treasure.

According to the plantation's supervisor, Wesley Nohara, 10 percent of the pineapples are jet-shipped to the mainland for fresh sales. These "must taste good and look good—appearances are very important."

The second year's growth, even though sweeter, is unacceptable for export since the fruits often grow not quite so upright and the tops become curved. Subsequent growths produce smaller, less visually perfect, but sweeter fruit.

He demonstrated finding a juicy pineapple by thumping his right-hand thumb and third finger on the palm of his left hand. "That is what a juicy one sounds like," he said of the rich hollow sound.

When asked about the wives' tale that a sweet pineapple's leaves easily come out when pulled, he responded, "I do not believe that."

For the East Coast market, the demand is for first year, large and slightly green, tart pineapples. "We would not eat them like that here," said Nohara, "and if we did have a tart one, we would sprinkle it with the coarse Hawaiian sea salt crystals to make it more palatable."

Their remaining pineapples are canned under store brand names, always stamped on the top 100 PERCENT HAWAIIAN. In Maui, the lowest paid worker gets $9 an hour. For seasonal picking, many laborers are imported from Arizona. Other pineapple companies such as Dole and Del Monte have moved most of their operations to third world countries, where a full day's labor is about $3.

The rows in each section are planted from the leafy green tops of the fruit forty-two inches apart. These mature into a continuous, spiny jungle. Pickers walk along a section behind a truck with a long conveyor belt. They will pick the perfect pineapples for designated uses. "Hawaiian pineapples are the best in the world; our quality is superior," said Nohara.

On this commercial plantation, it takes about twenty-four months to produce the first fruits. Usually two or three growths of pineapples are picked. Then the land is left fallow, completing the four to five year cycle.

The United States's Winter Fruit Supplier

The distance from Las Vegas to New York is almost the same as the length of Chile, 2,700 miles. Chile's many different climatic zones, the opposite of North America, create conditions for consistently high-quality fruits, which account for more than 14 percent of the world's fruit export market. More than one-third of the exports, about 56 million boxes of fruits, are sent to the United States. The value of this exceeds 1 billion dollars annually. That is quite a substantial quantity of Thompson, Flame, and Ruby grapes, berries, melons, kiwis, oranges, peaches, nectarines, plums, and cherimoyas.

The Sunshine Railroad, Queensland, Australia

On a six-day cruise-on-wheels, two car-loads of vacationers traveled from Cairns to Brisbane by luxury train. Initially, we were pampered with history, nature, and Aussie anecdotes by the tour guides. Then all the Aussies popped in with their own versions. There were few minutes free from laughter with these wonderful people.

We traveled through the subtropical paradise, covering several hundred miles a day on the narrow gauge track as we visited interesting sites along the way, lunched, and stopped early to stay in a hotel or resort. Two nights were spent at the Great Barrier Reef Daydream Island Resort. Naturally we went snorkeling and made the sunset cruise.

"G'd on ya, mate" (for well done) quickly became our favorite saying. And by the time the trip ended we had collected almost every-one's favorite recipe for Pavlova, the meringue national dessert of Australia.

Note: The Sunshine Railroad Tour: Trips, all-inclusive except alcoholic beverages. Six-day trips start from Cairns on Sunday or from Brisbane on Monday and cost around $1,000.

Daydream Island, Queensland Fresh Pineapple Fritters

*E*VERY *bite of a Queensland pineapple is a reminder of the glorious golden sunshine in this semitropical state of Australia. On Daydream Island, in the Whitsunday Islands, Graham Seymour uses fresh pineapple to create these special fritters. After a dip in this simple batter, it is cooked on a buttered griddle and served with a festive sprinkle of confectioners' sugar and a sprig of mint.*

S E R V E S   4

1 pineapple, peeled, cored, and sliced
    about ½-inch slices

½ cup all-purpose flour

2 to 4 tablespoons sugar (depending on
    the pineapple's sweetness)

1 teaspoon baking powder

½ teaspoon salt

¼ cup milk

1 egg

½ teaspoon vanilla

1 tablespoon butter

confectioners' sugar, garnish

fresh mint, garnish

In a mixing bowl combine flour, sugar, baking powder, and salt. In a measuring cup mix milk, egg, and vanilla. Quickly stir wet ingredients into dry. Dip pieces of pineapple into batter.

On a lightly buttered griddle over medium heat cook until browning just begins or for about 4 minutes. Flip over and cook an additional two minutes. Garnish with a dusting of confectioners' sugar and a sprig of fresh mint.

Chilean Plum Cheese

*F*OR A *dramatic presentation, serve with a wide selection of sliced fresh fruits. It is also quite good on rolls and bagels.*

YIELD: 1¾ CUPS

4 large plums, halved and pitted

½ teaspoon almond extract

⅓ to ½ cup confectioners' sugar (depending on tartness of plums)

8 ounces low-fat cream cheese

In a food processor or blender, pulse fruit, almond extract, and sugar until it is the consistency of applesauce, about 2 minutes. Add cream cheese and process until all ingredients are well blended, about 2 minutes. Transfer to a serving dish. Refrigerate for at least 1 hour before serving.

Indian Coconut Cilantro Chutney

*T*HIS *addictive fresh chutney is the perfect accompaniment to Indian Dosai with Curried Potatoes (page 184). And it is so easy to make.*

YIELD: 1¼ CUPS

1 cup coconut milk

1 bunch cilantro

2 green chilies, deseeded

juice of 1 lemon

Mix all ingredients together in a blender or food processor.

Note: Both canned and powdered coconut milk make an acceptable chutney. Also try the newer reduced-fat version of the canned coconut milk.

Unusual Fruits: Durians and Cherimoya

Some fruits are not only attention grabbers, but also objects of derision and scorn. Perhaps the queen of the difficult fruit is the durian, the "smelly" fruit of Asia. It grows on a tree to about the size of a volleyball. To find a ripe durian, just follow your nose.

On the back roads of Kuala Lumpur, I found a vendor hacking them open with a machete-type knife and tossing the hard green shells over his shoulder into a haul-away dumpster. I liked its slippery texture and promise of cool refreshment with lots of liquid, but the smell was gagging.

The smell factor is reason for hotels hanging signs in lobbies that read "No durians in the rooms, please." And there is no way to mask the smell. Gas, for some, is an additional problem from durians. Malaysians suggest that the seed pods outer cover be used in drinking water as an antidote.

Another fruit with questionable character-istics is the ackee. In Jamaica, ackee and salt cod is the national dish. Eating ackee can be like Russian roulette unless one knows when it is perfectly ripe and how to remove the seeds.

Chile is a major source of our winter fruits in the United States. Many are exotic, tropical, juicy, and refreshing. At the Holiday Inn Crowne Plaza, Santiago, Chile, the morning buffet had one of those edible centerpiece displays with a softball-size cherimoya.

Cherimoya, also called custard apple, has a bumpy, unfriendly, exterior. The fruit, which looks tough, is very sensitive. Taking a very aggressive dining stance, I selected the fruit from the center display, placed it on a plate, then smilingly asked my waiter to demonstrate how to eat it. He told me to slice it, scoop out the flesh with a spoon, and avoid the seeds. Its tastes are multilayered—first like a pineapple, then smooth creamy pear, then a vanilla pudding. With more investigation it starts to taste like a cross between mango and melon. This enigma fruit is nothing but delicious.

Seville Marmalade
from Dundee, Scotland

*S*UCH *a deal I got on these oranges," the conversation might have begun in the 1700s when James Keiller brought home to Scotland his bounty from a Spanish ship that had sought refuge from a storm. Unfortunately, as many promising deals are not what is anticipated, these oranges were dreadfully bitter.*

Janet, his wife, who was well versed in Scottish frugality and abhorrence for waste, boiled them, added sugar, and created one of the world's finest marmalades.

YIELD: 8 HALF-PINTS

4 (about 2 pounds) Seville oranges, thinly sliced, seeds removed

2 lemons, sliced, seeds removed

7 cups water

5 to 6 cups sugar, approximately

In a large saucepan bring fruit and water to a boil. Cook until peels soften or for about 25 minutes. Measure fruit and liquid. If it is fewer than 5 cups, add that much extra water. Add 1 cup sugar for each cup fruit.

In saucepan, stirring often, bring fruit, liquid, and sugar to a boil for about 15 minutes or until a candy thermometer reaches 220°F. Fill sterilized jars up to ¼ inch from the top. Wipe top. Secure lids with screw tops. Place in boiling-water canner for 5 minutes.

Note: Chivers Hartley, Department M, The Orchard, Histon Cambridge, United Kingdom CB4 4NR, offers an excellent base for Seville Marmalade available at Williams-Sonoma. You just add sugar and cook for home-made marmalade.

Nuevo Vallarta Fresh Salsas: Red and Green

DAVID CUEVAS, breakfast chef of the Radisson Plaza Sierra Nuevo Vallarta in Navarit, Mexico, always serves huge bowls of piquant salsas at breakfast. The secret to their success is the use of perfectly fresh ingredients, particularly vine-ripened red tomatoes. Treat these gently in the food processor to ensure the sauces are chunky, not mushy.

YIELD: 2 CUPS

RED SALSA

3 large tomatoes

1 onion

1 garlic clove

4 cilantro sprigs, stems removed

3 serrano peppers, blistered, peeled

½ teaspoon salt

GREEN SALSA

10 tomatillos, paper husks removed

4 serrano peppers, deseeded

1 onion

1 garlic clove

3 cilantro sprigs, stems removed

½ teaspoon salt

½ teaspoon black pepper

juice of 1 lime

Place all ingredients for either red or green salsa in food-processor bowl. Pulse until lightly chopped with a definable character.

Hot Pepper Jelly

*T*HIS *recipe was adapted from the* Kerr Kitchen Cookbook: Home Canning and Freezing, *an excellent resource for the fundamental techniques of making jams, jellies, preserves, marmalades, and conserves. After experiencing the ease of jelly making you will wonder why you have not tried it before. The heat of this jelly is a function of the pepper used. Use New Mexico green chili peppers for a mild-mannered jelly and habañeros or Thai red bird chilies, if you dare, for the killer stuff. Jalapeños and serranos pack a nice wallop and are readily available in the markets.*

Jessica Adler Hall of Bounty from the Farm shared a valuable tip with me: Use red peppers that are the ripe form of the green peppers. Their extra time sunbathing creates a glorious flavor base. She uses wines in her jellies, rather than water (see Notes), for even more flavor.

Y I E L D :   3   H A L F - P I N T S

6 ounces hot peppers, stems and seeds removed

3 cups sugar

1 cup cider vinegar, 5 percent acid

3-ounce pouch liquid pectin (don't use dry pectin)

Process peppers in food processor, adding a small amount of vinegar if necessary to make a smooth puree.

In a medium-size pan over high heat bring peppers, sugar, and vinegar to a boil. Stir constantly and boil for 10 minutes. Remove pan from heat and stir in pectin. Bring back to a boil and cook 1 minute, stirring constantly.

Remove from heat. Skim any foam. Pour into sterilized half-pint jars up to ¼ inch from the top. Wipe tops and place lids on jars. Screw bands. Filled jars are processed in boiling water for 5 minutes.

Notes: Do not touch your eyes or mucous membranes when working with peppers. Use gloves.

Jessica Adler Hall produces the most delicious hot pepper wine jelly. Her secret is to use only ripe, red peppers and quality Virginia wines. Bounty from the Farm is at 12384 Perry Mountain Lane, Viewtown, VA 22746-9603.

Hot-Air Ballooning over Albuquerque

From the basket of the Rainbow Ryders hot-air balloon, Albuquerque's spanking new subdivisions looked exactly like a landscape architect's drawing. And down in those neighborhoods, the dogs fulfill their nominal roles as protectors. Roused to action, dogs of every description ran to the yards, nervously looking up at the intruder and barking.

Hot-air ballooning is not a silent sport. Setting off the burners is as relaxing as standing next to a freight train traveling at seventy-five miles per hour.

The crews assemble the balloons at the crack of dawn, rolling out the colorful balloon fabric that they attach to the elegant woven baskets crafted with fine leathers. Wind currents are kinder and gentler at this hour. Plus the timing is perfect for champagne breakfasts after the flight. Bagels, cream cheese, and lox were standard, but on this day we were also treated to flaky croissants with the New Mexican touch—sweet pepper jellies with varying heat levels.

Receiving my certificate of initiation into the hot-air ballooner's group from the captain, I reveled in the crisp, warm, morning air. I looked from the flat desert to the morning light dancing in the shadows of the nearby mountains. Nibbles of croissant with pepper jelly were washed down with champagne and orange juice, signaling another great new day.

For more ups and downs, we hiked with Mary and Ray Summers's Southwest Wilderness Trails llama outfitters up into the Sandia Mountains, where breakfast is freshly cooked over the open fire. Popular menus include green chili quiche, shrimp and crab burritos, or red snapper veracruz.

214

Honey

Honey, perhaps the root of our sweet tooth, is one of the oldest recorded foods, evidenced by a painting in Spain's Araña Cave, near Valencia, which purportedly dates from the Stone Age. But the bees have been in honey production even longer, for ten to twenty million years. References are found dating from the twenty-first century B.C. in Sumerian and Babylonian cuneiform writings, the Hittite code, and the sacred and ancient writings of India and Egypt.

In Sumer, Assyria, and Babylonia, honey was poured along with wine over the foundations in sacred buildings and on stones holding offerings. In ancient Greece honey was offered to gods and spirits.

The Olympic athletes in ancient times used honey as an ergogenic aid for strength and endurance. Figure-conscious Egyptian women—perhaps even Cleopatra—had honey every morning at breakfast for weight control.

That one little teaspoon of the amber, sticky, heavenly sweetness is the lifetime production, typically one month, of twelve worker bees, the sexually undeveloped females. And for one pound of honey the bees must visit more than two million flowers, flying a combined distance of fifty-five thousand miles. But these little insects are efficient. To fuel a bee's around-the-world flight, only one ounce of honey is needed.

A colony may have up to sixty thousand workers. *Apiarists* (beekeepers) help produce scores of different varieties, labeled by the flower(s) from which it was collected. Side-by-side tastings of honey, such as the one I attended at the Wisconsin State Fair, reveal that honey's different varieties are just as pronounced as grape varieties. Colors range from almost white to dark amber with flavors from mild to quite strong. Basswod honey is white and strong. Clover and alfalfa are mild. Buckwheat is dark and full-bodied. Other popular sources are fireweed, orange blossom, tulip poplar, tupelo, and sage. Any honey labeled "wildflower" is from undefined sources. In Australia, eucalyptus is the major source. The prized French Gâtinais and Narbonne rosemary honeys are pure white. Especially prized is the Hymethus honey from Greece.

In the United States, breakfast is the biggest meal for honey, with the majority being spread on biscuits, toast, bread, rolls, muffins, hot cereals, drizzled on pancakes and waffles, and used to sweeten yogurts.

In many parts of the world creme or spun honey, a crystallized form, is preferred. A dramatic buffet presentation, such as seen at the Coconut Beach Resort in northern Queensland, Australia, is the entire wax comb balanced on end—a wax sculpture of overwhelming complexity. Each person has to figure out where to take their pieces. The comb is eatable and delightful to chew.

Honey's life is indefinite. But if sugar crystals form, the remedy is fast. Place about one cup of honey in the microwave. Zap for two to three minutes on high, stirring every thirty seconds. Store honey at room temperature.

Honey can be substituted for up to half the sugar in a baked recipe. Honey, due to its high fructose content, provides more sweetening power. For each cup of honey reduce the liquid by one-fourth and use one-half teaspoon of baking soda to counteract its pH of 3.9. Reduce oven temperatures by twenty-five degrees Farenheit for a product using honey.

French Flower, Fruit, and Herb Captured in a Jar

All the flowers and herbs in France's Provence are not destined for perfume. Many join local fruits for confitures—jams. Rosemary, lavender, jasmine, and the petals of fifty-four different flowers are used along with apricots, strawberries, blueberries, cherries, red currants, and black currants. Since 1920, Confitures Curtelin has been producing mostly by hand, in small intensely quality-controlled batches, the

champagne of jams. Finished jars of these jewels often have slices of fruits such as oranges in the marmalades, meticulously arranged around the glasses' interior. When the jam is added, it creates a glorious visual work of art.

Dulce de Leche

Another morning condiment, quite good on rolls and pancakes, is *dulce de leche.* As made in Argentina, this amber condiment is so sweet that, eaten in vast quantities, it might make your teeth hurt. It is guaranteed to tame even the wickedest of sugar demons. Made of caramelized sugar and milk (originally goat but now cow), it is a spreadable golden glop made by a long, slow cooking process. Whether spread on toast or tucked into a pastry, it is ubiquitous in South America and Mexico but under different names, such as *doce de leitre* in Brazil, *arequipe* in Colombia, *manjar blanco* in Chile and *cajeta de leche* in Mexico.

A good reference book for making dulce de leche is Lynelle Tume's *Latin American Cookbook* (Chartwell Books, 1979).

CHAPTER ELEVEN

Wet, Wild, and Wonderful Beverages

COFFEE: CONTROVERSIES, CULTS, AND CONVENTIONS

Coffee is more than just a beverage. It is one of the world's most valuable agricultural commodities. Coffee is believed to have originated in Ethiopia and was consumed by the Arabians. In Turkey, according to Muslim law, a husband's failing to provide his wife with coffee is grounds for divorce. The Islamic Turks' siege of Vienna is thought to have introduced coffee to Europe. The adoption was quick, and the fashionable cafes swiftly started pouring the black liquid, perhaps presaging the chic coffeehouses of today.

Opinions on coffee are as varied as those on world politics, sex, and religion. It is a continual and lively topic of conversation and argument, backed by empirical experimentation in millions of sites. Coffee styles approach cult status.

There are those who like coffee with added flavors and those who despair when flavors are added. Shops selling beans that are wise to this battle have two separate-but-equal grinders; one for flavored and one for plain. There is nothing worse for a coffee purist than to have flavor notes muddy up the complex tastes that coffee already sports.

Then there are the caffeinated versus decaffeinated wars. Heaven forbid the two beans mix. In our house we start the day with a 50 percent brew and increase the percentage of decaf beans to 100 percent by the end of the day.

Degrees of roasting are also controversial. Roasting changes raw green beans into shades of dark. Roasting brings out the tantalizing aromas—which, to some, are more evocative than the taste itself. Dark roasts produce a stronger flavor with the beans almost approaching black. The darker the roast, the lower the acidity. Some contend that dark roasting kills some of the volatile flavors.

The darkest roast, black and oily, is French, where sometimes the individual characteristics of the bean are hidden, but the acidity is almost dissipated. The Italian roast is a step lighter than French, and the result is a bit sweeter. Next down is the city roast. Lighter roasts appeal to the mellow drinkers. The lightest is cinnamon roast, which is high in acid and typically included in "nongourmet supermarket" coffees.

Preparation

Coffee preparation methods brew constant controversy. There are gadgets, machines, and paraphernalia enough for all coffee sporters. The drip machine is quite convenient, but most machines are variable in their water temperature. The paper filters have a tendency to remove some flavors and coffee oils, but the expensive gold mesh filter promises to get around that problem.

The coffee press or plunger is wildly popular in England and Australia, and some say that it produces too mellow a product. Start with the water too hot, or plunge before the recommended two to four minutes, or have the grounds too fine, and a failure is guaranteed. If the product stays in the pot too long, it continues to brew, even after plunging, and bitterness results.

Methods requiring boiling, such as percolator or cowboy coffee, create too bitter a product. Many are willing to use a coffeemaker that automatically starts brewing in the morning even if that means using last night's stale water. Of course, serious coffee fanatics always use fresh water. Bubbles are better; flat is just that. Some folks will use beans ground only nanoseconds before brewing; must not loose any of that aroma. Others do not care when it was ground.

Coffee now appears dressed for questionable success in a round bag akin to a tea bag. Some love the convenience of the coffee bags, but it is an absolute shock to others. Many think that instant coffee in a screw-top jar is the answer.

Getting the most flavor from beans requires following a few simple rules. Store beans in an airtight container. Use the freezer for longer term storage. Grind just before brewing. Tradition suggests using two tablespoons of coffee for each six-ounce cup of water, although that may be way too strong if using gourmet beans. Start off with one tablespoon of coffee per cup.

There does seem to be agreement that the water temperature should be between 195°F and 205°F, the water neither too hard nor too soft. After brewing, it should be immediately enjoyed and never left on a heating or warming element and, heaven forbid, never reheated! If it must be held, a vacuum carafe is the only possibility.

The lingo in domestic coffee shops is becoming fairly well established, particularly with the Italian names. It is considerably more chic to request a latte rather than a cup of strong coffee with two-thirds milk.

While there are some common coffee phrases, there exist delightful international variations. In Australia an order of "short black" is an espresso. Add more water and it becomes a "long black." In most countries "American" coffee is the weak, watery version, labeled "insipid" by many. Turkish coffee is a small thick cupful, often highly sweetened.

To make proper Turkish coffee, a long-handled pot, called a *cezve,* is placed over low heat with one cup of water and one rounded teaspoon of powdered coffee per person. When it comes to a boil, it is removed from the heat and left to rest for several minutes. The process is repeated three times, which eventually creates a froth. Sugar is usually added just before serving; the Turks like the coffee very, very sweet. The froth and liquid are divided among the cups. In France and Italy, the brews are very potent, as they also are in Venezuela.

Out in the American West cowboys developed their own stylings that today still have a following. Stephen Pedalino, executive chef of the Mountain Sky Ranch in Montana, detailed the instructions for cowboy coffee. Start with cold water and add ground coffee—a dark roast, but not quite French. (The resort

has its own Sacajawea blend roasted by a local beanery.) Bring to a boil over the open fire. Let simmer for about seven minutes, then pull off to the side. Add crushed eggshell—the albumen clinging to the inside of the shell helps temper and clarify the finished brew—and a pinch of salt to reduce harshness. Pour into tin cups.

In the Middle East, Bedouin tribes have unique coffee rituals. These nomadic tribes living in the harsh deserts and limestone-covered earth travel with sheep and goats, desperately searching for enough grazing land. But when a visitor comes to the front door, it is time for coffee. The rhythm from the coffee pounder in the ancient metal-trimmed grinding pot is unique from one Bedouin tent to another. The beating will continue for about twenty minutes, calling neighboring men to celebrate coffee with a visitor—coffee here is a man thing.

Men will discuss the problems of the world in the long Bedouin tents. The more poles in the tent, the more important is the man. First a long-handled ladle roasts beans, which are cooled in a wooden shaker. The brass mortar and pestle grind the beans. Cardamom is pulverized and added for a unique taste.

In Paris, the price of a basic cup of coffee, espresso without milk, must be listed. In many cases that will include where the cup is taken. Standing at the bar is the lowest price, in the salon inside at a table next highest, and on the terrace typically the most expensive. Waiters, particularly in the toney cafes, are the masters of intimidation. If you pop into the bar and order the coffee, they will haughtily suggest that you sit on the terrace and they will bring the coffee.

Variety

The beans grown in tropical climates have absorbed the sun's rays and the earth's essence. In many third-world countries, the "good" stuff is saved for export—it is too expensive to consume. Coffee bean cash crops are too vital to their economies for them to drink the coffee themselves.

Brazil and Colombia, the two largest coffee-producing countries, grow Arabica beans, but the majority are standard and not very special. These beans are more fragile and flavorful than the Robusta beans also grown in South America.

Arabicas have two-thirds less caffeine with perfect acidity.

Coffee bean varietals are similar to grape varietals. They are sensitive to the growing conditions of soil and environment as well as to the stock. A coffee tree (or bush) grows five years before it produces. Each tree yields two thousand beans, just enough to produce a single pound of roasted coffee. The beans, a pair inside each coffee cherry, like most quality products, should be picked when ripe. This is an expensive procedure because it requires hand-picking.

The mellow, soft, Jamaican Blue Mountain coffee commands fifty dollars a pound in the United States. Jamaican Blue has sold for more than fifty dollars a cup (that is the brewed cup of coffee, not a cup of beans) in Japan. Why? It is a nice mellow, low-acid coffee. But better yet, it has a marketing hype that the Japanese—and plenty of Americans—adore.

The cognoscenti will drop the names, along with big bucks, for primo beans beyond the Blue Mountain ones, including Yergacheffe from the Sidamo region of Ethopia, the Harar region of Ethiopia, Mocha Mattari from Yemen, Antigua and Huehuetenango from Guatemala, and Tarrazu (particularly those grown at the La Minita Estate) from Costa Rica.

Accompaniments

In Switzerland, coffee is always accompanied by chocolates. Milk chocolate ones are so convenient—just drop in one or two. No need to add milk or sugar or flavorings to the beans. With a small spoon, one can incorporate the additions or eat them in a semimelted state. A challenge for chocoholics is to add more and see how long they can keep melting the chocolates before having to refresh the coffee itself.

In the United States in the morning, coffee often precedes the food. Down under in New Zealand and Australia, one would never dream of such behavior. Food is first served, then the coffee, which is considered a much gentler approach to the stomach.

In the United States the estimated daily caffeine intake is 227 mg or two to three six-ounce cups of brewed coffee. Some live by a concentrated hit of espresso; others need the bottomless cup.

According to the *New England Journal of Medicine,* caffeine withdrawal (even

from over-the-counter medications) may result in headache, drowsiness, fatigue, nausea, vomiting, depression, anxiety, and disrupted motor performance.

Decaffeinated coffee, made from the unroasted green bean treated with a bath of methylene chloride to remove caffeine, is steam-cleaned to remove the chemical. Another approach, considered preferable by some, but inconclusive in health studies, is the steam-only method, called the water-process method.

To simplify coffee making, buy quality whole beans in small quantities. I like to buy small bags of different beans to mix and match. The beans are stored in heavy freezer bags with as much air removed as possible, because oxygen is the major culprit in flavor degradation. Mostly I grind before brewing, but I often grind several batches and store them in a rubber-sealed ceramic container so I can brew an early morning cup without waking others in the house. And I use fresh, cool tap water. It is nicely balanced water with no fishy taste. I put the brewed coffee in a vacuum carafe. When it is not hot enough, yes, I will zap it in the microwave.

Not being a devotee of flavored coffees, but willing to serve the stuff to friends, I assiduously clean the drip coffeemaker and grinder with baking soda to eliminate every bit of noncoffee flavors. In some households domestic tranquillity is also heightened by using the bottles of coffee flavorings. Add a hit directly to a brewed cup of traditional coffee.

HOTEL COLÓN TRYP'S COFFEE BAR

The typical breakfast in Seville, Spain, is coffee or tea with a roll or toast. Coffee is the heavy morning activity—some have twelve to fourteen cups a day. In Spain, some children start taking coffee very young. It is not unusual for thirteen-year-olds to have coffee daily.

Seville claims to have more bars per capita than any other European city. These bars are where friendships are made and cemented into lifelong relationships and where the business of business is done. Enrique Ysasi Fdez, De Bobadilla, director of the Hotel Colón Tryp, emphatically states that most important deals and arrangements are debated over coffee, not in the office. "When we talk, we talk over coffee."

Coffee breaks are revered. When calling a businessperson who is out for coffee, the receptionist never uses the euphemism that the person is "in a meeting." They honestly report that he or she is out for coffee. If a government worker is on a break, a queue forms and the clients wait until the coffee break is over. Working people usually take between twenty and thirty minutes for a coffee break. There is no disturbing someone during coffee, it is simply not done.

Even though most bars have high wooden stools, the patrons stand. The clients at a local bar are religiously loyal and would change bars only under distressing situations. The bartenders know the clients' usual orders and never forget. The bartenders also know if you want a glass of water on the side (popular in Seville but not in Madrid) and how strong you like your coffee prepared and exactly what you like in it if anything. They know if the coffee is taken solo (with nothing) or *corto de cafe* (a short cup) or *largo* (a long cup, using both spigots from the espresso machine in one glass). For those who do

not want too much caffeine, there is the *leche manchada,* simply a splash of coffee with a cup of milk.

All drinks are the same price—thank goodness, or the bartenders would go crazy because the number of ways their customers take coffee probably exceeds the number of bullfighting fans.

BRAMAH TEA AND COFFEE MUSEUM

Just across from London's Tower Bridge in the Butler's Wharf area is the Bramah Tea and Coffee Museum, which honors "two of the worlds most important commodities, through examination of their contribution to both global economies and cultures." Here also is a shop selling the highest quality Bramah teas and coffees, caddies, and other related items. The cafe provides an opportunity to taste many different beverages.

The founder, Edward Bramah, spent his life immersed in most phases of this business from working on a tea plantation to supplying commercial machines and coffee. He was a collector of tea and coffee paraphernalia, and an author and lecturer on the subject.

He wrote of the changes in the industry, "We had some momentous changes to tea and coffee in the 1960s and to see 90 percent of all our tea presented in tea bag form and 90 percent of our coffee as instant does not fill me with much joy. The detriment of the product came to be a shameful business."

One section looks at the growth of television advertising aimed at the British tea-drinking public by Nestlé and General Foods. They pushed their instant coffees into the market with nightly messages that were eventually successful.

Absolutely delightful is the giant collection of teapots, more than one thousand, ranging from whimsical to elegant, including the world's largest teacup, which is larger than a bathtub.

TEMPESTUOUS TEAS

The serving of tea has spawned the creation of exquisite cups, ceremonial bowls and earthenware pots, silver services, samovars, furniture (the tea table preceded the coffee table), houses, polystyrene containers, and fortune-tellers. Tea has even been used as a currency in ancient China.

It seems that this started when a few *Camellia Sinensis* leaves serendipitously blew into the water being boiled over an open fire, burning branches of that plant. The year was 2737 B.C. and the man was Chinese Emperor Shen Nung of China. The result, of course, was the first cup of tea and the birth of the most widely consumed beverage in the world.

The emperor enthusiastically consumed the drink, proclaiming it gave one "vigor of body, contentment of mind, and determination of purpose." Its cultivation, in mountainous areas in mineral-rich soil, and consumption spread throughout the Orient—at first, a beverage for royalty (the peasants were still drinking barley water), then for the masses.

More than twelve hundred years ago, the Tang Dynasty scholar and poet, Lu Yu, taught the ideal way to brew tea. Fresh water must first be obtained from a slow-moving mountain stream. It is boiled until it is possible to hear "the sounds of breakers majestic." One-quarter ounce of tea leaves in a pure white porcelain cup are covered with boiling water. This water is discarded and more water added. This should be slowly sipped.

In Imperial China, gentlemen and businessmen gathered in a neutral teahouse to conduct business, to settle disputes, to gossip, and for *yum cha,* or tea drinking. Men of leisure would bring along their caged pet birds. No food was served following the guidance of a third-century imperial physician, Hua To, who proclaimed "Eating food and drinking tea at the same time only results in excessive weight gain." And the Chinese considered obesity the height of rudeness.

In fourteenth-century Japan tea "joints" were awash with gambling, dancing women, and debauchery. At the same time the Buddhist priests used tea in religious worship.

Chado, the Way of Tea, developed almost to cult status under Sen-no Rikyu in the sixteenth century. The precise rules led to the creation of separate teahouses, austere gardens, unsymmetrical and non-repetitive interior decorations. Shogun Hideyoshi wished to rid himself of his tea master, Rikyu, and "allowed" Rikyu to kill himself. Rikyu's family finally had its fortunes returned and his three grandsons faithfully expanded their grandfather's ways by creating three separate schools of

tea ceremonies. One branch, Urasenke, is still practiced today.

After a light breakfast of miso soup, rice, and seaweed served at a small *ryokan* (inn) outside Kyoto, our hostess inquired whether we would like to have a tea ceremony. Her young daughter, learning the ritual steps, wanted to practice.

"Of course, what a treat," we responded.

After thirty minutes the young girl returned with her mother and conducted the ceremony. Her painstaking efforts surely emulated the rituals of the priest of tea and the glances toward mother for approval were richly rewarded.

While the Japanese tea ceremony is the most ritualized and stylized, rules are equally important in making Australian billy tea. At Ross River Homestead, a cattle and guest ranch, the world's thinnest cowboy with a long braid complete with feather, made damper (a quick bread made in a Dutch oven cooked in the ashes) and billy tea. Billy is the trusty tin pot that sits over the fire. After the water comes to a boil, leaves are added and steeped. Then the action begins by swinging the pot three times in a complete

circle (centrifugal force keeps the contents inside) before serving in thin tin cups.

The cups are rinsed in a basin of water ready for the next guest who is asked "Wanta cuppa?" The sliced damper sits under a dishcloth on the table while flies swarm on the open tin of golden syrup.

Not until the seventeenth century did the Dutch traders introduce tea to Europeans, where it became wildly popular and spread to other continents. The British East India Trading Company, after significant bloodshed, became the dominant traders. In eighteenth-century Colonial Williamsburg the traditions closely followed those of the mother country. The lady always poured the beverage, and the silver service set contained a pitcher for milk, a bowl for sugar, and a "slop" bowl for the tea leaves after brewing.

In the United States, the British traders' financial bungling was to be saved, in part, by the three-pence-per-pound tax levied by the British on tea purchased by Americans. The Sons of Liberty in 1773 brewed a tempest by dumping 342 large chests of tea in the harbor.

Preparation

Today tea styles and uses vary around the world. In Morocco's shops it is common to establish a relationship over tea before engaging in another ritual, bargaining. Taking the first glass, by tradition, means that the person is committed to three. Mint is often added to the second pot. In winter months if mint is scarce, the herb might be sage or wormwood.

In India *chai*, or teas flavored with spices, sugar or honey, and milk, is an ancient favorite of yoga practitioners. It may be served either hot or cold. In the United States chai has become quite popular and uses Assam black tea, milk, and ingredients such as cardamom, cinnamon, vanilla bean, ginger, cloves, honey, and sugar.

In Russia, heated water from a brass, copper, or silver samovar is poured into cups partially filled from a separate pot of brewed tea leaves called *samovar*. The original Russian samovar is from Tula, made in 1778 by Ivan and Nazar Lisitsyn. The brew is sipped from glasses with silver holders. The Russians add jam or hold a sugar cube between their teeth while sipping.

Tibetans create an attention-getting beverage by adding both yak butter and salt to leaves that have been steeped for almost an hour, creating a rather rancid-tasting beverage. This is served in brass cups.

England's rule of one teaspoon of tea per cup, plus one teaspoon for the pot, is still the guiding standard for much of the Western world. Fresh water is brought to a rolling boil, poured into the teapot, and permitted to steep from three to seven minutes. One pound of tea yields about two hundred cups more or less, depending on its brewing strength.

Variations

Asians prefer green teas that are unfermented and light green with a mild taste. Occidentals prefer black tea, a fully fermented leaf, which produces an amber liquid with full flavor. Oolong Tea, the middle range, is partially oxidized and today quite popular in China.

Of the three major green teas, jasmine (made with the flowers and green leaves) is a sweet, flowery blend. James Bond fans may remember his drinking Yin Hao jasmine, one of the most expensive teas in the world. Popular in the West is gunpowder tea with each leaf rolled into a small tight pellet. Dragon well is an excellent green tea with a toasty, herbal aroma.

The blends of leaves create many versions of black tea. Assam, the malty tea from India is a popular breakfast tea and particularly tasty with milk. Sri Lankan tea, a pungent taste with lemony aroma, is rich and brown in color and good hot or cold, with or without milk, or with lemon. Darjeeling, grown in the Himalayan foothills, is the "champagne of teas" with a muscatel flavor and perfumy aroma. English breakfast is a blend of Indian and Sri Lankan black teas served in the morning, with or without milk or lemon. Irish breakfast tea is a heady blend of African teas (primarily from Kenya), good with milk and sugar. Earl Grey is a blended Chinese black tea scented with the fragrant herb bergamot. Lapsang Souchong is a smoked tea from the Fukien province of China.

Despite its marketing, orange pekoe refers to the size of a tea leaf and is not a type of tea.

Most of the popular oolong teas are from Taiwan. Formosa (meaning

beautiful island) oolong has a peachy flavor and low astringency. The Formosa Pouchong is scented with gardenia or jasmine blossoms and recommended without milk before bedtime. From China and Taiwan comes black dragon, a fruity-tasting delicate brew.

Tea is in disfavor with some since it contains both caffeine, about one-third of that in coffee, and tannin. Tannins, some contend, interfere with the digestion of proteins.

ALL THE TEA IN TAIWAN

Tea grower, producer, and chef, Kou Shu Min and wife, Chang Ming Ye, at the Mountain Village of Giant Dragon Restaurant in Taiwan, offer tea tastings in their inn located below the famous Wu Lai waterfalls.

Min explained the tea-tasting process. "Smell the tea's fragrance. Take a small amount in the mouth. Swirl around for ten seconds, letting the liquid excite all tastebuds. Swallow with some air and breath out through the nostrils."

Min is creating foods exploiting the virtues of green tea's fragrance, such as steamed-in-green-tea prawns. The stylings are light, healthy, and beautifully presented—reflective of Japanese (who occupied the island from 1895 to 1945) and native Taiwanese cooking. Dishes enhanced with fresh tea leaves are reminiscent of the French's restrained use of fresh herbs.

The house tea wine produced by Min is not for the timid. Laughingly Min related, "When the earth and sky meet, one understands tea wine's potency and when the imbiber says 'I'm the only thing awake because the sky and earth go 'round and 'round,' he has had enough."

"Tea is healthy and its medicinal properties, particularly cholesterol reduction, are being scientifically studied at Taiwan's Tea Experiment Station," said Min.

THE IMPERIAL HERBAL TONICS AND APHRODISIACS

Food and medicine are inseparable in the Imperial Herbal Restaurant. Chinese herbal physician, Dr. Li Lian Xiang, diagnoses physical ailments, according to three-pulses in each wrist. He expertly recommends foods for now and herbal mixes to go. No appointment is necessary during restaurant hours.

The physician/herbalist from Tianjin, prescribes, mixes, and weighs herbs for customer's requesting a diagnosis. A dead serpent coiled ceremoniously on the counter faces customers waiting for their individually prepared packet of herbs. Behind is a series of tin-lined antique wooden drawers each meticulously filed with herbs. On top are glass jars brimming with herbal concoctions and wines. No fee is charged—rather money is discreetly left in a small red envelope on the counter.

Blending requires experience and high-quality ingredients. In the Metropole Hotel's third-floor restaurant, only the finest, certified herbs are used. "The Chinese herbal approach is cheaper, slower, but has no side effects," claims Mrs. Wang-Lee Tee Eng, the force behind the first herbal restaurant outside the People's Republic of China. "Sometimes the herbal medicine is not tasty, but our foods are. All herbs are safe. They must be taken consistently over time to feel the effect."

The Chinese herbal system was developed by Li Shizhen (1517–1593) who,

according to Mrs. Wang, painstakingly worked on the encyclopedic research for twenty-seven years. His empirical works were recorded on fifty-two scrolls, providing the basis for nutrition and health over the centuries.

Eastern herbal medicine is an integral belief. It is rare to share a meal with a Chinese group without being reminded what is good for the eyes, for the skin, and for the rest of the body.

Business is good. "Those who believe in herbal medicine keep coming back, according to Mrs. Wang. "When Chinese medicine is good, the word spreads fast."

Mrs. Wang, glows with an inner beauty, a peaceful contentment with her life and the special contributions the herbal restaurant provides to others. In the restaurant she teams her fervent belief in herbal medicine with practical financial skills honed from a business-school education at Toronto's York University.

Medicine as food often lacks gustatory appeal. But most of this restaurant's food/medicine is a palate pleasure with prices comparable with other restaurants. The modern cooking styles reflect healthier

Western cooking trends—reducing fat, using natural and fresh foods, and eliminating all monosodium glutamate.

Based on northern Chinese cuisine, the dish of fresh and dried scallops in an egg whites cloud, spiked with polygonaceous herbs (from the buckwheat family) and ladybell root, tastes ethereal and is good for the skin. For helping in wound healing, particularly following operations, there is sweet-and-sour snake head fish with lily bulbs (lily bulbs are of bonus value for the lungs). Try the giant prawn in spicy chili teamed with walnuts. Walnuts, the longevity fruit, are recommended for both the kidney and the brain. Creamy eggplants with crunchy pine nuts help the body rid toxins while relieving pain. The beverage menu has tonic soups and liqueurs, cooling herbal tea (for heat, sore throats, coughs, and colds), and health drinks. Popular is the acclaimed aphrodisiac wine.

Aware that there are many paths to health, Mrs. Wang uses Western medication for her family when needed: "Western medicines often work faster." But for herself, she always tries the traditional Chinese herbal approach first.

MIZPE HAYAMIN SPA RESORT HERBAL TEA BAR

Since prehistoric times, man has sought the curative powers of herbs and plants by making teas and infusions. From medicine bags of healers all over the world, herbs provided relief, when used properly. Much of this work today is incorporated into both Eastern and Western branches of pharmacology and medicine.

The build-your-own herb tea bar at the Mizpe Hayamin Spa Resort, in Rosh Pina, Israel, presents natural dried herbs and mints. The bar is stocked with mugs and strainers and fresh steaming water so guests may personalize a blend suited to their own tastes.

One is cautioned "Do not mix together many sorts of teas!" No magic blend will prevent or cure all the ills that mankind has been able to manifest. The herbs, many grown on the expansive property, claim to treat the following:

chamomile—colds, aids digestion, clearing the respiratory system, and insomnia

verbena—infectious feverish diseases, influenza, headache, nervous disorders; an expectorant

sweet balm—nervous disorders, depression, hysteria, insomnia, digestive problems, stomach, menstrual, and tooth pain; a diuretic

thyme—digestion; an expectorant

lavender—nerve weakness and dizziness, muscular pain; use flower for heart and kidney ailments

oregano—inhibits intestinal fermentation

rosemary—soothes pain; a nerve sedative; a disinfectant; strengthens muscles; disinfects and strengthens hair roots

wormwood—intestinal worms, digestive disorders, and stomach problems

zatar (Thymbra)—digestive disorders

Moroccan Mint Tea

THIS refreshing tea is served with the mint leaves in special 4-ounce glasses. The glass, fiercely hot, is taken in the right hand with the thumb on the top and the fingers balancing the bottom. Wooden holders are also available. Moroccan-grown leaves are fermented. A popular brand is Extra by La Menara.

SERVES 4

1 tablespoon black, fermented Moroccan loose tea leaves

boiling hot water

large handful fresh spearmint leaves

4 tablespoons sugar

To the kettle add tea leaves. Cover with boiling water. Return to heat and steep 2 minutes. Add a large handful of fresh spearmint leaves, stir, and steep 2 more minutes. Stir in sugar.

The Perfect Cup of English Tea

*T*EA *devotees love nothing more than having perfection in a cup. This is not typically found at 35,000 feet. The tea bag and the polystyrene container are the lowest common denominator and the bane of an airline passenger who tries to create a drinkable substance with these and the paltry two-thirds cup of lukewarm water.*

Loose tea is best. There is more caffeine per pound in tea than in coffee, but 1 pound of tea yields 200 cups; whereas 1 pound of coffee makes 40 to 50 cups. And remember, the finer the quality of tea leaves, the finer the cup of tea. Serve with milk or lemon and sugar.

1 TEAPOT

boiling water to preheat pot

1 teaspoon loose tea per serving
plus 1 for the pot

1 cup boiling water per serving

Fill teapot with boiling water. Empty teapot. Add tea leaves. Fill pot with boiling water. Steep 5 minutes. Pour through strainer into a warm cup.

The Ascent to Machu Picchu and Coca Tea

While runners in the ancient Inca civilization managed to run fresh fish from the coast of Peru up to Machu Picchu for the Inca rulers in fewer than two days, the tourist may find the journey more challenging.

Two major obstacles delayed my planned journey. The first is quite common, the wind shears at the Cuzco airport. Planes usually have only a brief window early in the morning for landing. It took three 3 A.M. trips to the Lima airport before I could actually fly into Cuzco.

Eventually we all boarded the plane and successfully completed the trip to Cuzco. There we encountered our second obstacle—the daily train ascending to Machu Picchu was canceled indefinitely because of the actions of the antigovernment, terrorist group,

The Shining Path. A possible alternative would have been the three-to-four-day hike accompanied by the sure-footed Sherpa guides.

Not to worry. Our guides drove us to the colorful Sunday market in the village of Chinchero. And here we were treated to fresh coca leaves, crushed and brewed like tea. This tea is the antidote of choice for altitude sickness. After several glasses I did not suffer any of the altitude symptoms and I did not feel the high that supposedly comes along with coca.

One leaf has less than the effect of caffeine. Note that the 1961 United Nations' treaty banned international commerce of the leaf except for pharmaceutical use and for use as a flavoring agent. (This original ingredient in Coca-Cola was eliminated years ago.)

I did notice that the natives were chewing the coca leaves for a bit quicker high, along the lines of the Papua New Guinea natives who chew beetle nuts.

Chocolate Science: Insights from a Biochemist and Chef

Chocolate's complex and addictive flavors account for its universal appeal. The numerous compounds present in chocolate depend on genetics, environmental conditions, harvesting, and processing to create those flavors. Theodore Pary, certified executive pastry chef, corporate chef, and director of research and development AMERO Food Manufacturing Corporation, knows all about the science of chocolate. He will quickly tell you that chocolate is so complex with its four hundred flavors that it cannot be reproduced by a biochemist.

Pary studied at the Culinary Institute of Paris and earned a degree in biochemistry. For decades his studies of the chocolate industry, from cacao bean growth through production, has made the world a better place for consumers to eat chocolate.

The beans grow in a tropical climate twenty degrees north and south of the equator.

When picked, the pods are opened, exposing their white mucilaginous pulp to oxygen, which starts the fermentation. This process creates heat and acid, which develop the flavor and the deep red color. "No fermentation, no flavor. No fermentation, no color," says Pary.

The next step is drying. In South America, Mexico, India, Malaysia, and Africa, millions of beans are dried to their brown color. Then brokers carefully select their beans, which are submitted to the FDA for inspection. Next, the beans are steam roasted, producing different roast types in a process similar to coffee beans. The "chocolate" flavor is associated with low roast. High roast results in a bitter taste. Each factory's roasting procedure is highly confidential.

After roasting, the shells are removed, leaving the nibs. These are ground to extract cocoa butter, creating chocolate liquor. Chocolate liquor, sugar, lecithin, and vanilla are combined in a huge mixer. This blend is processed in a roll refiner to reduce the particle size. The last manufacturing step is conching, where the substance becomes smoother, more palatable, and more mellow—more wonderfully chocolate.

Mousse-in-a-Cup: Fit for a Queen

CACAO beans were brought back to Europe by the New World traders. In short time they enhanced the product with sugar, starting the world's passionate love affair with chocolate. Adding milk created a beverage enjoyed today by both children and adults.

In the Hotel le Crillon, one of the truly luxurious venues of Paris, is Les Ambassadeurs, the two-star Michelin rated restaurant. Chef Christian Constant's cadre of chefs prepares a beverage much closer to chocolate mousse than to the thin hot cocoa of my childhood.

The waiter, immaculately attired in jet-black suit and stiffly starched white shirt, politely queried, "Café, tea, ou chocolat, Madame?" The Hotel le Crillon is situated near the Place de Concorde, where the guillotine operated during the French Revolution. Being so close to the site of Marie Antoinette's infamous end, I opted for her favorite late-1700s breakfast beverage—chocolate.

The hot chocolate is a beverage so rich, creamy, and heavenly that one's natural inclination is to look upward toward the Crillon's painted ceiling, perhaps to a divine source of inspiration.

The breakfast meat selection is quite extraordinary with ox tongue, sliced veal, rare roast beef, Parisian ham, chicken, and smoked salmon. A bevy of fresh juices includes squeezed plum juice. In addition to aged Gouda and other hard cheeses are a number of soft, beautiful breakfast cheeses and yogurt. Bowls of cereal and freshly sliced fruits provide a closer touch to the morning fare of the nonroyals. Also on the buffet is chocolate cake, pastries, a kingly kuglehoff studded with raisins, and a golden brioche.

Chilling in a silver bowl are bottles of mineral waters, including Perrier and a bottle of Tattinger champagne. The Tattinger family's holdings include the Crillon as part of the Concorde Hotel group, as well as Baccarat crystal, Haviland china, and Antal Gouillant perfumes, along with other distinctive lines.

The Crillon's staff of 40 chefs works in one of the most beautifully sumptuous kitchens in the world—a decor quite unlike *the usual commercial, somber stainless steel. The sides of the cooktops are all in marble surrounded with brass. The work tables are surrounded with brass rails, all receiving daily hand polishing.*

For a beverage suitable to all this grandeur, the potent, rich chocolate from the Isle of Guanaja is cooked with sugar and cream to create the "starting elixir." In the morning a magic portion of this is mixed with heavy cream and heated. Immediately it is placed in the silver service pot and presented in royal style. Hot milk is passed for anyone not quite brave enough to handle this mousse-in-a-cup.

4 ounces dark, bittersweet chocolate

1 cup sugar

2 cups heavy cream

hot milk, to taste

In a heavy pan or double boiler, melt chocolate, sugar and ½ cup of cream. Stir until completely mixed and creamy for about 5 minutes. Just before service time add remaining cream and heat. Pass hot milk separately for individual blending.

Wet, Wild, and Wonderful Beverages

237

Moroccan Milk Plus

*T*HE *number of possible additions to milk is amazing, including fresh fruits, vegetables, or nuts. All that is needed is a blender. While the Moroccans serve this drink at room temperature, believing that cold liquids are unnatural and unhealthy, our testers preferred these drinks chilled.*

SERVES 1

6 ounces milk

one or more of the following: ⅓ cup ground almonds, 1 banana, 1 pear, ½ avocado

In a blender process milk with selected enhancements. Pour into a glass.

Indian Lassi

*O*N A *hot day, nothing cools quicker than this yogurt drink. Often this accompanies* parathas, *a flaky, fried, whole wheat bread for the morning repast. For a flavored drink, add about 1 cup fresh fruit such as mango, bananas, berries, or cantaloupe.*

SERVES 2

1 cup plain yogurt

1 cup water

¼ cup sugar

mint leaves, garnish

Place all ingredients in blender and process. Garnish with fresh mint.

"Water, water everywhere, but who knows which drop we should be drinking," said Arthur von Wiesenberger, water master, at the International Toast to the Tap '95, held annually in the spa town of Berkeley Springs, West Virginia. This is the largest and longest running water competition in the world and is held at the rustic health spa, Coolfont, nestled in the Appalachian foothills.

Von Wiesenberger is the author of *The Pocket Guide to Bottled Water* (Chicago: Contemporary Books, 1991) and *The A to Z of Water Tasting Terms* (Santa Barbara: Best Cellar Publications 1995), and is perhaps the world's leading authority on water.

Prior to water tastings von Wiesenberger spends several hours training judges. He teaches a water vocabulary as precise as that used in the analysis of wines. He does not permit the judges to have coffee, alcoholic beverages, and spicy foods before the tasting. And he does not permit them to wear any scents or to chew gum. Discerning palates must be clean palates. These tastings are much more difficult than wine tasting because threshold differences, particularly among bottled, noncarbonated waters are subtle.

In double-rinsed, hand-buffed glasses, judging categories were appearance (hoping to find no suspended particles), odor (losing points for chlorine, plastic, sulfur, must, or metal), flavor (seeking for a clean taste void of salt, chemicals), refreshing mouth feel, a thirst-quenching aftertaste (devoid of residue), and an overall impression of desirability to have as an everyday drinking water.

Water experts agree that the taste of water can tremendously affect food products such as coffee, breads, and desserts. Water stored in plastic containers can absorb odors and flavors from nearby substances; glass is a better storage container. For maximum drinking pleasure, serve waters at sixty degrees Farenheit without ice.

239

Orange juice is a morning institution—a bright, sunny, refreshing way to start the day. Besides coffee and tea, it is, perhaps, one of the most universally consumed morning beverages.

At the El Minzah Hotel in Tangiers, Morocco, pitchers of freshly squeezed juice are served at room temperature because cold drinks are not considered healthy. Small pitchers are frequently replaced with more of the fresh product. Many natives consume vast quantities of orange juice. One gentleman claimed that he drinks at least one liter a day to keep fit and promised "it works."

The bars in Italy and Spain have colorful baskets filled with bright oranges, and the attendant will squeeze a glass of liquid gold right in front of your eyes.

Chilling the juice or the oranges, as in Morocco, is not popular and may detract from its liveliness.

In the Hotel Tryp Colón, Spain, the freshly squeezed juices are prepared for international guests who demand their juice cold. Six large glass pitchers in silver buckets of ice. In Andalusia, Spain, *jugo de naranza* (orange juice) is not consumed in the morning except by ladies, it is said, who need a laxative.

In France, Kate Ratcliffe, the charming American who runs both a school of Gascogny cuisine and the graceful charter barge, the *Julia Hoyt,* always squeezes her own, claiming that she cannot purchase any decent juices in the markets. What a delightful, bright way to get vitamin C.

Raspberry Orange Smoothie

*T*HIS *fast breakfast in a glass is perfect for those wanting only a liquid start, especially refreshing on a hot day. Everything goes into the blender. Pulse, and it's ready. Try other flavors with fresh berries or fruits in season.*

SERVES 4

2 cups buttermilk, low fat

2 cups fresh raspberries

1 cup frozen orange juice concentrate

½ cup ice cubes

2 tablespoons sugar

1 teaspoon vanilla

mint leaves, garnish

Place all ingredients in a blender. Cover and process until smooth. Pour into chilled glasses and garnish with mint.

Pop the cork on a bottle of champagne and breakfast is instantly an elegant celebration. This was the coronation drink of kings and even Napoleon who crowned himself in the Reims Cathedral.

And toast Dom Perignon, the saintly monk and cellar master at the Abbey of Hautvillers, Epernay, France. Historical wisdom credits Dom Perignon in 1668 with being the first to blend grapes of different locations (the cuvee) to make "the devil's wine," *vin du diable*. Of equal importance was his discovery of the more secure cork to replace the piece of wood wrapped in oil-soaked hemp. He purportedly adopted this idea from traveling Spanish monks who were using water gourds with cork stoppers.

Even so, champagne bottles remained potentially explosive. In the eighteenth century, masks were worn in summer for protection from the exploding glass. With stronger bottles capable of handling the carbon dioxide pressure from fermentation, champagne became a less dangerous drink.

"Creating the champagne is part man and part nature," stated Patrice Gourdin, spokesman for Moet et Chandon. Nature provides the lousy weather in the Champagne region with fog coming in from England. It is only ninety miles east of Paris. "With the poor chalky soil, cool weather, the vines have to suffer. It is this struggle that produces good grapes. We want crisp wine with lots of acidity."

Moet et Chandon in Epernay was founded in 1743 by Claude Moet. The company joined forces with Pierre-Gabriel Chandon in 1832. Today they are the largest vineyard owners in Champagne with 2,125 acres. More than one-third of bottles sold in the United States is from Moet et Chandon, whose holdings have expanded to Argentina (1960), California (Domaine Chandon, 1973), and Brazil (1974).

Until 1840 champagne was a sweet wine with added sugar, until Londoners requested the wine be made without sweetener. Today, in general, the driest wines go to the United Kingdom, while the slightly less dry to the United States. The French prefer dry, the Scandinavians sweet, the Venezuelans dry and sweet; the rest of South Americans prefer dry.

It takes almost four pounds of grapes to make a single bottle of champagne. It is a labor-intensive process. The best time to pick grapes is at dawn, gently with scissors.

Champagne is best stored in a cool (50 to 55°F), dark cellar with high humidity, free from vibration. It is best served chilled to 45°F. Chill in a refrigerator for two to three hours or immerse in a bucket with water and ice for thirty to forty-five minutes. Pour glass about two-thirds full. Do not keep in a refrigerator more than one week.

The proper glass is the flute, which came into use before champagne even existed. Flutes were first made at Murano, near Venice, in the late sixteenth century for Rhine wines and English ales. This still is the premier glass, allowing for a slow, steady stream of bubbles.

In 1663 the coupe was designed especially for champagne, but it lets the bubbles dissipate too fast. The saucer-shaped glass, fashionable during the Victorian era, is too shallow and too wide. Sometimes called the "Marie Antoinette" after her breasts, the glass has no point for prompting the formation of bubbles, in which case, the wine goes flat.

Botticelli: Pomegranates and Sparkling Wine

VITTOREO DALL'O, the food and beverage director at the Villa San Michele overlooking Florence, presents this bubbly morning cocktail for special occasions, but only in the autumn when the pomegranates are fresh. The color is a muddy Siena pink, which starts the day in grand style in this restored villa with its facade designed by Michelangelo in the sixteenth century.

SERVES 6

1 pomegranate

1 bottle Italian spumante (or other sweet sparkling wine), chilled

sprigs of fresh mint, garnish

Break open pomegranate into a fine mesh strainer. Using the back of a strong spoon smash seeds, forcing juice into a bowl. Mix juice with spumante. Pour into champagne flutes. Garnish with fresh mint.

Villa San Michele's Room Service: High above Florence

Room service at the Villa San Michele in the Fiesole area of the Tuscan hills just outside Florence is a place to contemplate the peace and serenity that Franciscan monks enjoyed for more than four hundred years. This land was a holy place dedicated to St. Michael. But all the finest earthly appointments were used—Carrera marble altar, stone fireplaces, tapestries by Arazzo, frescoes on the walls, and the curved X-shaped chairs known as "chairs of Savonarola."

Our suite was built into the limestone wall covered with wisteria, overlooking the central formal Italian gardens, enclosed with cypress trees. In the center were the lemon and orange trees heavy with fruit. The large terra cotta vase of fresh flowers decorated the suite's table that was spread with the custom-made fine linens. On the tray was buffalo mozzarella, made fresh and imported from the southern part of Italy. For a starter came two glasses of freshly squeezed pomegranate juice matched with Italian spumante (page 244).

Room service is not the best way to start the day in this resort. The long terrace loggia is a rapturous setting for breakfast, with the rising sun's rays dancing and creating marvels on the golden walls of the villa. Below the double-groined vaulted ceiling, the antique wooden side tables are set with the breakfast buffet: chunks of Parmigiano-Reggiano, soft fresh Pecorino and local cheeses, paper-thin slices of Parma ham, salt-free Tuscan breads, soft rolls with a golden egg wash, toast, croissants, apple turnovers, yogurt cake, pound cake filled with modest dots of candied fruit, fresh fruit tart, ripe figs and melons, confiture, and choices of all the typical morning beverages. The cappuccino had the best head of steamed milk I have ever seen.

After breakfast one can climb up the stone-walled path to the small town of Fiesole, where there is a Roman theater, archaeology museum, and small church. If you delay enough and walk around to the panoramic view site it may be appropriate to stop for a fresh slice of focaccia topped with green olives, tomatoes, anchovies or eggplant, and roasted red peppers from the bakery shop. It is sold by weight to perfectly fit your appetite or eyes.

When the morning-after-the-night-before hits those who have imbibed beyond their limits, even the idea of breakfast is a torture. Morning starts with drinking water, popping one or two fizzes or a couple of aspirin, and the vehement promise never to do that again.

It became quite obvious in looking for the ultimate hangover cure that, while none emerged as a winner, many ideas were in strong contention for possible soothing ideas.

My hunch was that Hedonism II, an all-inclusive (including unlimited alcohol) Jamaican resort known for its adult wild parties, including nudity and drinking, would lend a clue. So over I went to chat with the bartender to discover his suggestions.

"Well, I really do not have one," he confessed. But he did suggest having a bloody Mary like so many other hangover fighters, "the hair of the dog that bit you."

Soups, universally, get the nod for the hangover. One popular Mexican T-shirt claims: "Menudo, the breakfast of champions." Menudo is made of tripe. The broth is enriched with calves feet, then thickened with hominy and spiced with fresh green chilies. To keep things really going, it can be garnished with fresh wedges of lime and chopped onions. The hot tortillas included as a side are also considered quite soothing.

Al Lucero, author of *The Tequila Book* (Berkeley, CA: Ten Speed Press, 1995) and owner of Maria's, which serves traditional New Mexican cuisine in Santa Fe, said on the topic of menudo and hangovers, "It smells awful and tastes awful and if you psychologically can get beyond the fact that you are eating the lining of a cow's stomach, then maybe it will work. But I have never tried it."

While Maria's serves menudo at their New Year's Day Hangover Brunch, which starts fashionably after noon, they take a more pleasing approach overall, with huevos rancheros, breakfast burritos, Chimayo red chili made with pork, green chili with either chicken or pork, and if you can face it, menudo. Some of these heat-seeking items operate under the theory that the pain caused will keep the mind off the original hurt.

Another traditional beverage, according to Lucero, is Sangrita, a tomato juice mixture in a shot glass with jalapeño or Tabasco, lemon juice, Chimayo red chili powder and salt and pepper. Fill a separate shot glass with tequila. Drink the tequila shot then down the tomato mixture. That is all there is to it. The Chimayo chili is not terribly hot, but it is very flavorful. The New Mexico approach is *sabroso,* meaning flavorful. Chili does not have to make your eyes water.

A similar tripe soup, *iskembe corbasi,* is the Turkish hangover cure, sold in iskembecis, which are open all night long. A similar tripe soup has followers in Persia.

The Thais suggest Thai Jasmine Rice Soup with Shrimp (page 168).

Finnish farmers, famed vodka drinkers, claimed to have developed a product, called Rassol, that is *the* answer to hangovers. It is the briny beverage used to

pickle cucumbers and cabbage. This is traditionally drunk at breakfast after the pickles are eaten. Some even suggest those pickles should be washed down with a bottle of vodka.

A legendary morning hangover cure revealed by a tour guide at the lush Coyaba River Gardens and Museum in Ocho Rios starts with one pound of allspice berries in a quart of Jamaican white rum. Patiently let it rest for several months. Then drink to chase away a hangover. It can be applied topically to relieve insect bite itch; or drink if relief is not speedy enough.

And then the list of hangover preventers goes on and on. There's always the old saying in college circles regarding the mixing of potent alcohols: "Beer on whiskey, mighty risky. Whiskey on beer, never fear."

Coating the stomach by drinking a glass of milk or eating a bowl of mashed potatoes is a popular preventive measure. And an aspirin after a night of heavy drinking may ameliorate the next morning's malaise.

Maria's Ten-Step Bloody Mary

O N *NEW YEAR's Day, Maria's New Mexican Restaurant in Santa Fe serves this phenomenal Bloody Mary with their Hangover Brunch. The secret is to make each drink fresh and not to use a mix:*

S E R V E S   1

ice cubes

1½ ounces vodka

Worcestershire sauce

Tabasco sauce

salt and pepper, to taste

½ lime

Sacramento tomato juice

1. Fill a 16-ounce glass with ice cubes.
2. Pour in vodka.
3. Add 2 dashes Worcestershire sauce.
4. Add 7 shots Tabasco sauce.
5. Add salt and pepper.
6. Squeeze in juice of ¼ lime.
7. Fill glass with Sacramento tomato juice.
8. Stir.
9. Squeeze in juice of another ¼ lime.
10. Sprinkle salt and pepper on top before serving.

Liberian Ginger Beer

GINGER beer, refreshing from the bite of fresh ginger perfumed with the headiness of cloves, wakes up the sleepiest folks. From Liberia, it is also a suggested tonic for unhappy stomachs. The spicy concentrate is mixed with sugar and water just before serving.

Ales and beers made of ginger are quite popular all over the African continent. Another approach is to crush or mince one pound of peeled ginger, cover with water adding two cups of sugar. Simmer over a low heat for several hours or until most of the water has evaporated. Refrigerate and serve chilled adding additional water as desired.

This recipe was inspired by Ida Daniels, who runs a catering business specializing in Liberian cuisine in Richmond, Virginia.

SERVES 6

6 ounces fresh ginger, crushed with the side of a knife

4 cups water

1 fresh clove

sugar, to taste

Soak ginger in water overnight. Add clove and soak for another night. Remove ginger and clove. Discard. Mix ½ cup of this concentrate with sugar and additional water to taste and serve chilled.

Israeli Kiwi Tropical Surprise

THE Israelis are not known to be prodigious consumers of alcohol. The annual per capita consumption is only 4.5 liters. But in the glorious Hills of Galilee, the Amiad Winery operated by the Kibbutz Amiad makes delicious sweet wines from fruits such as kiwi, pear, blackberry, kumquat, jeijoa, and loquat, all grown on their property. This is their suggested drink for a special morning. After all, the kibbutz salespersons claim that their wines aid in digestion and help clean out the system.

SERVES 1

1 part vodka

3 parts kiwi wine

3 parts freshly prepared tropical fruit juice (such as pineapple, mango)

Stir all ingredients with crushed ice and serve with kiwi slice.

Breakfast Menus from Around the World

C an you tell where you are by what is served for breakfast? The growth of business travel and large international corporate hotels have made it possible to have the American or the English breakfast in most corners of the world. It is nice to enjoy the comforts of home, but when it comes to breakfast you miss out on lots of fun, and good adventuresome eating, if you are forced to stay in a corporate hotel for breakfast.

Some breakfasts are the everyday; some are very special occasion ones.

The menus are included so you can see the country context in which breakfast is enjoyed. Both classic breakfast traditions and new trends and food ideas are included in the recipe chapters. You can create delightful breakfast and brunch occasions featuring particular countries. Mixing and matching from one country of origin is highly encouraged. With the internationalization of food, that is just what is happening everywhere in the world.

Ingredient Sources (page 265), has mail order information for difficult to find ingredients.

ASIA

Japan

Miso-Shiru (Miso Soup) (page 171)

Rice and Nori, Roasted Seaweed

Raw Egg, Cooked Fish–Salmon

Assorted Crunchy Pickled Vegetables

Condiments, Pickled Red Plums
(Umeboshi)

Green Tea

Kohi (Coffee)

Texas Toast, Jam

China, Hong Kong, and Taiwan

Chinese Congee (Jook) (page 165)

Sesame Pancakes with Optional Egg

Soy Milk, Sweet or Salty with Condiments

Hot Pepper Sauce

Red or Green Tea

Korea

Kimchi

Korean "New Mother" Seaweed Soup
(page 169)

Rice

Assorted Meats and Vegetables

Barley or Rice Tea, Tea

Thailand

Rice with Meat, Vegetable

Thai Jasmine Rice Soup with Shrimp
(page 168)

Condiments

Tea

Malaysia and Singapore

Nasi Lemak: Fragrant Coconut-Infused Rice,
Chicken Rendang, Spicy Prawn Sambal,
(pages 33–35)

Turkey Sausage (page 37)

Borneo Longhouse Steamed River Fish in
Rice Wine (page 46)

Roti Jala, Lacy Coconut Pancakes with
Tropical Fruits (pages 134–35)

Hot Sambals

Roti Canai, Paper-Thin Griddle Bread
(pages 140–41)

Dosai, Idils (page 184)

Congee, Soups and Porridges
(page 165)

Fruits and Durians (page 209)

AUSTRALIA AND SOUTH PACIFIC

Australia

Eggs and Bacon, Tomato

Toast, Scones, Muffins, Marmalade and Vegemite (page 64)

Baked Beans on Toast

Ham, Peanut Butter or Vegemite (page 64)

Muesli, Fresh Fruit

Bacon, Sausage, Steak

Bondi Beach Couscous with Figs and Honey (page 158)

Daydream Island, Queensland Fresh Pineapple Fritters (page 207)

Milk, Orange Juice, Coffee, Tea

New Zealand

Golden Kumara Hash Brown on Ginger Scented Sauce

Bay of Islands Oyster Flan on Kumara Hash Browns (page 52)

Bay of Islands Kerikeri Orange and Macadamia Nut Piklets with Fresh Orange and Maple Syrup (page 132)

Huka Lodge Noodles with Venison Sausage and Fresh Mango Chutney (page 187)

Marmite on Toast (page 64)

Egg, Tomatoes, Wild Mushrooms

Muesli, New Zealand Style (page 148)

New Zealand Fruit Compote (page 201)

Lamb Fry

New Zealand Whole Orange and Apricot Muffin (page 117)

Coffee, Tea

Papua New Guinea

Sweet Potatoes

Papua New Guinea Sago Pancakes (page 198)

Greens and Fruits

EUROPE AND THE UNITED KINGDOM

United Kingdom

Perfect Hyde Park Scrambled Eggs with Smoked Salmon (page 18)

Salmon Kedgeree

British Isles Grilled Kippers (page 49)

Grilled Tomatoes, Mushrooms, Bacon, Black Pudding

Alverton Manor Brioche Loaf with Glacé Fruit (pages 81–82)

254

English Cheddar Cheese Scones (page 123)

Scottish Oatmeal (page 156)

Seville Marmalade from Dundee, Scotland, (page 210)

Jams, Toast

The Perfect Cup of English Tea (page 233), Coffee

WESTERN EUROPE

Iceland

Cheese

Buttermilk with Fresh Fruit

Rye or Pumpernickel Bread

Cucumbers and Tomatoes

Spain

FIRST BREAKFAST

White, Crusty Bread, Pastries

Buttered Toast and Jam

Coffee with Milk, Hot Chocolate

Spanish Potato Tortilla: The Tapa that Came to Breakfast (pages 176–77)

Andalusian Garlic, Olive Oil, and Fresh Tomato Slices on Crusty Bread (page 68)

Churros (doughnut) and Hot Chocolate

SECOND BREAKFAST

Ham, Sliced Sausage, Tapas

Sandwich with Crusty Bread

Beer

Portugal

Fresh Bread, Butter, Fruit Preserves, Cheese

Caldo Verde: Portuguese Green Soup (page 162)

Broa, Portuguese Corn Bread (page 103)

Bolo Real, The Portuguese Royal Pumpkin Cake (pages 108–09)

Coffee, Tea

France

Croissant, French Baguettes (page 106)

Butter and Jam

Pastries

Cafe Au Lait, Espresso

Mousse-in-a-Cup (pages 236–37)

Chicken Paté Gascon (page 39)

Gascon French Country Ham (page 55)

Italy

Crisp Rolls

Roman Breakfast Pizzas

Ricotta and Bittersweet Chocolate Chunk
Tort (pages 112–13)

Botticelli: Pomegranates and Sparkling Wine
(page 244)

Cappuccino

Germany

FIRST BREAKFAST

Rolls, Ham or Honey

Coffee

SECOND BREAKFAST

Rolls, Cheese, Sausage

Mineral Water, Apple Juice, Beer

Austria

FIRST BREAKFAST

Rolls, Coffee

SECOND BREAKFAST

Two Long, Thin Vienna Sausage with
Mustard on a Hard Roll

Viennese Marzipan Breakfast Cake
with Chocolate Chips and Ginger
(pages 110–11)

Mozart Zopf (bread in five braided
strands)

WEEKEND BREAKFAST

Fresh Fruit

Soft-boiled Eggs

Leberwurst and Cheese with Dark Breads

The Netherlands

Dutch Currant, Raisin, Citron, Whole
Grain Buns (pages 92–93)

Dutch Whole Grain Rolls with
Mushrooms, Red Peppers and Cheese
(pages 94–95)

Coffee

Switzerland

Croissants with Butter and Jam

Rolls, Meats, and Cheese

Coffee with Chocolates

Scandinavian Countries

Open Sandwiches

Thin Breads, Crisp Flat Breads

Danish Pastries, Copenhagen Style
(pages 84–85)

Swedish St. Lucia Buns (page 86)

Swedish Sunflower Carrot Rye Bread
(page 89)

Stockholm's City Hall Hot Rye Flakes with Ligonberries (page 157)

Smoked Fish Platters

Vegetables, Salads

Cereals

Coffee

EASTERN EUROPE

Hungary

Hard Crusty Rolls, Butter, Jam or Honey

Salami, Ham or Sausage

Cheese, Eggs

Fresh Green Pepper Rings and Tomato Slices

Fruit Juices

Tea or Coffee Au Lait

Milk or Cocoa

Poland

FIRST BREAKFAST

Oatmeal, Hot Wheat Cereal, Millet

Bread and Butter

Bagels, Cream Cheese

Sliced Meats, Mild Cheese

Croissants, Jam, Butter

Grain Coffee from Roasted Wheat or Barley with Chicory

Warm Milk or Hot Cocoa for Children

SECOND BREAKFAST

Sautéed Wild Polish Mushrooms (page 61)

Hot Soup, Sandwich and Soup for Children

Russia

Black Bread

Butter, Jam

Kasha with Milk, Sugar and Butter

Breakfast Blini with Ham and Sour Cream

Sandwich with Cheese, Ham or Salami

Herring and Caviar

Milk

Coffee or Tea with Lemon and Spoonful of Fruit Jelly

SUNDAY BREAKFAST

Boiled Potatoes in Oil and Vinegar

Rye Bread

Beef or Pork Sausage

Indian Tea

Greece

Fresh Fruit, Honey

Cheese, Bread and Sweet Yeast Breads

Thick Strong Coffee

ISRAEL, TURKEY,
MIDDLE EAST, AND INDIA

Israel

NON SABBATH

Olives, Cheese, Bread, Havlah

Yogurts, Vegetables, Fruits

Pita Bread with Zatar and Olive Oil
(pages 75–76)

Middle Eastern Minted Labani Balls
(page 65)

King David's Warm Cheese Cake
(pages 114–15)

Shashuka 1 (page 22)

Shashuka 2 (page 23)

Oatmeal and Chickpea Cookies for Ethiopian
Children (pages 120–21)

Israeli Kibbutz Morning Salad
(page 193)

Israeli Kiwi Tropical Surprise (page 250)

Herbal Tea (page 230), Coffee

SABBATH
(NO COOKING PERMITTED)

Olives, Yogurt, Breads

Cheeses

Smoked and Pickled Fish

Tea and Coffee

Turkey

Bread, Cheese, Olives

Yogurt with Honey, Jams

Salads, Fruit, Vegetables

The Young Turks Healthy Cheesy Herbed
Toast (page 63)

Simit, The Turkish Sesame Rings
(page 104)

Spicy Turkish Tomato Lentil Soup
(page 164)

Tea and Coffee

Middle East

Pita, Middle Eastern Flatbreads (page 105)

Dibs (page 64)

Bedouin Herdsman

Bread

Bowl of Coffee

Jordan Peasant Breakfast
Bowl of Soup, Humus

Arabic Coffee

Lebanon
Pita Bread, Cheese, and Olives

Flat Bread with Zatar Spices and Onion

Soup

Strong Arab Coffee

Uzbekistan
Kumys or with Sharp Creamy Cheese

Flat Bread, Nan

Tea

Afghanistan
Giant Chapatis

Tea

India

NORTHERN
Spiced Rice

Bread, Puris

Spiced Samovar Tea

SOUTHERN
Idils with Sambal

Buttermilk or Curds

Indian Dosai with Curried Potatoes (pages 184–85)

Indian Coconut Cilantro Chutney (page 208)

Tropical Fruit

Indian Lassi (page 238)

Coffee

AFRICA, EGYPT, AND MOROCCO

Africa
Eggs, Bacon, Sausage, Toast

Porridges Including Mealie Meal

Sweet Potatoes

Liberian Ginger Beer (page 249)

Egypt
Falafels with Pita Bread

Egyptian Fool Midammis, Fava Beans with Tomato, Eggs, Olive Oil, and Lemon (page 188)

Lettuce, Tomato, Carrots

Black or Green Olives

Feta Cheese

Eggs

Coffee

Morocco

Breads

Moroccan Mint Tea (page 232)

Moroccan Milk Plus (page 238)

Juices

Tea or Coffee

NORTH AMERICA

Canada

Eggs, Canadian Bacon, Tomatoes

Toast, English Muffins, Jams

French-Canadian Mashed Potato and Saltcod Cakes

Fresh Nova Scotia Maritime Fish Cakes (page 51)

Cape Breton Gaelic Oatcakes (page 119)

The Unicorn's Souffléd Pancake with Strawberry-Honey Sauce (pages 130–31)

Coffee, Tea

United States

Eggs with Bacon, Sausage

Toast, Rolls, Biscuits, Muffins, Pastries

Fruits, Cereals, Juices, Yogurt

Coffee, Tea, Milk, Water

101 Waffle Whimsies (pages 135–37)

Buttermilk Pancakes (page 127)

Hot Whole Grain Porridges (page 155)

Bittersweet Chocolate Almond Spread (page 66)

Western

New Mexican Green Chile and Cheese Eggs (page 19)

Breakfast Burrito with Red and Green Salsa (page 71)

Big Bear Lake Potato Pancakes with Fresh Watemelon Salsa (page 178)

New Mexican Green Chile Breakfast Potatoes (page 179)

Tortillas (page 145)

Polenta, Pork, Posole, and Poached Eggs (pages 56–57)

California Coddled Eggs with Cheese, Fresh Dill and White Wine (page 27)

Mountain Sky Guest Ranch Pecan Rolls (page 101)

Grand Teton Lodge Oven-Baked French Toast (page 125)

Hawaii

Loco Moco: Eggs with Hamburger, Sticky Rice and Gravy

Pan-Seared Mahimahi with Herb and Fruit Sauce (page 47)

Trilogy Cinnamon Buns (pages 98–99)

Pancakes with Aloha (page 133)

Saimin, Hawaiian Noodle Soup (page 172)

Maui Spam Musubi, Sticky Rice Balls (pages 190–91)

Kapalua Pineapple Chile Compote (page 203)

Kahakuloa Valley Taro Garden Patties (pages 182–83)

Malassadas, Hawaiian Portuguese Holeless Doughnuts (page 102)

Guava, Pineapple, Likilo'i, Papaya Juices

Papaya, Pineapple Slices

Kona Coffee

MEXICO AND CARIBBEAN

Jamaica

Jamaican Escoveitch Snapper (pages 42–43)

Ocho Rios Green Banana Porridge (page 159)

Steamed Fish with Scotch Bonnet Pepper Sauce

Scrambled Eggs with Salt Cod and Ackee, Calaloo

Homestyle Papaya Johnnycakes (page 144)

Eggs, Sautéed Plantains, Breadfruit

Herb Teas (Cerasee or Mint), Coffee

Mexico

FIRST BREAKFAST

Sweet Roll

Cafe con Leche

Hot Chocolate or Atole (Cornmeal Beverage)

SECOND BREAKFAST

Mexican Chicken Chilaquiles (pages 20–21)

Mexican Eggs with Nuevo Vallarta Fresh Salsas (page 211)

Mexican Two-Squash Soup with Avocado and Lime (pages 160–61)

Huevos Rancheros (page 21)

Beans, Tortillas (page 145)

Fruit or Juice

Cafe con Leche

SOUTH AMERICA

Crispy Hard Rolls

Butter, Jam, Fruit-Cherimoya
(page 209)

Chilean Plum Cheese (page 208)

Dulce de Leche (page 216)

Coffee

Venezuela

Scrambled Eggs with Tomatoes

Venezuelan Corn Arepas (page 142)

Fried Plantains with Shredded White
Cheese

Stuffed Empañadas

Stewed Baby Shark (on the Coast)

Llaneros Steak (in the Highlands)

Carne Mechada

Sausages, Ham

Black Beans (page 188)

Fruit Juices

Queso Blanco, Queso Palmita

Coffee

Glossary

Al dente. Cooking "to the tooth" or until still crisp or not mushy, particularly with vegetables and pasta.

Bain Marie. To cook in a water bath by placing cooking dish inside another dish containing water to ensure even and reduced heat. Also a container of hot water used to keep food hot.

Bake. To cook food with dry, hot air.

Blanch. To cook quickly and partially in boiling water or hot oil.

Blend. To combine two or more ingredients together, forming a single identity.

Boil. To cook in liquid that is bubbling.

Caramelize. To heat sugar or an ingredient containing sugar until browned, creating a unique taste.

Chinoise. Cone-shaped strainer (shaped like a Chinese hat), particularly useful for straining stocks.

Confectioners' sugar. Powdered sugar, particularly useful in baking and pastries.

Deglaze. To add liquid to a cooking pan to collect all cooking flavors and particles accumulated in the pan.

Fold. To gently incorporate an ingredient containing air into a heavier substance, such as beaten egg whites into a cake batter.

Food Danger Zone. The temperature range at which bacteria grows rapidly on food, from 40 °F to 140°F.

Fry. To cook in hot fat.

Garnish. To decorate or enhance a dish with edible products.

Grand Marnier. Orange liqueur.

Julienne. To cut into matchsticks, approximately ⅛ × ⅛ × 2 inches.

Liaison. Binding agents such as cream, butter, or eggs to thicken and enrich soups and sauces.

Marinate. To soak food in seasoned liquid to infuse flavors or tenderize.

Mise en place. Having all ingredients and utensils prepared before cooking and assembling a recipe. From the French "everything in place."

Mix. To combine ingredients evenly.

Nonstick pan. Cooking pan treated with special surfaces to which foods will not adhere. Requires plastic or wooden utensils to prevent scratching.

Parchment paper. Baking paper that will not burn in the oven and will keep items from sticking to the pan.

Pipe. To squeeze through a pastry tube.

Plastic film. Wrap for covering foods to isolate flavors and for conveniently forming ingredients into shapes. Also used for poaching foods such as sausage.

Ramekin. An individual soufflé dish often made of porcelain, usually 3 or 4 inches in diameter.

Reduce. To concentrate flavors by boiling off a quantity of liquid.

Roast. To cook with dry heat, usually refers to meats and vegetables.

Sauté. To quickly cook over high heat with very little fat or oil, comes from the French term meaning "to jump."

Scaling. To measure dry ingredients, such as flour, by weight for the ultimate in accuracy.

Simmer. To cook in a liquid that is below the boiling point.

Soufflé dish. 1 or 2-quart porcelain or earthenware dish with straight sides for baking or chilling ingredients.

Stir-fry. To quickly cook over intensive heat in a small amount of oil while constantly stirring ingredients in the pan. Often used in Chinese cooking in a wok.

Stock. Liquid with extracted flavors from cooking with meat, fish, poultry, vegetables, and seasonings.

Temper. To gradually change the temperature of an ingredient by adding a small amount of the warm ingredient to the cold one such as with cold eggs before adding to a warm sauce. Without tempering, the eggs would cook rather than mix with other items.

Unmold. To remove from a pan by retaining the shape of the contents.

Vegetable spray. Pressurized or pump vegetable oil mixed with lecithin that is sprayed lightly on utensils' surfaces to prevent food particles from sticking.

Virginia ham. Specially dry-cured and smoked hams from Surry County or Smithfield that are very salty and sliced paper-thin for flavoring.

Whip. To incorporate air into a substance, such as air into whipped cream.

Whisk. To beat with a wire implement, a whisk, until well mixed.

Zest. Outside portion of citrus fruit that does not include the white layer or pith.

Ingredients Sources

HERBS AND SPICES

Penzeys, Ltd.
P.O. Box 1448
Waukesha, WI 53187
Phone (414) 574-0277
Fax (414) 574-0278
(Fresh bulk, herbs, spices, and seasonings)

EUROPEAN PRODUCTS

Zingerman's
422 Detroit Street
Ann Arbor, MI 48106
Phone (313) 769-1625
Fax (313) 769-1235
E-mail: zing@chamber.ann-arbor.mi.us
(Importer of cheeses: Italian, Dutch, English, Swiss, French, Spanish; olive oils from Italy, Spain, France, Israel; vinegars, breads, loose teas; meats: Spanish chorizo, corned beef)

Foods of All Nations
212 Ivy Road
P.O. Box 3422
Charlottesville, VA 22901
Phone (804) 977-1877
Fax (804) 977-8610

Lisbon Sausage Co., Inc.
P.O. Box 2028
New Bedford, MA 02740
Phone (508) 996-6451
(800) Amarals
Fax (508) 994-0453
(Portuguese sausages)

Brits
13 East Eighth Avenue
Lawrence, Kansas 66044
1-888-38BRITS
Phone (913) 843-2288
E-mail brits@fastlane.com
www.highlandraill.co.uk/fish1
(kippers, Scottish salmon)

TURKISH, MIDDLE EASTERN, ISRAELI

Sultan's Delight
P.O. Box 090302
Brooklyn, NY 11209
Phone (800) 852-5046
Fax (717) 745-2563

Greater Galilee Gourmet, Inc.
2118 Wilshire Blvd., Suite 829
Santa Monica, CA 90403
Phone (310) 459-9120
(800) 290-1391
Fax (310) 459-1276
(Israel, Persia, spices, oils)

ORIENTAL

Anzen Oriental Foods and Imports
736 NE MLK Jr Blvd.
Portland, OR 97232
Phone (503) 233-5111
Fax (503) 233-7208

Spice Merchant
P.O. Box 524
Jackson Hole, WY 83001
Phone (800) 551-5999
Help line for recipe assistance
(307) 733-7811
E-mail 71553.436@compuserve.com
(Chinese, Japanese, Indonesian, Indian, Thai)

The Oriental Pantry
423 Great Road
Acton, MA 01720
Phone (508) 264-4576
Orders (800) 828-0368
Fax (617) 275-4506
(China, Japan, Thailand, India, Philippines)

PLANTS AND SEEDS

Evergreen Y. H. Enterprises
P.O. Box 17538
Anaheim, CA 92817
(Oriental seeds, seasoning mixes, soup mix, cooking sauce, teas, cookbooks)

The Rosemary House
120 South Market Street
Mechanicsburg, PA 17055
Phone (717) 697-5111
Fax (717) 697-3222
E-mail: RosemaryHs@aol.com
(herbs, spices, teas, plants, seeds)

BAKING SUPPLIES

King Arthur Flour Baker's
Catalogue
P.O. Box 786
Norwich, VT 05055-0876
Phone (800) 827-6836
(complete baking supplies, grains, flours)

International Contacts

Alexander and Baldwin Sugar
Museum
P.O. Box 125
Puunene, Maui, Hawaii 96784

Alverton Manor
Tregolis Road
Truro, Cornwall TR1 1XQ
United Kingdom

Baba Nyonya Heritage Museum
50 Jalan Tun Tan Cheng Lock
Malacca, Malaysia

Bounty from the Farm
Jessica Adler Hall
12384 Perry Mountain Lane
Viewtown, VA 22746-9603

Bora Özkök's Cultural Folk
Tours
9939 Hibert St., Suite 207
San Diego, CA 92131-1031
Phone (800) 935-TURK

Bramah Tea and Coffee
Museum
The Clove Building
Maguire Street
Butler's Wharf, London SE1 2NQ

Jane Butel's Cooking School
800 Rio Grande Blvd., NW #14
Albuquerque, NM 87104

Chateau de Lassalle
Hotel and Restaurant
Club Gascogne
La Plume, France

Colonial Williamsburg
Foundation
P.O. Box 1776
Williamsburg, VA 23187-1776

Conditori La Glace
Skoubogade 3-5
DK-1158 Copenhagen,
Denmark

Confitures Curtelin, 17 Rue
L.I.D.
BP 636
06517 Carros CEDEX, France

Daydream Island Travelodge
Resort
Whitsunday Islands,
Queensland, Australia
Private Mail Bag 22
Mackay, QLD., Australia

Divan Hotel
Cumhuriyet Caddesi No. 2
80200 Elmadg
Istanbul, Turkey

ENATUR Central Reservations
Portuguese Posadas
Av. Santa Joana a Princesa 10
1700 Lisbon, Portugal

The Gazebo Pancake House
Capitol Landing Road
Williamsburg, VA 23185

Grand Hotel
Blasieholmshamnen 8, Box
16424
103 27 Stockholm, Sweden

Grand Lido
SuperClubs
Negril, Jamaica

Gripsholms Värdshus and
Hotel
Kyrkogatan 1, Box 114,
S-647 00 Mariefred
Sweden

Hacienda Antigua Bed and
Breakfast
6709 Tierra Drive NW
Albuquerque, NM 87107

The Half-Moon Golf, Tennis,
and Beach Club
PO Box 80
Montego Bay, Jamaica

Hassler Hotel
Trinti de Monte
Rome, Italy

Hayman Island Resort
Whitsunday Island
Australia

Hayman Resort
Hayman Island, Great Barrier
Reef
Queensland 4801 Australia

Hotel De Crillon
10 Place de la Concorde
75008 Paris
France

Hotel du Vin
Lyons Road
Mangatawhiri Valley
New Zealand

Hotel Melia Caribe
La Guaira Carabelleda,
Venezuela

Hotel Raphael
17 Av. Kleber
75116 Paris
France

Hotel Royal Riviera
3, Avenue Jean Monnet, 06230
St. Jean-Cap-Ferrat
France

Hotel Santa Fe
1501 Paseo de Peralta
Santa Fe, NM 87501

Hotel Tryp Colón
Canalejas 1, 41001 Sevilla
Spain

The Hyde Park Hotel
66 Knightsbridge
London, SW1Y 7LA

Holiday Inn Crowne Plaza
Ave Bernardo O'Higgins 136
Santiago, Chile

Holiday Inn Halifax Centre
1980 Robie Street
Halifax, N.S. Canada B3H 3G5

Huka Lodge
TAUPO
New Zealand

The Hyde Park Hotel
66 Knightsbridge
London, SW1Y 7LA

Jackson Lake Lodge
The Grand Teton, WY 83012

The *Julia Hoyt* Luxury Barge
Kate Ratcliffe's Gascon Cooking
School and Tours
PO Box 888
Mendacino, CA 95460

Ka'anapali Beach Hotel
2525 Ka'anapali Parkway
Lahaina, Maui, Hawaii
96761-1987

Kimberley Lodge
Bay of Island
P.O. Box 166 Pitt Street, Russell
Bay of Islands, New Zealand

King David Hotel
23 King David Street
Jerusalem 94101
Israel

Maria's New Mexican Kitchen
555 West Cordova Road
Santa Fe, NM 87501

Marina Mandarin
6 Raffles Bouvelard
Marina Square
Singapore 0103

El Minzah Hotel
85, rue de la Liberté
Tangiers, Morocco

Mizpe Hayamin Kibbutz
Sea of Galilee
Israel

Mountain Sky Guest Ranch
P.O. Box 1128
Bozeman, MT 59715
Phone (800) 548-3392

Park Lane Hotel
Hong Kong

Parkroyal, Wellington
Grey and Featherston Streets
Wellington, New Zealand

Pastelaria Rosa D'Ouro
Rua de Belem, 116
1300 Lisbon, Portugal

Pousada do Castelo, Obidos
2510 Obidos, Portugal

Pousada dos Loios
7000 Évora, Portugal

Pride of Rainy Lake
Voyageurs National Park Boat
Tours, Inc.
International Falls, MN

Radisson Moriath Spa and
Resort
Dead Sea
Israel

Radisson, Nuevo Vallarta,
Paseo de Cocoteros #18
Navarit, Mexico

Radisson SAS Royal Viking
Vasagatan 1
Stockholm, Sweden

Radisson SAS Scandinavia
Hotel Copenhagen
Amager Boulevard 70
DK-2300 Copenhagen S,
Denmark

Rastle's Hotel
1 Beach Road
Singapore 189673

Rail Europe
Rail Europe for reservations
schedules on all European
trains, Eurail passes and related
products: (800) 4-EURAIL

Rainbow Ryders Balloons
10305 Nita Place NE
Albuquerque, NM 87111
Phone (800) 725-2477

The Regent of Kuala Lumpur
160, Jalan Bukit Bintang
55100 Kuala Lumpur, Malaysia

Renaissance Hotel
Jalan Bendahara
75720 Melacca, Malyasia

Rio Grande Super Tours
2301 Yale SE A2
Albuquerque, NM 87106

The Ritz-Carlton Kapalua
One Ritz-Carlton Drive
Kapalua, HI 96761

Ron Spahn Bread and Breakfast
Big Horn Mountain
P.O. Box 579
Big Horn, WY 82833

Saint Louis Barge, Burgundy
Canal
Contact: Ellen Sack,
the Barge Lady
101 West Grand Avenue,
Suite 200
Chicago, Il 60610
Phone (800) 888-0071

Sans Souci Hotel Club and Spa
SuperClubs
P.O. Box 103
Ocho Rios, Jamaica

Santa Fe Cooking School
116 W. San Francisco St.
Santa Fe, NM 87501

Sarawak Travel Agencies
No. 70, Pandungan
Kuching, Sarawak
(Trips to Borneo Longhouse)

Simpson-in-the-Strand
100 Strand
London, WC2R 0EW

Skamania Lodge
P.O. Box 189
Stevenson, WA 98648
Phone (800) 221-7117

Sonoma Restaurant
4411 Main Street
Philadelphia, PA 19127

The Spa at Doral
4400 NW 87th Avenue
Miami, FL 33178

Sturebadet
Sturegallerian 36
S-114 46 Stockholm
Sweden

Sunshine Rail Tour

Taranga Bed and Breakfast
Arrow Junction, RD 1
Queenstown
New Zealand

Thermal Hotel
Lake Balaton
Heviz, Hungary

Trans Niugini Tours
Sepik Spirit
P.O. Box 371
Mount Hagen
Papau, New Guinea

Trebah Garden
Mawnan Smith, Near Falmouth
Cornwall, TR11 5JZ
United Kingdom

Trident Villas and Hotel
P.O. Box 119
Port Antonio, Jamaica, W.I.

Unicorn Inn and Restaurant
The Nobel Family
RR#1 South Gillies
Ontario, Canada POT 2VO

Villa San Michele
Orient Express Hotel
Via Doccia 4, 50014 Fiesole
Florence, Italy

Wainwright Inn Bed and
Breakfast
43113 Moonridge Road
P.O. Box M4-6
Big Bear Lake, CA 92315

The Wayfarers
172 Bellevue Avenue
Newport, RI 02840
Phone (800) 249-4620

Index

270

271